UNDERSTAI

A concise introduction

Tim Oliver

M000190038

First published in Great Britain in 2018 by

Policy Press
University of Bristol
1-9 Old Park Hill
Bristol BS2 8BB
UK
t: +44 (0)117 954 5940
e: pp-info@bristol.ac.uk
www.policypress.co.uk

North American office:
Policy Press
c/o The University of Chicago Press
1427 East 60th Street
Chicago, IL 60637, USA
t: +1 773 702 7700
f: +1 773-702-9756
e:sales@press.uchicago.edu
www.press.uchicago.edu

© Policy Press 2018

British Library Cataloguing in Publication Data
A catalogue record for this book is available from the British Library.

Library of Congress Cataloging-in-Publication Data
A catalog record for this book has been requested.

ISBN 978-1-4473-4639-5 (paperback)
ISBN 978-1-4473-4638-8 (hardcover)
ISBN 978-1-4473-4641-8 (ePub)
ISBN 978-1-4473-4642-5 (Kindle)
ISBN 978-1-4473-4640-1 (ePDF)

Cover design by Hayes Design

For Cerys

Contents

Contents

List of figures, tables and boxes

Figures

List of figures, tables and boxes

Tables

Boxes

Abbreviations

AV	Alternative vote
BBC	British Broadcasting Corporation
CAP	Common Agricultural Policy
CETA	EU–Canadian Comprehensive Economic and Trade Agreement
CFSP	Common Foreign and Security Policy
CJEU	Court of Justice of the European Union
CSDP	Common Security and Defence Policy
DCFTA	Deep and Comprehensive Free Trade Area
DExEU	Department for Exiting the European Union
DIT	Department for International Trade
DUP	Democratic Unionist Party
EAGF	European Agricultural Guarantee Fund
EC	European Community
ECHR	European Convention on Human Rights
ECJ	European Court of Justice
ECSC	European Coal and Steel Community
EDA	European Defence Agency
EEA	European Economic Area
EEC	European Economic Community
EFTA	European Free Trade Association
EMS	European Monetary System
EPP	European People's Party
ERDF	European Regional Development Fund
ERM	European Exchange Rate Mechanism
ESA	European Space Agency
ESTA	Electronic System for Travel Authorization
EU	European Union
FTA	Free trade agreement
GCSE	General Certificate in Secondary Education
GDP	Gross domestic product

HMG	Her Majesty's Government
IMF	International Monetary Fund
LSE	London School of Economics and Political Science
MEP	Member of the European Parliament
MFN	Most favoured nation
MP	Member of Parliament
NATO	North Atlantic Treaty Organization
NHS	National Health Service
OSCE	Organization for Security and Co-operation in Europe
QMV	Qualified majority voting
SDP	Social Democratic Party
SNP	Scottish National Party
TEU	Treaty on European Union
TTIP	Transatlantic Trade and Investment Partnership
UK	United Kingdom
UKIP	UK Independence Party
US	United States of America
USSR	Union of Soviet Socialist Republics
WTO	World Trade Organization

About the author

Dr Tim Oliver is a Senior Lecturer at Loughborough University London, a Jean Monnet Fellow at the European University Institute in Florence and an Associate of LSE IDEAS, the foreign policy think tank of the London School of Economics and Political Science. For several years he was a senior lecturer at the Royal Military Academy Sandhurst and he has also taught at LSE and UCL. He has worked in the House of Lords, the European Parliament and held research and visiting positions at New York University, the SAIS Center for Transatlantic Relations (Washington DC), the RAND Corporation (Washington DC) and the Stiftung Wissenschaft und Politik (Berlin).

Acknowledgements

This book began as a series of lectures given while I was a Visiting Scholar at New York University in the autumn and winter of 2016. My thanks to Professor Mike Williams, head of the NYU Program in International Relations, for the chance to talk Brexit in New York. My time at NYU was part of a Dahrendorf Fellowship at the London School of Economics, where I was working on transatlantic relations. This book was completed while a Jean Monnet Fellow at the European University Institute, Florence. Thanks to my research assistant, Alex Boyles. Thanks also to those who reviewed earlier drafts of the book, not least the anonymous reviewers. Their comments and feedback improved the book immensely. Finally, my thanks to Stephen Wenham and Jamie Askew at Policy Press for their immense patience as I finished this book.

Copyright acknowledgements

ONE

Studying Brexit

Introduction

Brexit is the most important and controversial topic in modern British politics. It confronts the UK with a series of questions and debates about its identity, society, political economy, trade, security, international position, constitution, legal system, sovereignty, unity, party politics and the attitudes and values that define it. While questions and debates about these topics took place before the vote to leave the EU, the referendum's debate and result have brought them together in a way that could make Brexit a rare turning point that profoundly transforms Britain.

Brexit, however, is not a single event or process or entirely about Britain. It is a series of overlapping processes and debates taking place at and involving multiple actors in Britain, the remaining EU, the rest of Europe, and around the world. It is its wide-ranging nature and complexity that makes Brexit one of the most important and difficult political issues to define and analyse.

To introduce you to Brexit this book is divided into eight chapters. This first chapter looks at what Brexit is and how to study it. There are many ways to define and examine Brexit. Indeed, it is never out of the news in the UK and often a topic of discussion elsewhere. How then is it possible to define and study something that can touch on so many issues and is in a constant state of flux?

Chapter Two looks at UK–EU relations before the referendum. This chapter looks at the history of Britain's relations with European integration and also sets out some basic details about why the EU was founded and how it has evolved. To understand why Britain voted to leave the EU it is necessary to first understand why it joined and what its membership of the EU has been like. Has Britain been 'an awkward partner' in the EU, one that has blocked integration, sparked arguments and struggled to come to terms with membership? If so then this might explain Brexit. Or has it been a 'quiet European'? There is a case to be made that Britain has also been a constructive player in European integration, albeit in ways the British people especially have rarely appreciated.

Chapter Three looks at the renegotiation of Britain's EU membership, which David Cameron sought after winning the 2015 general election, and the referendum campaign that followed. The chapter examines why the referendum was called, what the UK–EU renegotiation was about and what it secured, and what happened during the campaign.

How the British people voted in the referendum is the topic of Chapter Four. This chapter sets out various studies and polling that show how the British people cast their votes. Showing how the British people voted is reasonably straightforward. Explaining why they voted as they did and for what, however, is more difficult, although it is the more important task if Brexit is to be defined and implemented.

Chapter Five looks at what happened in Britain after the vote to leave the EU. The vote triggered a series of processes within the UK that are playing out between cabinet ministers, within and between the political parties, in both chambers of the Westminster Parliament, between Westminster and devolved and local governments, in the courts, in British society and throughout the business community.

Chapter Six looks at how the rest of Europe responded to Brexit. Brexit, it should not be forgotten, is not simply about Britain. No member state of the EU has ever left the Union. This has presented the EU with unique challenges for itself and in relations with the UK. The chapter explores the scenarios for how Brexit may unfold, setting out the series of deals that may or may not be negotiated between the UK and the EU. It is important to appreciate that Brexit is one of several challenges facing the EU. To understand Brexit it is necessary to examine how it fits into these other challenges.

Finally, Brexit fits into wider international changes, which are the subject of Chapter Seven. Britain's vote changes not only Britain and the EU, but also their places in the world. What does Brexit mean for relations between the US and Europe? Are Brexit and the election of Donald Trump as US president a sign of a backlash against globalisation? And what do other powers such as Russia or China make of it?

In the Conclusion the book returns to some of the key questions set out at the end of this Introduction, which serve as a guide for how to study Brexit as it unfolds.

Why Brexit matters

Before unpacking Brexit, it is important to address the question of why to study or think about it. What is it about Brexit that fascinates so many, that worries or excites so many others, and that gets so much attention in the British, European and international media? There are three reasons.

Ideal topic through which to understand a changing UK

If you can understand Brexit, then you gain a good grasp of the leading debates about the UK's politics, economics, society, identity, culture, history, constitution, security and foreign policy. As discussed in Chapter Three, Britain's EU referendum showed how Europe had in some respects become a proxy for many other issues in UK politics. Brexit is also crucial to understanding where the UK is headed because it seems likely to be what historians term a 'critical juncture', this being an event or development in the history of a country that leads to significant change to its unity, identity, society, political economy, and place in the world.

Britain's relations with the EU (and Europe more broadly) have long been a central issue in debates about the future of Britain. It is one of the reasons why the issue of Europe has been so divisive. Some people resent or fear the connections and influence the EU has over the UK. Others see it as part of a future the UK cannot ignore.

The UK and Brexit are a fascinating case study for the social sciences

The UK has long been a good case study in political science, international relations, and political economy, including in theoretical discussions in these areas. In international relations the UK is no longer a global power such as it was in the days of the British Empire, but it has not become a small, regional or local power. This means we are not studying a regional power but something between that and a global power, one in a state of transition and which therefore reveals much about how states respond to changes to their place in the world.

In political science the UK is a good case study if you want to look at the process of European integration (the history of the UK–EU relationship is one of the most researched topics in the history of the EU), electoral systems (Britain now has a large range of different electoral systems such that it has become a laboratory for different electoral systems), constitutional matters given the UK's uncodified constitution is in a constant state of flux, which might lead to its breakup in the form of Scottish independence. Britain's political and economic movements such as Thatcherism, Keynesian economics, or Brexit itself have been watched carefully around the world.

Brexit also provides an opportunity to test academic theories and models used in social sciences to understand the world. What might Brexit mean for the many models of European integration? What do the various theories of bureaucratic politics tell us about Brexit? Do existing models and theories of economics and trade offer an adequate analysis of Brexit?

Provides pointers to the future of the EU and global politics

Brexit offers a chance to analyse how the EU is changing because it is in part explained by changes in the EU and not just the UK, for example the growing role of the Eurozone in the EU. Brexit is unprecedented for the EU. No member state has ever withdrawn from the EU. Some overseas territories such as Greenland have left, but Denmark (of which Greenland is a self-ruling part) did not withdraw. But a member state, and a member state as big as the UK, leaving the EU is not something that can be easily overlooked.

How the EU responds to Brexit, how its internal balance of power changes, what it means for the EU's place within Europe and the wider world are big questions that will shape the future of the EU and the rest of Europe. It is important to realise that how the EU responds to Brexit will also be an important factor for understanding what happens to the UK. Any UK–EU Brexit deals will not simply be about what the UK wants. They will also be about what the EU wants.

Brexit has also been linked to developments such as the election of Donald Trump, the emergence of 'post-truth politics' and a decline in public commitments in the West to globalisation. Brexit can therefore be used as a way of studying wider trends across the world.

How to study Brexit

As the defining issue of British politics, not a day goes by without the emergence of some new speech, debate, statement, book, report, analysis, or policy proposal related to Brexit. That means anyone seeking to understand Brexit can face a challenge that will overwhelm them with news and analysis. A way is needed to sift through all the developments in order to focus on those that are most important. That means we need to ask four questions.

What is Brexit?

In 2016, 'Brexit' was included for the first time in the *Oxford English Dictionary*, which defined it as 'The withdrawal of the United Kingdom from the European Union'. The word is an example of a portmanteau, a type of compound noun formed by fusing together two words. Who actually coined the word is disputed, but most date its first use to 2012 and connect it to the then popular use of the word 'Grexit', to mean Greek exit from the Eurozone.

It has not passed unnoticed that Brexit is technically inaccurate given it is the UK that will be leaving the EU. Britain is part of the United Kingdom of Great Britain and Northern Ireland. Unfortunately for those on the other side of the Irish Sea, 'UKxit' just doesn't work as well. The word also is one of many coined to describe the UK's' exit from the EU. Just as Brexit is an ongoing process and not a single event, so too has there been a continual outpouring of new words and phrases as Brexit has slowly unfolded. Some popular Brexit terms include 'Bremoaner' and 'Brexiteers'. Less than helpful ones include 'Bramageddon' and 'Bregret'. At the end of the book is a 'Brexicon' in which are set out some of the key terms and words used in the Brexit debate. A longer list of some of the more obscure and bizarre Brexit words can be found in Oliver (2016a).

However, merely defining the word 'Brexit' and associated terms, only gets us so far. The definition in the *Oxford English Dictionary* has no specific time frame or focus in terms of policy of explanation for why Brexit happened. As discussed in Chapter Six, while Article 50 – the article of the EU's treaties that sets out how a member state can leave – provides a two-year time frame for exit negotiations, the full range of negotiations and the practical implications of Brexit are likely to take much longer, and require a longer-term historical analysis to fully understand and explain. This also points to how Brexit is about more than the 'withdrawal'. A fuller understanding of Brexit requires not only an examination of why the British people voted as they did, but also an analysis of the range of processes in the UK and elsewhere that have been set in train by the vote to leave.

When is Brexit?

If Brexit is a series of overlapping processes and debates taking place in Britain, the remaining EU, the rest of Europe, and around the world then these processes and debates are not limited to a certain time frame. Voting in the referendum only took place between the hours of 7am and 10pm on Thursday 23 June 2016, although it had been possible to vote by post for several weeks before this. The official referendum campaign began on

15 April. But analysing developments from 15 April to 23 June 2016 provides only a partial analysis of Brexit.

As Chapter Two shows, the history of UK–EU relations offers several reasons as to why Brexit happened and where UK–EU relations might go next. Historical analysis can go back quite far. There are books that take a very long-term view such as that by Brendan Simms (2016) entitled *Britain's Europe: A Thousand Years of Conflict and Cooperation*. Focusing on more recent developments can still involve the struggle to narrow down dates to focus on. Britain might have joined the then European Economic Community (EEC) in 1973, but its attempts to join can be traced back to the 1960s. While Euroscepticism has been present in UK politics since before Britain joined the EEC, it was in the opposition to the Maastricht Treaty of 1992 that many parts of contemporary UK Euroscepticism began. While it was the Conservative government of David Cameron, elected in May 2015, that held the referendum, David Cameron committed to a referendum during the previous Conservative-Liberal Democrat coalition government.

As discussed further below, Brexit is a series of processes that have been unfolding since the result of the referendum became clear in the early hours of 24 June 2016. Some of these processes will take longer than others, with some potentially being open ended. This book, after an historical overview in Chapter Two, focuses largely on developments from 2015 to the start of 2018, with Chapters Five to Seven also offering some speculation about the longer-term changes. Some speculation is to an extent inevitable given this book is being written as Brexit is unfolding. However, as the later chapters show, while it is not possible to examine Brexit in terms of outcomes, examining Brexit as a series of processes helps provide some clarity about the past, present and future of this complex issue.

How do we break down and analyse Brexit?

As should be clear by now, Brexit is not a single event or solely about the UK's withdrawal from the EU. While Chapters Three and Four provide an analysis of why the British people voted for Brexit, and Chapter Two some historical background to explaining that vote, it is in Chapters Five to Seven that the book opens up Brexit by focusing on three sets of processes: those unfolding within the UK; those at the European level, including UK–EU Brexit negotiations; and the wider international implications. Those processes are summarised in Table 1.1. In the individual chapters the book examines not only the issues, but who the key participants are in each.

Can we theorise Brexit?

As a topic in a constant state of flux and unfolding in so many different ways, it is easy to become caught up in the latest news and gossip about Brexit and lose sight of the overall picture. A way is needed to sift through all the developments to focus on those that are the most important. This is where theory can play an important and necessary role. Many students, to say nothing of decision makers or members of the general public, recoil at the word 'theory'. It can suggest abstract rather than practical thinking. Yet everyone uses theoretical approaches and does so every day as a way of making sense of the world and our lives in it.

Theories do many things, one of which can be as a tool to narrow down the chaos and complexities of life so as to focus on what is the most important and see connections between that which is observed. It means that when using theory there is a need to be clear about what it is about Brexit that is to be the focus. There are three general theoretical approaches that can be used, each of which has a different focus.

First, theories of international relations offer a range of ways of looking at Brexit, mainly through analysing the state. This is especially true of what are known as 'realist' approaches to international relations. There are a wide range of realist theories, but the focus is on viewing a country's place in the world or Europe as defined by the distribution of power around the globe. Realism includes an appreciation of the role decision makers' outlooks and thinking play, but where a key element of the theory remains decision makers – and therefore their state – act in calculated, rational ways to maximise the national interest.

Various realist theories of European integration have sought to explain how and why European states have integrated and

Table 1.1: Brexit processes

Britain's Brexit	
Process	**Issues**
Brexit narrative	What the vote by the UK's population meant. 'Brexit means Brexit' means …?
UK government	Developing and implementing a strategy for Brexit, managing the administrative challenge.
Parliament and the judiciary	Scrutinising and approving the Brexit process, its aims and outcomes.
Party politics	Positioning the parties to manage Brexit and fit with their ideological outlooks.
The Union	The role of devolved and local administrations in Brexit; the place (and identities) of Scotland, London, England, Wales, and Northern Ireland in the UK.
UK society	Healing divisions from the referendum, stimulating debate about Brexit, the place of immigration in the UK and developing a new immigration system.
The economy	Choices over the UK's political economy, winners and losers from Brexit.
Europe's Brexit	
UK–EU: Article 50 and an exit deal	The Divorce: Exit agreement for the UK covering (mainly) UK budget contributions, Northern Ireland border, and the status of UK and EU citizens.
Brexit transition	The Moving Out: a transition arrangement for the UK out of the EU. Or is it an implementation period or an extension to the negotiations?
New relationship	The new relationship: agreement between the UK and EU over a new relationship.
Brexit and the 27 other EU member states	Facing a Britishless EU: remaining EU member states need to reach agreement over what to offer the UK and over what time frame, potentially with countries ratifying any agreement individually.
Rebalancing the EU	The future of the EU: the new balance of power within the post-Brexit EU, the Eurozone's place in the EU, and European integration, disintegration or muddling through.
EU in Europe	EU in Europe: ideas about the future of the EU's relations with non-EU European countries, EU-EEA/EFTA relations, and European geopolitics.
EU's daily business	Continuity: how to let the UK and the rest of the EU continue normal non-Brexit business until the UK withdraws.
The world and Brexit	
Britain in a multipolar world	Seeking new trade links, agreeing schedules at the WTO, defining Britain's role in the world, UK–US relations.
UK–EU cooperation in the world	How to continue cooperation on foreign, security and defence matters, UK and Europe in transatlantic relations.
The EU in a multipolar world	The EU in the world, Russian and Chinese views of Brexit and Europe's place, Western unity.

formed institutions to bind them together. Neofunctionalist theories, for example, explain how activity and cooperation in one area spill over into other areas, in turn encouraging states to undertake further integration (Haas 1958).

Andrew Moravcsik's (1998) 'liberal intergovernmentalism' offers a more nuanced approach, arguing that European integration is driven forward by the economic and security interests of the various member states. Moravcsik's theory also examines the negotiations and bargaining that go on within the member states as they seek to position themselves at the European level.

This book often adopts an approach that will be more familiar to students of international relations. Sometimes the UK will be referred to as if it is a single, unified actor. This is often far from the case, with the UK's referendum being a good example of the strong divisions that can exist inside a state and which play a prominent part in defining whatever policy that state seeks.

Second, the theoretical focus could instead be on the role of ideas, which is especially true of constructivist approaches. Constructivism is not a theory as such, more a way of focusing on how the norms, conventions and rules which make up politics are created and shape the behaviour of states. It is not only material capabilities that matter but also how 'we' view our place in the world (Wendt 1992).

As such, constructivists focus on how identities and norms are formed and their role in policy making, for example by socialising officials and decision makers (Checkel 2001). Constructivists can often point to some form of correlation between ideas and outcomes, but that does not mean causation. Many constructivist theories have struggled to prove a direct link between ideas and outcome (Moravcsik 2001).

Finally, there are theoretical approaches that look more to institutions and bureaucratic politics. Such theories often focus on how the output – the policy or a stated position – is produced from within the bureaucratic and institutional setup of a state or organisation. As such, politics and policy are shaped by what the institutions and networks know what to do and can do with the procedures at their disposal (Pollack 2009).

One particular approach here is that of 'policy networks', where the focus is on exploring the behind-the-scenes negotiations and networks that often shape policy through a bargaining process of resource exchange (for example over information, money, ideas, legitimacy) (Peterson 2009). The complexity of Brexit has meant that often a lot of debate about Brexit has focused on processes rather than policy.

There are a range of other theories and models which do not easily sit in the above categories, but which offer insights into Brexit. Cognitivist approaches look at the mindsets – the psychology and role of emotions – of decision makers (Rapport 2017). The beliefs and personalities of each mean they react differently to the same situation.

Sociological theories of structure and agency provide a way of examining the limits that shape the world (the structures) but also the ability of a state to change the world around it (the agency) (Outhwaite 2017). Economic debates, not least about the various models employed to analyse what Brexit could mean, appear frequently in debates about Brexit (Bailey and Budd 2017).

There is also a growing literature that looks at what Brexit means in terms of gender or the situation of marginal groups; both in terms of their future rights and by looking at the marginal role they played in the referendum campaign (Guerrina and Murphy 2016).

Finally, Brexit and the Eurozone crisis have, in recent years, helped create theories of European disintegration (see Webber (2014) and Rosamond (2016)) or 'differentiated integration' that analyse how a changing, multi-speed EU works (Schimmelfennig 2015).

Key questions

As should be clear by now, Brexit is not a single event, a single process, just about Britain, only about Britain leaving the EU, or something that will be over in a short period of time. Set out below are three sets of questions that you should keep in mind as the book proceeds and which will also be useful in trying to think about Brexit as it unfolds. They are discussed in more detail in the Conclusion.

Causes

1. Why do you think 51.9 per cent of those who voted chose Leave?
2. Why do you think 48.1 per cent of those who voted chose Remain?
3. Was Britain destined to leave the EU?
4. What effect has Britain's membership of the EU had on it and vice versa?
5. Should David Cameron have called the referendum or was there another way to handle what he termed Britain's 'European Question'?

Consequences

1. Has the EU referendum settled or changed Britain's 'European Question'?
2. What does Brexit mean for the rest of the EU?
3. How have non-EU Europe and the rest of the world responded to Brexit?
4. What have been the UK and EU's strategies for Brexit and how should they be approved and scrutinised?
5. Who wins and loses from Brexit?

Meaning

1. 'Brexit means Brexit' means what?
2. What theoretical approach best explains and analyses Brexit?
3. How can the success or failure of Brexit be measured?
4. Is Brexit a 'critical juncture' for the UK and/or the EU?
5. Is Brexit something that is unique to the UK or something symptomatic of wider trends?

Books on Brexit

You will find at the end of each chapter 10 further readings on the topics covered in that chapter, listed alphabetically according to the surname of the first author. Below are listed 10 recent books and special issues of academic journals that provide good overviews of the topic of Brexit.

Cambridge professor of law, Kenneth Armstrong's *Brexit Time: Leaving the EU – Why, How and When?* (CUP, 2017) is divided into four sections examining the world before the vote, the vote itself, preparing for Brexit, and Brexit itself.

David Bailey and Leslie Budd's *The Political Economy of Brexit* (Agenda, 2017) looks not only at the political economy of Brexit, but also at such issues as the unity of the UK and the future of the EU.

The *British Journal of Politics and International Relations* published two special issues (Vol. 19(3) and 19(4)) on Brexit in August and November 2017. Contributions cover a wide range of topics such as the causes of Brexit through to the implications for Britain's place in the world.

Harold Clarke, Matt Goodwin and Paul Whiteley, *Brexit: Why Britain Voted to Leave the European Union* (CUP, 2017). A very detailed analysis of the referendum. Required reading for anyone interested in why Britain voted as it did.

Geoffrey Evans and Anand Menon (the head of the ESRC's UK in a Changing Europe research programme) *Brexit and British Politics* (Polity Press, 2017) explains the outcome of the vote by looking at longer-term trends in British politics.

Brexit: What Everyone Needs to Know by David Allen Green (OUP, 2018) sets out what you need to know by answering 41 questions about Brexit.

Lee McGowan, *Preparing for Brexit: Actors, Negotiators and Consequences* (Palgrave, 2017) looks at the way the Brexit negotiations have unfolded since the referendum to the summer of 2017.

William Outhwaite's *Brexit: Sociological Responses* (Anthem Press, 2017) builds around a sociological approach a broad-ranging analysis.

Political Quarterly issue of April–June 2016 (Vol. 87(2)), published during the referendum campaign, contains a wealth of articles looking at UK–EU relations. The July–September 2016 issue (Vol. 87(3)) contains some of the earliest post-referendum analysis published in an academic journal.

Julie Smith, *The UK's Journey into and out of the EU: Destinations Unknown* (Routledge, 2017). A good overview of Britain's European journey.

TWO

The history of UK–EU relations

Introduction

An understanding of Brexit first requires an understanding of the organisation the UK is exiting from. This chapter briefly explains why the EU was founded, what its main institutions are, what it has developed into in terms of a political and economic union, and what it does. The chapter then turns to the history of Britain's part in the EU. Relations have not always been smooth, with Britain being labelled an 'awkward partner' as a result of a number of factors, such as its late membership. At the same time the UK has played a constructive role, albeit more as a 'quiet European' than an openly enthusiastic one. This history of a two-faced approach towards the EU helps explain why in January 2013 Prime Minister David Cameron committed the Conservative Party to seeking a renegotiated UK–EU relationship that would then be put to the British people in an in/out referendum. As the chapter shows, his decision reflected the deeply divisive issue that Europe had become in both the Conservative Party and UK politics more broadly.

Why the EU was founded

There are two deceptively simple questions to begin understanding Brexit: why was the EU founded and what does it do? Understanding why the EU exists makes it possible to understand why Britain joined and to appreciate the long history behind the tensions that have defined Britain's relations with

European integration and which were an important background factor in Brexit.

The EU is one of many overlapping organisations, institutions and networks that shape, facilitate and structure the politics, economics, society and security of Europe. There are several other prominent organisations, some of which extend beyond Europe but which are largely focused on it. The Council of Europe was established in 1949 and today consists of 47 member states which range from the UK to Russia. Unlike the EU, with which it can sometimes be confused, it does not make binding laws. However, its most famous body is the Strasbourg-based European Court of Human Rights, which enforces the European Convention on Human Rights (ECHR). Originally proposed by Sir Winston Churchill, the ECHR is an international treaty drafted after the Second World War, which is designed to protect human rights across Europe. As a signatory to the ECHR, the UK, like other signatories, accepts that the European Court of Human Rights acts as the highest European court on matters of human rights. The ECHR was incorporated directly into UK law through the Human Rights Act 1998, allowing UK citizens who feel their human rights have been breached to take their case to a British court rather than having to seek justice from the court in Strasbourg. As the Council of Europe is a separate organisation from the EU, Brexit does not mean the UK will withdraw from the Council of Europe or the ECHR, although the idea of withdrawing from the ECHR has been raised by some Eurosceptics in the past.

Other pan-European organisations include the Organization for Security and Co-operation in Europe (OSCE), which focuses on security issues such as arms control and election monitoring; the North Atlantic Treaty Organization (NATO), the world's largest and most powerful military alliance; and the European Economic Area (EEA), and the European Free Trade Association (EFTA), both of which are discussed later. There are also lots of technical and sector-specific organisations such as the European Space Agency (ESA) or the European Atomic Energy Community (Euratom), both of which have close relationships with the EU. Finally, there are smaller, regional and bilateral networks, such as the Visegrád Group (an alliance within the EU of the Czech Republic, Hungary, Poland and Slovakia).

While some of these pre-date the EU and some, such as ESA, are not technically (or wholly) part of the EU, it is the EU that has emerged as the predominant organisation for European politics, economics, social matters and non-traditional security such as policing or environmental security (NATO remains dominant on traditional military security). Why, then, was the EU founded? There is no single reason to explain European integration, but six can be identified.

Franco-German reconciliation

The EU and European integration, especially in the early years, was driven forward by the French and Germans coming to terms with their past history of conflicts, the last two of which formed core parts of the two World Wars. The EU has therefore been a political framework through which France and Germany have managed their differences. This was in part built on the appropriation of some of the institutions established by Vichy France and Nazi Germany to combine their industries, albeit this time with the intention of avoiding nationalism and war (Brunet 2017). The resilience and strength of this relationship – also known as the 'Franco-German axis' – has often been referred to as the motor of European integration. If the two agree on a proposal for the future of the EU then its chances of moving forward are very high.

Pressure from the US

US decision makers in the post-war era were in no mood to once again find their country intervening in a European conflict between France, Germany and Britain. Their fighting had also led to a situation in which at the end of the Second World War the US was the dominant power in Western Europe and much of the rest of the world. US decision makers soon realised they had an interest not only in European unity to avoid further conflict, but also in the unity of Western European states in the face of the USSR in what would soon become known as the

Cold War. Since 1945 the UK has pursued a close relationship with the US in part because it has been a keen advocate of US involvement in European security and politics as a way of maintaining a balance of power that the UK has not been able to achieve on its own. While NATO was an important part of the US commitment, securing peace in Europe through economic and political integration was also seen as an important way for securing peace. This lay behind US backing – including financial payments – for the early stages of European integration.

The threat from the USSR

The Soviet threat in the early years of the Cold War motivated countries in Western Europe to cooperate in both their defence and their economic survival. After 1945 Europe was left divided into East and West, with Germany – and its capital, Berlin – divided by the victorious allies into the separate countries of West and East Germany. The idea of Western European unity, however, was unsettling to many leaders and publics, not least because it involved the idea of rebuilding, reintegrating and rearming West Germany. Germany is the heart of Europe economically, politically, demographically and geographically. If it is weak, then Europe's centre is weak. At the end of the First World War the victorious allies had made the mistake of punishing Germany to the point where its weakened state dragged down the rest of Europe. At the end of the Second World War there was a realisation in Western powers that this could not happen again. But reintegrating West Germany meant bringing back to life a large part of a country many people still feared. A way was needed to do this that bound West Germany to the rest of Western Europe. The West Germans themselves were keen to bind themselves to their Western allies in order to show that they were prepared to be reintegrated with the rest of European society. The beginning of European integration was found in the idea of a European Coal and Steel Community (ECSC) which would bring together these two industries (which were crucial to war fighting) from Belgium, Luxembourg, the Netherlands, West Germany, France and Italy.

A reaction against nationalism

Nationalism was widely blamed for having twice driven Europe into two World Wars, which tore the continent apart. If nationalism could be replaced with Europeanism, the argument went, you could overcome deep national divisions which, unless addressed, would at some point in the future drive the countries of Europe to fight one another again. Eurosceptics disagree with this. They argue it was not nationalism that drove European states to fight one another but the lack of democracy in many European states. Nevertheless, for those who pushed the early phases of European integration, it was nationalism that concerned them the most.

Strengthen the nation states of Western Europe

Alan Milward, an historian of European integration, neatly summarised the purpose of European integration in the title of his most famous book: *The European Rescue of the Nation State* (Milward 1992). For smaller countries – Belgium, Luxembourg, the Netherlands – but also the larger ones such as West Germany, France and Italy, European integration was about strengthening European states in the face of two challenges. First, they had found themselves weakened by war and now dwarfed by global powers that shaped their politics, most notably the US and USSR. Second, the economic experiences of the Great Depression meant they wanted to avoid a recurrence of this and the protectionism that had exacerbated it. They also needed the economic stimulus to grow their economies to pay for welfare states. By pooling their sovereignty they could enhance and collectively expand their security and economic well-being, and thus their sovereignty. In time this argument would also be used to explain how the EU allowed its member states to face the challenges of globalisation. By working together they could achieve more in the world, for example on environmental or regulatory matters, than they could by working alone.

Reverse the decline of Europe and its member states

At the end of the Second World War the future seemed to belong to continental-size powers such as the USSR and the US. Europe's only hope appeared to be by matching this through cooperation. This connected to some longer-running hopes by some of creating a United States of Europe that would be a third power in the world. This idea can be traced back to before the World Wars.

Similarly, there is also a long history of European states hoping to leverage their international standing by joining with or aligning with other European states. Hopes that France could use European integration to enhance French power in the world (and over Germany) have long been an underlying aim of French participation. As discussed in Chapter Seven, Britain has also sought to use the EU's collective might to boost its own claims to global power.

What the EU does

The EU has evolved from a European Coal and Steel Community of six countries in Western Europe to a European Union of 28 countries that today covers most of Europe, is run by multiple institutions and holds a wide range of responsibilities and powers. It has grown through a series of treaties and agreements, the most important of which are set out in Table 2.1. Further key dates in the EU's development can be found in the timeline at the end of the book.

One of the problems when discussing the EU's history is that the organisation has not always been the 'European Union'. The ECSC led, in 1957, to the European Economic Community. This was also known as 'the common market'. This was the organisation the UK joined in 1973.

As a result of the EEC's responsibilities and work expanding, it was in 1992 renamed the European Community (EC). In the same year, the Maastricht Treaty created a European Union, of which the EC was a part. From 1992 onwards, it became more common to talk of the EU, not the EC. It was not until the Lisbon Treaty that the EC was formally merged into the EU.

Table 2.1: Key treaties and agreements in the EU's development

Date	Event
1951	Treaty of Paris is signed establishing the European Coal and Steel Community between France, West Germany, Italy, the Netherlands, Belgium and Luxembourg.
1957	The Treaty of Rome is signed establishing the European Economic Community and the European Atomic Energy Community.
1968	EEC members agree a customs union, removing all import duties between them.
1979	The European Monetary System (EMS) and Exchange Rate Mechanism (ERM) are established.
1985	The Schengen Treaty is signed, abolishing borders between some EEC member states.
1986	The Single European Act is signed.
1992	EEC renamed the EC. Treaty of Maastricht is signed, creating the EU.
1997	Treaty of Amsterdam is signed.
2000	Charter of Fundamental Rights is established.
2001	Euro becomes the currency of 12 member states.
2001	Nice Treaty signed.
2003	Convention on the Future of Europe prepares a draft constitutional treaty.
2005	Constitutional treaty is abandoned after rejection in referendums in France and the Netherlands.
2007	Lisbon Treaty signed and is ratified by 2009.

Explaining the EU's growth

As touched on in Chapter One, there are a number of ideas and theories that explain European integration (Rosamond 2000). Some neofunctionalist theories point to integration being the result of 'spillover' where cooperation between states in one area leads to the need for cooperation in another. Liberal integovernmentalism, on the other hand, points to how integration has been driven by the convergence in the interests of member states, especially the largest states. Institutionalist theories point to the growing power of the EU's institutions to bind the EU together, or how these institutions have facilitated cooperation between member states that grows deeper over time as interests increasingly align. Finally, constructivists focus on how identities and norms are formed and their role in policy making, for example by socialising officials and decision makers.

Whatever explains the process by which European integration happened, it has led to a Union that today does a wide range of things. This can be seen in a review Britain's Conservative-Liberal Democrat coalition government commissioned in 2011–13. Called a 'Review of the Balance of Competences', it was the most comprehensive review ever undertaken of the effect of the EU on a member state, and is discussed further in Chapter Three. Drawn up over the course of two years, and based on a wide range of evidence submitted from around Britain, Europe and the world, the final 32 reports (see Table 3.1) covered an extensive list of topics. It gives a good indication of the extent of the EU's work and powers, but it should not be overlooked that the extent of the EU's 'competences' – or powers – varies considerably from area to area.

The work of the EU

If there is one goal the EU works towards it is to create and maintain political, economic and social unity across Europe. As the preamble to the EU's treaties put it, its aim is to create 'an ever closer union amongst the peoples of Europe'. What that means in terms of an end destination is much disputed. For some it means a United States of Europe, for others it will remain a union of states with the EU facilitating cooperation between them. It does mean the EU is more than an economic union, and that some political cooperation and unity is an integral part.

The process of European integration began, as discussed above, in the form of a project to integrate coal and steel. It was from this, and other projects such as that to cooperate on atomic energy (which created Euratom), that further integration – and projects – were subsequently built. These include creating a single market across Europe. This has entailed the creation over several decades of a single space for the free movement of goods, capital, services and people. To ensure that market works effectively the EU has the power to regulate common standards and works to remove national barriers.

There are several other projects which emerged from these efforts. Schengen, agreed in the 1980s and formally launched in 1995, has removed passport and other border checks between 26 European states. At the start it was not an EU policy, emerging instead outside of the then EEC because it had not been possible to reach agreement between all of the then EEC members on abolishing border controls. The aim was to remove barriers to both people and trade, with the result today being that millions of people each week cross between states without any disruption. It also means the members share a common visa policy and common checks on travellers entering and leaving the area. Having begun as a non-EU policy it was eventually absorbed into the EU (which also runs Frontex, the EU's border and coastguard agency, which maintains the EU's borders in coordination with the border and coastguard agencies of the member states of Schengen), but with some member states remaining outside it. The UK and Ireland, who have had a common travel area since Ireland became independent of the UK in 1922, stayed outside. Several new EU member states such as Bulgaria are also outside it, but obliged to join eventually as part of their membership of the EU. Several non-EU states such as Switzerland, Iceland and Norway are also members, a reflection of the close economic and social ties they have with their neighbours who are in the EU.

One of the best-known projects is the single European currency. The euro had long been discussed as a possible means by which EU member states could coordinate and integrate their economies further, with the aim of increasing trade and bolstering Europe's place in the world. Its creation also reflected a desire by Germany to bind itself economically to the rest of the EU when in 1990 the reunification of Germany – which since 1945 had been divided into West and East Germany – raised fears of German power. The euro has faced significant problems in recent years, in part because it was launched without the strong central political institutions necessary to tackle the economic and social imbalances that would face a currency union covering so many different countries. Debate continues today as to whether integration should now move forward in ways that create such institutions, although doubts exist as to whether member state governments – and their publics – would support this.

The EU also provides its members with a single voice in trade policy and some areas of international policy. The EU's combined GDP of €14.9 trillion makes it an economic superpower. It has waged trade wars with the US and negotiates trade agreements on behalf of its member states. That economic might can also be used to pursue certain collective international policy goals – whether in humanitarian aid or security – through a range of policies, the most prominent of which is the Common Foreign and Security Policy (CFSP). This encourages the EU and its member states to work together on matters such as international environmental agreements, pursuing certain international norms such as human rights, or in trying to influence the policies of other states around the world.

Finally, the EU's budget provides funding for a number of areas. As Figure 2.1 shows, in 2015 the EU spent around €140 billion across five broad budget categories (see Figure 6.1 in Chapter Six for analysis of what EU member states pay into the budget). Historically a great deal of funding has been directed towards agriculture and fisheries, and this remains the case with 'Sustainable growth' taking up 41 per cent of spending in 2015. This includes the European Agricultural Guarantee Fund (EAGF), which makes payments to farmers to provide them with a sustainable standard of living and ensure a stable food supply at affordable prices. The EAGF is one part of the Common Agricultural Policy (CAP), other parts of which include spending on rural development, aimed at developing rural economies.

The proportion of the EU's budget spent on areas such as agriculture has declined, with EU funding increasingly spent on two areas. First, 36 per cent of funding goes towards 'Economic, social and territorial cohesion'. This includes the Regional Development Fund and Social Fund, also known as 'structural funds' which are focused on local economic growth, training and business start-ups. Cohesion funding is aimed at areas of the EU where living standards are less than 90 per cent of the EU average. The second area focuses on 'Competitiveness' and includes spending on such programmes as Erasmus, which encourages Europeans to study, train and gain work experience outside their home country; infrastructure spending on key transport and energy networks; and Horizon 2020, which is the EU's fund for research and innovation, often going to universities and research laboratories.

Figure 2.1: EU spending in 2015

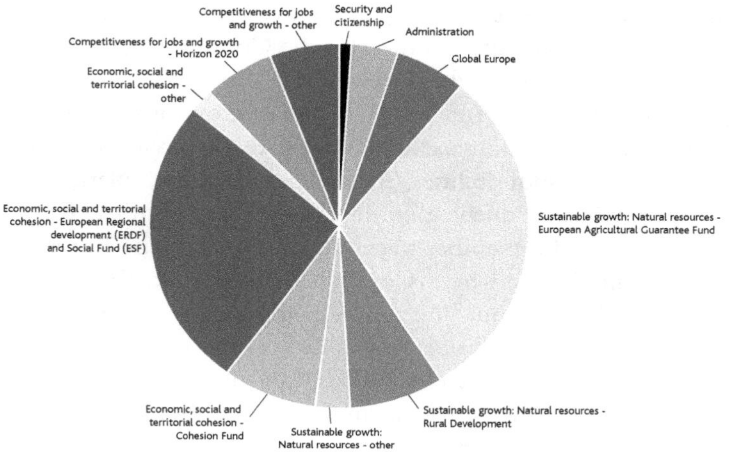

Source: House of Commons Library (2018).

The EU's main institutions

The EU is overseen by a complex range of institutions that, like the EU itself, have evolved as the Union has grown (Pinder and Usherwood 2013; Kenealy, Peterson and Corbett 2015). This can be seen in the most senior EU institution of all: the European Council. This is a summit meeting, which first emerged in the 1970s, that now meets at least four times a year in order to bring together the heads of government of the EU's 28 member states. It has been compared to the board of directors of the EU, but was not formally an EU institution until the Lisbon Treaty. It provides broad strategic guidance for the direction of the EU. It has its own president, currently former Polish prime minister Donald Tusk, who chairs proceedings. It has been at these meetings that some of the most important decisions about the EU have been made, such as over political and economic integration, budget disputes, treaty revisions, new member state applications, and major foreign policy issues.

The European Commission is the EU's executive and main bureaucracy, which develops EU policies and laws and is therefore the driving force behind many EU policies and initiatives. These policies and laws must first be approved by the

EU's member state governments in the Council of the EU and by the democratically elected representatives of EU citizens in the European Parliament. It is then for the Commission to oversee the implementation and enforcement of these policies and laws. The Commission is run by a College of Commissioners with 28 members, one from each member state, each with their own portfolio of responsibilities (such as competition, enlargement or energy). Each of these commissioners was nominated by a government of a member state and approved by the European Parliament. Headed by a Commission president, the current occupant Jean-Claude Juncker was appointed after the 2014 European Parliament elections as he was the lead candidate – also known as the 'Spitzenkandidat' – of the European People's Party (the EPP), which won the largest number of seats. The Commission also consists of about 30,000 staff. It is their job to work with hundreds of committees that connect with representatives of member state governments, specialists, special interest groups, elected representatives, corporate interests and civil society from across the EU. A great deal of what the Commission does depends on EU member states implementing laws and policies, the Commission lacking the power to do this directly within the member states. It is expected to take a pan-EU view and so avoid any national interest. It also represents the EU in some international arenas, these ranging from overseeing negotiations with aspirant members (or departing members in the case of Brexit) through to conducting trade negotiations for the EU.

The Council of the EU, also referred to as simply 'the Council' is the EU's key daily decision-making body. It consists of national government ministers meeting regularly in councils reflecting the topic under discussion. When they are not meeting, discussions are undertaken between the Permanent Representations of each member state, who are the delegations (rather like embassies) in Brussels of officials and diplomats from each member state. Compared to the Commission and the Parliament, the Council is more intergovernmental in nature. It is directed by a rotating six-month presidency, which is held by each member state in turn. Decisions are often reached through unanimity (and in some areas such as foreign policy this is required), but when this is not possible can be reached via a simple majority (mainly for matters of procedure) or through a process known as Qualified Majority Voting (QMV). QMV is a system of voting where each state's allocation of votes is based on their population. To be successful, however, a measure must be supported by a certain number of states who represent a certain percentage of the EU's population. The exact percentages depend on the type of proposal, but the most common requirement is that a vote in favour represents 55 per cent of the member states (16 out of 28) and 65 per cent of the total EU population. Once the Commission has proposed a new law, it is sent to the Council for debate and approval or rejection. The proposal is also sent to the European Parliament, with whom on a range of issues, the Council must reach agreement for it to pass.

The European Parliament is a democratically elected legislature of 751 Members of the European Parliament (MEP) elected every five years by every eligible EU citizen. MEPs are divided up among the member states roughly on the basis of population, with the largest – Germany – having 96 MEPs while the smallest member states – Malta and Luxembourg – have six. Meeting in Brussels and the French city of Strasbourg (the latter being an outdated requirement the Parliament itself has tried to abolish but which it is required to honour under the EU's treaties, on which France will veto any attempt at change), it cannot propose laws (this resting with the Commission) but in many areas shares with the Council the powers of approval and amendment. Through both its own efforts and as a result of various treaty changes, the Parliament has played an increasing role in running the EU, with it now having equal powers with the Council. The Parliament also plays a role in agreeing to the accession of new members (and under Article 50 must agree to the exit deal with a departing member state), to international agreements the EU enters into (such as trade agreements), has power over the setting of the EU's budget (and can reject it with a two-thirds majority), can question and approve the appointment of the president of the Commission and the College of Commissioners, and can, with a two thirds majority, force the resignation of the Commission.

Finally, the Court of Justice of the European Union (CJEU) is the supreme legal authority of the EU. Based in Luxembourg, it consists of three courts: the Court of Justice (also known as the European Court of Justice, or ECJ); the General Court; and the European Union Civil Service Tribunal. Each serves a different purpose. Of the three, it is often the ECJ to which people refer when talking or writing about the CJEU. It consists of 28 judges, appointed by each member state. The ECJ's main role is to ensure that national and EU laws, and any international agreements entered into by the EU, 'meet the spirit of the treaties, and that EU law is equally, fairly, and consistently applied through the member states' (McCormick 2014, 91). It can only rule on matters where the EU has competence, these mainly being economic matters. It has been crucial to the idea that the EU's laws and treaties take precedence over national laws in those areas where the EU has responsibility. One of its most famous decisions, the 1979 *Cassis de Dijon* case, established the principle of mutual recognition: that goods produced and marketed legally in one member state may be sold without further restrictions in all other member states. Decisions are supposed to be reached through unanimity, but votes are usually taken by simple majority. Enforcement of the Court's rulings rests with the member states – either their governments or national courts – with the Commission monitoring compliance.

What distinguishes the EU from every other international organisation are the supranational institutions of the European Commission, European Parliament and CJEU. The member states have transferred significant powers and responsibilities to these institutions, allowing them a degree of power over the running of the EU that is equal to, or in some areas more powerful than, that of the individual member states. At the same time, much of the focus of decision making remains with the intergovernmental institutions of the European Council and Council of the EU. Despite this, the EU's institutions – and in particular its supranational ones – have faced regular criticism that they are too powerful, distant, slow and unaccountable. Yet they have also been criticised for not being powerful enough (for example the EU has struggled to solve the Eurozone's problems because of a lack of the necessary enforcement powers and ability to centrally manage the Eurozone economy) and of having a decision-making process that, because of national restrictions, is so overly consensus driven that it could be improved by stronger and more centralised decision making.

Why the UK joined and joined late

When Britain joined the EEC in 1973 it did so after a period in which it had initially ignored European integration and then made two failed attempts to join. Why then did the UK join late? Why was it twice rejected? Why did it not try to shape European integration from the beginning? And what legacy did this create for UK–EU relations? It is not as if Britain was not involved in some way at the start. One of the fathers of European integration – and after whom the European Parliament has named one of its buildings – was Sir Winston Churchill. In September 1946 at a speech at the University of Zurich he talked about the need for a United States of Europe as a way of rebuilding Europe, of strengthening it after the devastation of the Second World War and creating unity in the face of what was to become the Cold War. Why then did the country he had until only a year before led as one of its greatest prime ministers decide against participating?

Power and prestige

Britain was a victor in the Second World War. It had not been defeated unlike large swathes of the rest of Europe. It might have been left exhausted and almost bankrupt, but as far as the British were concerned they were winners. At one point, Britain had stood alone as the last European holdout against Nazism. This embedded an idea in Britain of its 'standing alone'. To some extent that is true because it was the last holdout. But like the other two large victors of the Second World War – the US and the USSR – it has tended to overlook its dependence on others to win the war. Hitler's Nazi Germany was defeated by the combined efforts of the British Empire, the US, the USSR and a host of smaller allies.

Nevertheless, the British narrative of the Second World War was that it had been a victor and should be treated as an equal to the US and USSR. But this was not Britain as known today but Britain as the British Empire, on which Britain had drawn heavily in the war. The backbone of the British Empire was the British Indian Army, with forces from Canada, Australia, New Zealand, Africa and many other parts of the Empire serving to defend Britain and, especially in the war against Japan, the Empire. Regrettably that Commonwealth and imperial contribution to Britain's power and security can be overlooked by modern debates in the UK that can assume that Britain stood very much on its own.

Strategic lessons from the Second World War

The ability to draw on the support of the Empire and, crucially, the US, meant Britain had been able to resist the Nazis and in doing so reinforce a strategic outlook that dependence on alliances with other countries in Europe would be insufficient to protect Britain's security. The collapse of France, in particular, had reinforced this. The idea then in post-1945 of committing to the rest of Europe did not sit well with British decision makers, unless it was in the form of some commitment that directly engaged the US in European politics, and this was found in NATO. As the first NATO Secretary General (and former British Army general) Lord Ismay quipped, NATO was 'to keep the Russians out, the Americans in, and the Germans down'. Committing to some form of arrangement to bind Britain, France and West Germany in a political and economic union would have gone against the painful lessons Britain had recently learnt from the Second World War. As touched on further in Chapter Seven, this sense of Britain as the last holdout in Europe, and one that should always look outside of Europe for alliances that can shape the European and global order, lives on today.

Europe was only one of the three circles of British power

For all his lauding of a United States of Europe, Churchill himself was not wholly of the opinion that Britain should partake in any efforts at European integration. Instead he saw Britain as sat at the heart of three overlapping circles that defined its place in the world: Europe, the US, and the British Empire and Commonwealth. These three overlapping circles defined Britain's international relations, standing and role. But these three overlapping circles would soon be transformed.

The Empire and Commonwealth circle started to fade away with the decolonisation of the 1950s and 1960s. British trade had also long been shifting more towards the European and transatlantic marketplaces. The experiences of the Suez crisis in 1956, when Britain and France, with the cooperation of Israel, had tried to occupy the Suez Canal, which had recently been nationalised by Egypt, revealed how Britain was no longer the imperial power it had once been. The canal was seen as strategically important for the British Empire, being the gateway to British territories 'east of Suez'. British, French and Israeli military efforts went smoothly. But the US under President Eisenhower had not been informed and opposed the move as an unacceptable act of imperialism. Through pressure on the pound sterling the US caused an economic crisis for Britain that led it to quickly back down and withdraw its military forces. It was a humiliation that led to the resignation of Prime Minister Anthony Eden, who had also lied to the House of Commons over the invasion. It was a painful lesson that drove France to look more towards European cooperation and the UK towards staying close to the US.

Unsure of its role in the world

The fading of the Empire left the two circles of Europe and the US, but this was not something British politicians and decision makers were entirely comfortable with making choices over. In 1962, Dean Acheson, a former US Secretary of State, gave a speech at the US military academy at West Point that caused much angst in Britain. He said:

> Great Britain has lost an Empire and has not yet found a role. The attempt to play a separate power role apart from Europe, a role based on a special relationship with the United States, and on being head of a commonwealth which has no political structure, or unity, or strength, this role is about played out.

This did not go down well in Britain. Acheson was no enemy of Britain, being a life-long Anglophile. But his speech ran up against ideas in Britain that the country was, despite the debacle of Suez, still a global power. But note what Acheson said: 'The attempt to play a separate power role *apart* from Europe.' Acheson was asking why, instead of accepting that Britain was a European power and so engaging fully with the rest of Europe, Britain was instead pursuing a relationship with the US and a relationship with a Commonwealth 'which has no political structure, or unity, or strength'. That his speech was received with much hostility in Britain revealed how sensitive – and disputed – was the issue of Britain's decline and place in the world. Public reaction to Acheson mirrored the private reaction inside government a few years earlier to the report, *Study of Future Policy, 1960-1970* (Cabinet Office 1959), commissioned by Prime Minister Harold Macmillan to look at Britain's status in the world up to 1970. The report, which in retrospect is quite accurate in its predictions, made at the time for such bleak reading for those who thought Britain would remain a global power that Macmillan had it classified and banished to the archives.

Shifting economics

Britain's relative decline (relative because it continued to grow in wealth but others overtook it by growing more quickly) had also seen a shift in its trading patterns away from the Empire and towards the markets of Western Europe. This was a slow but painful transition that conflicted with the use of the pound sterling as a global currency used – in the sterling area – by a number of countries. But that group of states had long been declining, with Australia and Canada, for example, having long since looked more to the US than the UK.

Joining the EEC in 1973 meant Britain had to cut some of the remaining imperial preferences and markets with which it had maintained close relations, such as Australia and New Zealand. No other European state had witnessed such a profound shift in its trading patterns, in part because no other European state had (thanks to war) maintained such a global empire and international trading system.

In response to the growth of the EEC, Britain had in 1960 attempted an alternative model for European economic relations in the form of the EFTA. Originally consisting of seven countries – Austria, Denmark, Norway, Portugal, Sweden, Switzerland and the UK – it was designed as an intergovernmental approach to encouraging trade between its members that avoided having supranational institutions such as the European Commission and CJEU. However, it failed to deliver the same economic gains and, crucially, political links the UK wanted to secure with the rest of Europe.

Doubts on the Left and Right

Shifting from the Empire and Commonwealth to Europe angered groups and individuals on the Right who felt the Empire was being abandoned along with Britain's global ambitions. It also raised doubts for those on the Left. In the immediate post-war era Britain's Labour government had set out to build what Prime Minister Clement Atlee had told the Labour Party conference would be the 'New Jerusalem'. A combination of a universal welfare state and Keynesian economics had led to the nationalisation of certain key industries. Having seen off the Nazis, the British state would now be mobilised to defeat the giant evils of squalor, ignorance, want, idleness and disease. The security lesson learnt from the Second World War of independence and separation now translated into social policy.

Having nationalised the coal industry the Labour Party was therefore unlikely to consider integrating it with France or Germany. As deputy Prime Minister Herbert Morrrison is said to have argued: 'The Durham miners won't wear it.' The Westminster Parliament – defined by the idea that 'parliamentary sovereignty' means there is no higher authority in the UK – gave Labour the powers to affect widespread change to the political, social and economic landscape of Britain. While the degree to which US loans helped pay for such changes serves as a reminder that Britain's sovereignty may not have been as much as some believed, the idea of pooling that sovereignty with other West European states was for many a non-starter.

Britain's political and constitutional setup

Britain's late membership of the EU also then owes something to Britain's unique political and constitutional culture compared to many other Western Europe states. Britain does not have a codified constitution; instead its constitution has evolved in large part by decision makers making things up as they have gone along, albeit often (but not always) with reference to history and convention. This flexibility lies at the heart of a majoritarian system of government where whichever political party can command a simple majority in the House of Commons has control of Her or His Majesty's Government. That government then has almost unquestioned authority over the UK thanks to the centralised nature of the UK state, meaning that almost all power rests in Westminster and Whitehall.

The majority in the Commons that this centralised power is based on is often the result of a minority of votes across the country because of the first past the post electoral system used to elect MPs. This has contrasted with the proportional electoral systems used elsewhere in Europe which lead to more consensus-driven politics (as seen in coalition governments) and which are sometimes backed by federal structures that distribute power away from the centre, for example in Germany.

This has led to tensions between Britain and the rest of the EU over the nature and power of such institutions as the European Commission, where non-elected political appointees exercise power that is accountable via other means than those familiar in British politics. Efforts to reform and codify the EU's powers in various treaties have also clashed with a British tradition of pragmatic uncodified constitutional change. This, to some extent, reflects a tension between English common law (law derived from custom rather than legislation) and Roman (or civil) law used elsewhere in Europe (and as a mixed system in Scotland).

Cultural and demographic differences

On top of the political, economic, security and constitutional reasons for Britain's late membership there were also demographic, cultural and 'narrative' reasons connected to the history that has prevailed in Britain of it having an 'island story' rather than a continental one. The idea of Britain as a global power (albeit in relative decline) was still a widely held idea among the public, and especially decision makers, in the post-war era. It was also noticeable in economic statistics thanks to the UK's continued links around the world, clear in military and security commitments (and between 1949 and 1963 something that was felt personally by all healthy men aged 17–21 who undertook national service – that is, conscription that sent them to parts of what was still a worldwide empire), observable in a legal and constitutional system that had global links (through the use of common law and as the legal and constitutional centre of the empire) and also in terms of demographic and family links.

This personal, and especially family connection, remained clear up to and long after Britain joined the EU. In 2006 the IPPR think tank (Sriskandarajah and Drew 2006) looked into where Britons lived overseas for more than six months. Their work revealed three large concentrations: the rest of Europe, North America, and Australia and New Zealand. Large numbers were also to be found in South Africa, South Asia (especially India and Pakistan) and the Caribbean. If Britons resident in Ireland (with which the UK shares a common travel area) and Spain (home to a then estimated 761,000 Britons) are removed from the European calculation then Europe's share shrinks considerably.

The distribution reflects demographic links that connect Britain and what some term the 'Anglo-sphere' of the English-speaking world. That world is not only defined by links with what in the past was called the 'White' Commonwealth – Canada, Australia and New Zealand – but, thanks to immigration to the UK also connects it to countries in Africa, Asia and the Caribbean. This mix of cultural, demographic, political, economic and historical links help explain why Oxford historian – and a committed European and liberal – Timothy Garton-Ash (2001) concluded that '[t]he answer to the question "Is Britain European?" has to be "yes, but not only"'.

Late realisation

What delayed Britain's membership then was a combination of strategic outlooks, historical experiences, a different political and legal setup, economic, demographic and cultural links beyond Europe and an unwillingness to accept that relative decline meant Britain needed to think more about Europe than the wider world. The realisation that this could not be sustained and that Britain was also missing out on being able to shape what was fast emerging as the key organisation in European politics eventually moved UK decision makers towards applying for membership. Britain might have been doing well, and its people in the 1950s had, as then Prime Minister Harold Macmillan put it, 'never had it so good'. But the sense of global decline was palpable and by the 1970s the country was labelled – both at home and abroad – as the 'sick man of Europe' thanks to a series of economic booms and busts. This contrasted with the steadier growth the members of the EEC had experienced, which only added to a sense among UK decision makers of Britain's decline.

Repeated attempts at membership

Membership of the EEC became an economic, political and strategic concern for the UK, with the first attempt at membership made in 1961. It was eventually rejected in 1963 by France's President de Gaulle. For de Gaulle, Britain was not sufficiently European. The French rejection, along with another in 1967, did not represent the positions of the rest of the EEC, all of whom supported British membership. It might also have been less about how European Britain was and more about how de Gaulle feared Britain challenging French leadership in the EEC.

Nevertheless, that de Gaulle argued Britain was not European enough was telling. Britain's late applications and their rejection meant that when Britain finally joined in 1973 – as a result of de Gaulle leaving office in 1969 – it arrived late, frustrated by delays at getting in, and found an organisation already established to operate in a way that was more in fitting with politics elsewhere in Europe than the style found in Westminster and also designed (especially in its budget) to meet their needs, not Britain's.

The two-faced European

Pick up any book about Britain's membership of the EU and you will soon read about how that relationship has rarely been smooth. Brexit has taken this to new heights. Look more closely and you will soon see that the relationship has also been more constructive and positive than might first appear. Even opinion polling has shown support for UK membership fluctuating significantly, albeit with support for withdrawal never falling below 25 per cent (Ipsos Mori 2016). Britain has therefore often been seen as a two-faced European, sometimes also described as 'Janus faced' after the two-faced Roman god.

A good example of this two-faced approach can be found in a speech Margaret Thatcher gave in 1988 at the College of Europe in Bruges, a speech that has become known as the 'Bruges Speech' (Menon and Salter 2016). This speech is widely interpreted as an attack on the European project. One line in particular is often quoted: 'We have not successfully rolled back the frontiers of the state in Britain only to see them re-imposed at a European level.' This was in reaction to attempts, as she saw it, by some in the EEC to push forward integrated economic and social policies that would be underpinned by unnecessary regulations that would stifle business and competitiveness. This clashed with what had become known as Thatcherism, which, among other things, emphasised deregulation and the power of free markets. Such ideas were also found in the US in the form of 'Reagonomics', named after President Ronald Reagan. The speech was therefore interpreted in Britain as Thatcher defending an Anglo–American (sometimes referred to as 'Anglo-Saxon') economic order against a more corporatist, Keynesian and interventionist European one. This was used by her press secretary to feed a domestic message that Thatcher was standing up for Britain, arguing that it was a place apart from the rest of the EEC, and that it was being held back by it. These arguments have only grown among Eurosceptics since 1988.

There is, however, another side to the speech that looks at how it shaped the EEC and later the EU. British outlooks on the speech assume it was greeted with hostility across Europe. Yet Thatcherism and Reagonomics were part of a wider series of changes in the political economy of the West that also swept across much of Europe. The speech offered a perspective that aligned with frustrations found elsewhere in the EEC. As explored below, Britain, and Thatcher especially, had pushed for the creation of the single market to encourage competition across Europe, something other member states had also embraced. Look back on the ideas Thatcher set out in the speech – especially of a deregulated EEC with central institutions that were not the overpowering ones some elsewhere might have hoped they would become – and it soon becomes clear that such ideas have been central to debates of EU politics for the last few decades. Indeed, some of the problems the EU faces today – such as in the Eurozone – stem from not having central institutions that are strong enough to assert themselves against the sovereignty and powers of the member states. Despite this Thatcher is seen to epitomise Euroscepticism in the UK while also being seen elsewhere as the champion of the EU's single market. The case can therefore be made that, like the UK, she was an awkward partner but also, through some of her actions, a quiet European.

An awkward partner

Britain's late arrival, along with the vetoes that had delayed it, meant membership did not get off to the most positive of starts. In retrospect, it looked a fitting start to the often tumultuous membership that would follow. Britain, according to this interpretation of its membership, has been 'an awkward partner' (George 1998). As we will discuss in the next section, there are reasons to critique this. Not least, as the title of George's book alludes to, Britain has been 'an' awkward partner and not 'the' awkward partner it is sometimes described as (Daddow and Oliver 2016). The indefinite article 'an' matters. Britain has not been the only awkward member state. Other EU member states have also been awkward by, for example, rejecting treaties, failing to uphold EU law, or bringing the Eurozone to the verge of collapse. However, Britain's awkwardness certainly stands out for nine reasons.

Struggling to fit with the setup of the EU

An awkward relationship was to some extent assured thanks to the terms on which Britain eventually joined the EEC, a result of its late membership meaning it was beholden to both how the EEC had been setup and the terms of membership the other member states had been able to set for it. An appreciation of how difficult EEC membership could be in terms of changing this agenda or shifting policies appears to have only dawned on British decision makers once the UK was a member. In one of the biggest tensions, Britain found it had to pay into an EEC budget that had been configured largely towards agricultural interests elsewhere in the EEC and which left Britain contributing more to (and receiving a lot less back) than any other state except Germany, and this despite being at the time one of the poorest.

Trying to change the EU and fit in caused tensions in UK politics

In 1974 the British government changed from one led by the pro-European Conservative Edward Heath to a Labour one led by Harold Wilson. Wilson and Labour had submitted Britain's second application for EEC membership in 1967, but not without causing tensions within the Labour party. Wilson, faced with a slim parliamentary majority and a UK-EEC membership that needed adjusting, felt the best way to manage the issue was to seek a renegotiated relationship which would then be put to the British people in an in/out referendum. This was to be the first time a UK-wide referendum was held. The eventual renegotiation did secure some changes, with 'Structural Adjustment Funds' being created to pay for projects in some of the EEC's poorest regions, which included a number of areas in the UK. Overall, however, the situation remained much as it had before, with the renegotiation sold to the British people as a successful exercise in UK diplomacy at securing concessions.

The eventual referendum, held on 5 June 1975, saw 67 per cent of Britain that voted do so to remain in the EEC (on a turnout of 63.9 per cent). This provided Labour with only a short reprieve from its tensions over EEC membership. In the hope of maintaining cabinet unity, Harold Wilson had allowed ministers to campaign on differing sides. The divisions this helped bring to the surface added to pressures, not least from Labour's move towards a more Left-wing agenda, which led in the early 1980s to a group of pro-European Labour MPs splitting away to form the Social Democratic Party (SDP). By the 1983 general election Labour was campaigning for withdrawal from the EEC.

A transactional approach to membership

Labour's renegotiation and referendum were only the beginning of a history of demands for special treatment from the EU. Tellingly, Labour ministers viewed the UK–EEC relationship as a 'business arrangement' (Wall 2012, 516). Despite this, the 1975 renegotiation had not substantially reduced the amount the UK paid to the EEC. Relations were therefore again strained when in the early 1980s Conservative Prime Minister Margaret Thatcher pushed the EEC to restructure its budget so that the UK would not have to pay as much in. The 'rebate' which she secured for the UK's contributions followed fraught negotiations in which Thatcher famously declared that she wanted 'my money back'. To the rest of the EEC, especially other net contributors, this was evidence of Britain pursuing a purely national as opposed to collective approach to European integration. The rebate, and the way it was secured, has caused a degree of resentment ever since.

Britain has secured many opt-outs

Throughout its membership, Britain has been able to secure opt-outs and exclusions from common EU policies, most famously from the European single currency and Schengen. It was also able to negotiate an opt-out from some areas of cooperation in justice and home affairs and later from the 'Charter of Fundamental Rights', which was an attempt by the EU to create a bill of rights for itself. British officials often resisted the use of the word 'federal' to refer to anything within the EU because it carried connotations of a 'federal Europe', which in Britain had become associated with centralisation of power in Brussels and the emergence of a United States of Europe. The rest of the EU went along with many of these opt-outs, but not without unease.

There was therefore a sense of exasperation when, as explored in Chapter Three, David Cameron demanded as part of the UK's EU renegotiation of 2015–16, that the EU consider removal of a British exemption from the Treaty of Rome's preamble that made clear the contracting parties were 'determined to lay the foundations of an ever-closer union among the peoples of Europe'. Again, the words 'ever-closer union' had to some within the British debate come to mean the centralisation of power and creation of a federal United States of Europe. This is not to argue that other EU member states have been unable to secure exemptions. Denmark, for example, was also able to secure an opt-out from the euro along with other areas such as defence cooperation. But Britain was the member state that always made the most demands and disrupted the application of common EU ideas across the Union. The willingness of the EU to eventually acquiesce to Britain in a way it would not for other member states generated elsewhere in the EU a feeling of unfairness and special treatment, something the British themselves often failed to appreciate.

Has been the bane of many prime ministers' time in office

As touched on above, Britain's demands for special treatment stemmed from a domestic political debate that rarely embraced European integration and was often deeply divided over it. As a result, the issue of Britain's relations with the EU has caused problems for successive prime ministers and shaped their premierships. Divisions within Labour over Europe weakened both Harold Wilson and James Callaghan; Margaret Thatcher's downfall was in part because of divisions with her cabinet over Britain's attitude to the idea of a single European currency; it was the source of bitter splits and divisions within John Major's government; it caused tensions between the pro-European Blair and the more wary Gordon Brown; the vote for Brexit brought down David Cameron; and the problems of implementing Brexit have defined Theresa May's troubled premiership. No wonder then that British leaders have appeared weary of dealing with EU matters and confronting some of the causes that can make the relationship with the EU a troubled one.

Euroscepticism has defined public and media debate

Public opinion on UK membership has been erratic but support for leaving has never gone below 25 per cent (Ipsos Mori 2016). The British public has therefore never been consistently positive about UK membership. This has not been helped by a media which has moved from supporting membership, albeit with a long-running suspicion of motivations from elsewhere on the continent, to one which has been largely negative, alarmist and sensationalist about its claims of the effect Brussels and the EU has on everyday life in the UK (Daddow 2012).

This media and public suspicion has rarely been met by a strong pro-European message from leading politicians. Tony Blair, one of Britain's most pro-European prime ministers, was once described as an 'anti-anti-European' (Donnelley 2005) because he was willing to attack Eurosceptics but rarely willing to go beyond this by actively making a pro-European case to the British people. Like many prime ministers, when Blair did speak positively of Europe he did so when speaking elsewhere in Europe. Pro-European campaign groups have often been weak in comparison to the better-resourced and -organised Eurosceptic ones. The result has been a political culture in which UK politicians have been willing to take credit for any positive developments in the EU, but on the whole were more inclined to attack it to score easy political points and blame it for unpopular things they might have done anyway. There has also been a strong temptation to blame the EU for the UK's own problems. In 2013, Boris Johnson, then Mayor of London, argued that one of the benefits of leaving the EU would be that 'we would have to recognize that most of our problems are not caused by Brussels' (Johnson 2013).

Britain has been willing to say no

It has not just been in political debate where relations have been strained. Britain has also appeared to be awkward because it has been more willing than others in the EU to voice concerns, delay proposals and, ultimately, say no or veto a deal. It has often been said that other member states were prepared to hide behind that willingness and so allow the UK to play the 'bad cop' in European integration. As a large state Britain could not be easily ignored. Part of this willingness also stems from Britain's majoritarian and more confrontational political system, as discussed earlier. Compromises are publicly avoided, instead happening in the UK system in more private networks within and between government and Parliament (Russell and Gover 2017).

Britain has too often looked to the US

Britain's commitment to a 'special relationship' with the US has posed dilemmas when Europe and the US have moved in opposite directions. When faced with such a dilemma Britain has often been willing to side with the US, as happened under Tony Blair over his decision to back the US over the 2003 Iraq War. This might, as noted earlier, be in order to ensure the US remains committed to Europe, but this has also brought with it accusations that the UK is an American 'Trojan Horse' intended to undermine any EU efforts that do not align with those of the US. For example, efforts to create EU cooperation in foreign, security and defence matters have long been weakened by UK opposition, which stems from a concern that such efforts would undermine NATO and the US commitment to Europe.

Awkward because of its size

Britain is not the only member state to have joined after the EU was founded (19 other member states joined after Britain did in 1973), faced difficulties in joining (countries in Eastern Europe, for example, complained that their accession was a particularly difficult one), feel distant from the core (countries such as Bulgaria and the Baltic states worry about this), be an island with an insular outlook (Malta, Cyprus, Ireland), struggle with the EU's policies, budget or treaties (the citizens of France, the Netherlands, and Ireland have each rejected EU treaties in referendums), have links with the US (Atlanticism is a norm in European politics), seen large numbers of immigrants and asylum seekers (southern European states have been confronted with a far bigger refugee crisis in recent years), or seen a rise in Eurosceptic parties (the leaders of France's Front National have twice – in 2002 and 2017 – made it to the second round of the French presidential election). What has made Britain different and awkward has been the combination of these with its size. As one of the largest member states its votes, budget contributions, and positions matter more than those of many other member states. Whatever the cause of the UK's awkward behaviour, once triggered it cannot be easily ignored.

A quiet European

There are six counterpoints that show how Britain has been a more positive and constructive player in European integration than it is often credited with.

Popularity vs effectiveness

It would be a mistake to confuse popularity with effectiveness. You can be deeply unpopular (or at least have a public appearance of being so) or be seen as awkward, but still be effective and constructive at getting your way. There is little doubt that deeply divisive political differences exist in the UK about membership of the EU and that these have caused tensions with the rest of the EU, but that does not always affect what Britain gets done in Brussels. Britain is widely judged to have been one of the most effective players in getting what it wants: more opt-outs and exclusions than any other member state, a substantial rebate on the budget, renegotiation of its relationship in 1975 and again in 2016 (something no other member state has ever secured) and, as discussed in detail further below, success in shaping a large number of policy areas to British aims.

Has had to assert itself to be taken seriously

Britain's abrasiveness in the earlier phases of its membership was because it had to overcome an unwillingness to take seriously its position as a new member state, which is a common problem faced by all new member states. Britain challenged the accepted order of the EU, one which had been shaped around the needs of France and Germany. One of the strongest backers of Britain's membership had been the European Commission, whose leaders hoped Britain would act as a counter-balance to French efforts to lead the EU. There was therefore an unwillingness on both sides to come to terms with the UK as an EU member state.

Atlanticism is the norm in the EU

Atlanticism has long been a strong norm within European politics. In siding with the US Britain has not always been alone. When Britain decided to support the US over the 2003 Iraq War it was backed by a large number of governments in other EU member states (although, arguably, perhaps not their publics). This division led US Defense Secretary Donald Rumsfeld to talk of 'Old Europe and New Europe', with 'New Europe' including large numbers of new member states from central and Eastern Europe. Like Britain, and indeed most other EU states, they have looked first and foremost to the US for their defence and not to the EU. It was also for this reason that soldiers from Britain and a large number of other EU states fought in the war in Afghanistan. It was to show their countries' commitments to the future of the Atlantic alliance and the security it brings to them, the EU and Europe.

Britain has won on many policy areas

The favourite example of Britain shaping the EU, and one made repeatedly in Britain, is the role Britain played in creating the EU's Single Market and the advancement of economic reforms across Europe. That even some British Eurosceptics have been keen on the UK retaining access to the single market highlights how much some in Britain feel the country invested in the project. As noted earlier, Margaret Thatcher's extolling of the free market in her Bruges Speech was in line with the trend in the EU's political economy. Feelings that the EU had become a servant of Anglo-Saxon free-market economics were so strong in France that they played a part in France's 2005 referendum rejection of the European constitution. Other areas where Britain has been a strong advocate of the EU's work are as diverse as climate change through to animal rights.

Any complaints that Britain has been and can be outvoted in the EU ignores that a Westminster-style zero-sum mentality of win/lose is not how the consensus system of the EU (or of many other EU member states) works. It also ignores that the UK has been closer to most final EU policy outcomes than most other EU governments (Hix 2015b). That Britain has over the past few years found itself somewhat at odds with EU decisions reflects in no small part a disengagement by the UK government, but thanks to the consensus system Britain was on the winning side 87 per cent of the time (Hix and Hagemann 2015).

Has been a good enforcer of EU laws

Britain has not only been good at shaping EU policy, it has also been good at implementing EU law. Part of Britain's difficulties with the EU may stem from the fact that it is too often a good European when it comes to EU law, the enforcement of which has provoked a long litany of complaints in the media. The European Commission can take a member state to the CJEU for failure to fulfil its EU legal obligations. As Figure 2.2 shows, states such as Italy, Greece and Spain have typically had the worst records. The UK's record has long been a good one and during the period 2012–16 equalled that of Germany, the two having the best records of any of the large member states.

The EU's design reflects British aims

Britain's budget rebate might be seen as one of Britain's most awkward and destructive contributions because it enshrines a transactional approach to the EU of *juste retour*. This ignores that the EU has long faced, and will continue to face, awkward demands from its member states for *juste retour*. The UK has been one of the strongest backers of reforming a budget that once favoured *juste retour* for French agriculture, among others. Britain's strong support for EU enlargement, along with that of NATO, has brought about an EU that stretches across most of Europe.

Figure 2.2: Judgements concerning failure of a member state to fulfil its obligations (2012–16)

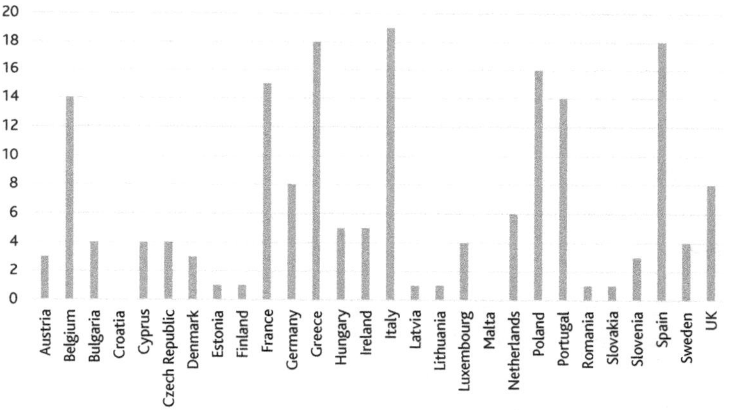

Source: Court of Justice of the European Union (2017).

Support for widening the EU was also premised on the idea it would prevent the deepening of the EU because it would make further integration more difficult. This has meant finding consensus within the EU has become increasingly difficult, creating problems for the EU when trying to manage problems such as those in the Eurozone. This can, to some extent, be blamed on Britain.

At the same time, most of the problems within the Eurozone cannot be attributed to the UK's behaviour. Nor can the need to agree a balanced relationship between the nine non-Eurozone members of the EU and the 19 within the Eurozone. This was not only about relations with the UK, although because of its size the UK was again at the forefront of tensions.

Conclusion

How then can it be explained that a country that on the one hand has often succeeded in getting what it wants from the EU has at the same time been home to such a divisive debate about Europe? There are three groups of reasons.

Historical legacies

UK–EU relations have been defined by a mix of Britain's imperial hubris, strategic lessons from the Second World War, economic links with global markets that dramatically shifted, late membership of an EU set up to serve other member states, and contrasting political and constitutional norms that have caused misunderstandings and tensions.

Finding a role

Being a member of the EU has never, despite what Dean Acheson hoped, been the primary role Britain sought to play in the world. Membership of the EU has not been seen as important to Britain's identity, sovereignty, or social and economic future as it has in many other EU member states.

A constraining public debate

Despite a referendum in 1975, the British public has rarely been engaged in detailed discussion about the EU. British politicians have wanted to avoid raising the topic, in part because of the tensions it confronts Britain with over the roles it wants to play in the world and also because it has become an increasingly toxic subject. It should not be forgotten that across Europe the past decades have seen a move from what has been called a 'permissive consensus' about European integration, in which European publics were content to allow integration, to a 'constraining dissensus' where publics have become more divided and unlikely to sanction integration (Hooghe and Marks 2009). British politics has shown this very clearly.

Further readings

Chris Bickerton, *The European Union: A Citizens Guide* (Penguin, 2016). Provides a penetrating analysis of the complex and byzantine ways in which the EU works.

Christopher Booker and Richard North, *The Great Deception: Can the European Union Survive?* (Continuum, 2005). Gives a strongly Eurosceptic take on Britain's relationship with the EU and the origins and history of European integration.

Timothy Garton-Ash, 'Is Britain European?' *International Affairs*, 77(1), January 2001. Looks at many of the questions surrounding Britain's identity.

Andrew Geddes, *Britain and the European Union* (Macmillan, 2013). A good introductory textbook on UK–EU relations.

Stephen George, *An Awkward Partner: Britain in the European Community* (OUP, 1998). One of the best accounts of Britain's often awkward relationship with European integration.

Daniel Kenealy, John Peterson and Richard Corbett, *The European Union: how does it work?* (OUP, 2015). A comprehensive overview of how the EU works, which combines theoretical analysis with detailed descriptions of the EU's institutions and policies.

John Pinder and Simon Usherwood, *The European Union: A Very Short Introduction* (OUP, 2013). A quick and accessible way to understand the EU, its institutions, its development and the debates that shape it.

Brendan Simms, *Britain's Europe: A Thousand Years of Conflict and Cooperation* (Allen Lane, 2016). Simms's history shows Britain (and before it, England's) struggle to shape Europe.

Stephen Wall, *The Official History of Britain and the European Community, Volume II: From Rejection to Referendum, 1963–1975.* (Routledge, 2012). The definitive history of Britain's application to join the EEC.

Hugo Young, *This Blessed Plot: Britain and Europe from Churchill to Blair.* (Overlook Press, 1998). A classic account of the failings of Britain's political elite to manage UK–EU relations.

THREE

The renegotiation and referendum campaign

Introduction

The chapter reviews developments from January 2013 to the immediate outcome of the referendum result. It outlines why David Cameron committed the Conservative Party to a renegotiation to be followed by a referendum, paying particular attention to the divisions Europe had caused within the Conservative Party but also to the wider changes in UK politics and the EU that added to pressure for some form of vote. Having been able to form a Conservative majority government after winning the 2015 election, David Cameron set about seeking a renegotiated relationship. The chapter explores his efforts to do so, looking into why he sought a renegotiation, what he sought to secure and what was eventually agreed. As the chapter shows, the renegotiation was not easy, but Cameron felt it would play an important part in securing the future of UK–EU relations and winning a referendum. Finally, the chapter turns to the EU referendum itself. Over several sections, the chapter looks at how the campaign unfolded, how the different campaigning groups were structured and what arguments each side put forward as the British prepared to vote in only their third ever nationwide referendum.

Why David Cameron committed to a referendum

On 23 January 2013 David Cameron delivered a speech at the London headquarters of Bloomberg (Cameron 2015). He extolled the connections between the UK and Europe, noting that Britain's history was not only one of an island story but also one deeply connected to the rest of Europe. He pointed to the tensions that had long been present, and identified some of the causes such as differing political systems, contrasting historical experiences, a changing EU and public unease at immigration levels. In particular, he argued that Britain's relations with the rest of the EU had been difficult because they lacked sufficient public backing. He therefore committed the Conservative Party to seeking a renegotiated relationship for the UK with the EU, which would then be put to the British people in an in/out referendum. This would happen if the Conservative Party won the next election, due in May 2015. As he concluded, 'it is time to settle this European question'. Many factors contributed to making the June 2016 referendum happen, but it is to this speech that the referendum can most clearly be traced back. The speech itself was the product of several developments.

Tensions within the Conservative Party

As we have already touched on, the issue of Europe had long been a source of tension within the Conservative Party, and more than anything it helps explain why Cameron committed to a referendum. The issue of Europe had played a big part in the downfall of Margaret Thatcher and the weaknesses and infighting of John Major's government from 1990 to 1997. Euroscepticism had become such a defining trait of Conservative Party politics that local constituency associations were rumoured to reject anyone for selection as a Conservative candidate if, when asked what they thought of the EU, they did not give a strongly Eurosceptic answer. The leadership of the Conservative Party itself had helped fuel this, with leading figures in the party openly fighting over the issue in the 1990s, especially over the ratification of the Maastricht Treaty. Margaret Thatcher herself came to encapsulate a Eurosceptic agenda, with her regretting some of the decisions she had made in office that had furthered European integration, such as the transfer of powers to the EU in the Single European Act. In the 2001 general election, William Hague, then Conservative leader, had campaigned – and lost – largely on a Eurosceptic 'save the Pound' message.

This was the party Cameron won the leadership of in 2005, a victory he secured in part by promising to withdraw Conservative MEPs from the European People's Party (EPP) group within the European Parliament. The EPP was made up of other Conservative and Christian Democrat parties from across the EU, including Germany's Christian Democrat Union, which was the party of German Chancellor Angela Merkel. Many within the Conservative Party were uneasy with what they saw as the EPP's support for further European integration. Many Conservative MEPs objected to the move, worried that such a development would deprive the Conservative Party and any Conservative government of contacts and information from such events and networks as pre-EU summit meetings of the EPP. Nevertheless, for Cameron, the decision seemed a sensible one in order to win over Eurosceptics within the party.

It was to be the first of a series of concessions he would make to Eurosceptics. Others included a commitment to holding a referendum on the Lisbon Treaty, which was to a large extent a repackaging of the European constitution that had been rejected by French voters in a referendum in 2005. This commitment became impossible to deliver on because the treaty had been fully ratified across the EU by the time Cameron became prime minister in 2010. The desire for a referendum on Europe of some kind, however, did not go away. In 2013 Conservative backbench MPs successfully put through the House of Commons a Bill for a referendum, which, though rejected in the House of Lords, did secure support from Cameron. However, such concessions failed to stem demands. William Hague, former Conservative Party leader and Foreign Secretary in Cameron's coalition government, once described Europe as a "ticking time bomb" in the Conservative Party. Cameron's concessions repeatedly failed to defuse the bomb.

The changing UK political landscape

Two developments in UK politics also played a leading part in Cameron's thinking. First, Conservative Eurosceptics were not happy when in the 2010 general election the Conservative Party failed to win a majority and opted to enter into a coalition with the pro-European Liberal Democrats. Being in coalition meant that in his Bloomberg speech, Cameron was committing his Conservative Party to a policy of an in/out referendum and not the UK government. He was, however, able to offer a series of further concessions to those within his party. As part of the coalition agreement drawn up by both parties, the government passed an Act of Parliament requiring a referendum to be held in the event of a transfer of new powers to the EU. The government also undertook a comprehensive review of the powers of the EU, in what was called the Review of the Balance of Competences, of which more below. On the issue of UK–EU relations it was as if the coalition consisted of three parties: the Liberal Democrats, Conservative Eurosceptics, and more moderate Conservative MPs surrounding David Cameron.

Second, if Conservative MPs were uneasy at being in coalition with the pro-European Liberal Democrats it was in no small part because of their concern at the rise of the UK Independence Party. UK politics has seen a number of Eurosceptic parties, such as the Referendum Party, which campaigned in the 1997 general election. But it was the UK Independence Party (UKIP) that emerged as the dominant party. Formed as the 'Anti-Federalist League' in 1991, it changed its named to the UK Independence Party in 1993. From 2006, and thanks in no small part to the leadership of Nigel Farage, the party was able to capture increasing attention, votes and in 2014 the defection of two Conservative MPs (Ford and Goodwin 2014). The party's emergence as a major force in UK politics was seen that year when it came top in the European Parliament elections, sending 24 MEPs to Brussels. This was the first time a party other than the Conservatives or Labour had come top in a national vote since the Liberals had last done so in 1906.

UKIP was soon seen as a clear example of a rise in populism, which is where a political party – and especially its leader –

claims to represent a suffering people against a corrupt elite and dangerous others (who are often foreigners). The party's forthright Euroscepticism, anti-immigration line, commitment to more traditional political values, and mix of British and English nationalism appealed not only to a number of Conservative MPs, but also to Conservative voters. Some Conservatives felt UKIP votes cost the party a majority in the 2010 election. Even if this can be disputed, the pressure the party felt from UKIP was palpable. Committing to an in/out referendum was one way in which some felt UKIP's rise could be curtailed.

Referendums in UK politics

It was not, however, just the Conservative Party feeling the pressure from UKIP or Euroscepticism more broadly. All three main UK parties entered the 2015 general election committed in differing ways to holding a referendum on Britain's relations with the EU. The most pro-European party of the three, the Liberal Democrats, had even fought the 2010 general election on a commitment to holding an in/out referendum, albeit in the event of a new treaty or transfer of powers to the EU. The party had committed itself to such a policy following the difficulty it had faced during the ratification of the Lisbon Treaty, when in 2008 several Liberal Democrat MPs rebelled against a party line of rejecting a referendum on the treaty. The party's eventual compromise was to argue that any vote on the treaty – or any future one – would be taken by many in Britain to be an in/out vote, and as such should be one.

The Labour party under the leadership of Ed Miliband had also begun to feel the pressure from UKIP, especially among traditional working class Labour voters who felt uneasy about Labour's support for immigration (and the Labour government's decision in 2004 to allow free movement from the new Central and Eastern European member states of the EU), and more broadly over such issues as globalisation and identity politics. Labour have been the only party to split over Europe, and some on both the Left and Right of the party remained uneasy at Britain's membership of an organisation they felt would constrain any Labour government's ability to deliver change.

When in 2007, Labour Prime Minister Gordon Brown argued for 'British jobs for British workers' it was pointed out that this policy could infringe EU laws that, in order to encourage pan-EU competition and equal status for all EU citizens, restricted such policies.

That in the 2015 general election all of the UK's main parties were committed in different ways to a referendum on the EU also reflected the growing use of referendums in UK politics. The 1975 referendum on membership of the EEC had been the first time a national referendum had been held, a decision that caused much debate about what it meant for the idea of 'parliamentary sovereignty'. If Parliament is sovereign then should it be bound by the result of a referendum? Referendums had subsequently been held on creating devolved institutions in Scotland (in 1979 and 1997), Wales and Northern Ireland, establishing a Mayor and assembly for Greater London, and devolving power to northeast England, along with a host of smaller referendums on local matters such as the creation of city mayors. In 2011 the second UK-wide referendum was held over whether to change the UK's electoral system from First Past The Post to the Alternative Vote. Scotland's independence referendum in 2014 had been the most contested, and one watched carefully by those focused on UK–EU relations because of its connections to sovereignty and identity politics.

While UK-wide referendums remained rare – the UK has now held three such votes – the increased calls for them and their use at regional and local levels were because direct democracy was seen as a positive way of prompting debate, engaging the public on a single issue in an in-depth way and promoting direct involvement (Tierney 2014). Referendums also have weaknesses, such that political elites and well-funded interests can exploit them, minority groups can be isolated (sometimes their isolated position can be exacerbated), the debate and choice can be oversimplified to a binary answer, they can become a vote on an entirely different matter to that posed on the ballot paper, and the political elite, often in the form of a parliament, will have to deal with an outcome they may disagree with. Another problem with referendums in the UK is that their constitutional standing remains vague. The UK's uncodified constitution makes no direct provision for referendums, meaning they are largely in the gift of the UK's prime minister and government. As a result, the incumbent government have a large say over the timing, the question, the subject and the electorate. The 2016 referendum, for example, could have included a requirement for a two thirds majority or for majorities in all four nations of the UK, but no such conditions were included.

It is important, therefore, to see referendums in the UK as political tools, far more so than in other countries where they may be called as a result of a constitutional requirement enforced by a Supreme Court and have set requirements such as the need for a super-majority of more than two thirds for a proposal to pass. As prime minister, Cameron's decision to call a referendum was something over which he had a great deal of power. As some of his biographers have noted, he could sometimes be prone to taking big political gambles. By 2015, when he pushed ahead with a vote, he had won two previous referendums – the 2011 AV referendum and on Scottish independence – and polling suggested Remain had a very good chance of winning. He used the power he had to call a referendum as a gamble that it would deal with the tensions within his party.

A changing EU

Finally, as Cameron himself argued in his Bloomberg speech, the EU was changing and Britain's relationship with it also needed to change. This was in large part because of developments within the Eurozone of which Britain had decided not to be a part. As the largest non-Eurozone member this meant Britain found itself outside a group of EU states that increasingly appeared to be the core of the EU. A taste of the tensions this could give rise to had occurred in December 2011 when Cameron vetoed a proposal to stabilise the crisis in the Eurozone called the fiscal compact. Cameron felt the move would harm the UK's financial services, but in doing so every other member state of the EU felt Britain was ignoring the greater good of the EU and so bypassed the veto by creating the fiscal compact separately from the EU's institutions. Britain was once again playing the part of an awkward partner, outvoted and isolated.

It appeared to point to a UK headed in one direction while the rest of the EU was headed in another. It helped add to an argument, as Cameron put forward, that the 'democratic consent for Britain's membership has worn wafer thin'. This, he argued, was because the British people's will to continue with the relationship had not been sought since 1975. During that time European integration, which had begun back in the 1950s, had turned the EEC the UK had joined into a European Union of 28 Member States with a single currency and a single market that allowed the free movement of goods, services, capital and, most sensitively of all in the UK case, people. Britain, as a quiet European, might have been an architect of this Union, but sustaining support was becoming, for Cameron, increasingly difficult. That said, the changes the EU had undergone had led to growing demands for referendums across the EU. Only in the UK, however, was this pushed as far as a vote on withdrawal. And the focus of Britain's debate was largely inward looking. Membership of the EU had long been seen, as Cameron himself admitted, as a means to an end, not an end in itself. If that end was some form of political union then the British people's support would need to be tested. As Sir John Major argued when he backed Cameron's policy, by settling the question the vote 'can be cathartic. It can end 40 years of political squabbles.' However, many wondered if this would be more about bringing a cathartic moment to the Conservative Party than the UK.

The UK–EU renegotiation

David Cameron's victory in the 2015 general election, in which the Conservative Party won a slim but working majority in the House of Commons, was unexpected by many. It meant Cameron now had to deliver on his commitment to a renegotiation and an in/out referendum. In June 2015 he informed the President of the European Council, Donald Tusk, that he would do this. Why did he seek a renegotiated relationship, what did he want and what did he get?

A renegotiation as a campaign tactic

As noted above, Cameron had made clear that a changing EU necessitated changes to the UK–EU relationship. But this was not the only reason. There was a simpler tactical reason. Britain's 1975 referendum had also been preceded by a renegotiation, a move that appeared to strengthen the hand of Harold Wilson, the then Labour prime minister. The deal might not have achieved as much as Wilson had hoped, with the issue of Britain's budgetary contributions left unaddressed until Margaret Thatcher negotiated a rebate in the 1980s. But in Britain's zero-sum, transactional approach to the EU a renegotiation meant winning concessions from the EU which could boost the standing of the prime minister and the case for remaining. Opinion polling pointed to a likely boost in support for remaining in the EU if Cameron could repeat Wilson's approach by securing such a deal (Goodwin and Milazzo 2015).

A renegotiated relationship would also provide Cameron with a justification for his own decision to back a vote to remain. He had made clear in his Bloomberg speech that if he did not secure a renegotiation that strengthened Britain's place in the EU then he would not support a vote to remain. Many wondered at his sincerity in making such an argument. But had he not made such a claim then it would have more than likely infuriated Eurosceptics, endangering his leadership. Refusing to rule out the possibility of withdrawing also made sense from a negotiating perspective because the rest of the EU could not think this was a bluff. Cameron's approach was one found across the Conservative Party, where a large number of MPs who had expressed Eurosceptic opinions in the past felt that leaving would be a step too far. A renegotiated relationship offered them a way of balancing their Euroscepticism with a pragmatic commitment to continued membership. Some Eurosceptics had also pushed for Britain to attempt reform, outlining their ideas in a series of reports (Business for Britain 2015). However, some expected such efforts to fail, in turn strengthening their case for a British withdrawal from an organisation they viewed as incapable of reform.

The renegotiation also provided Cameron time to decide the timing of the vote. As noted, UK governments have a large degree of control over referendums. The renegotiation did mean some delay to when the vote could be held, which risked the vote happening mid-term, when governments and their leaders are traditionally at their least popular. But this still provided Cameron and pro-European groups time to prepare for the coming campaigns. Cameron wanted a short campaign to avoid a protracted one as happened in the Scottish campaign, where 18 months of campaigning had allowed time for support for independence to grow.

Identifying areas for renegotiation

In committing his government to a renegotiation, Cameron might have made the argument that a changing EU necessitated a changed UK–EU relationship but it was far from clear what that entailed. He faced several limitations. The previous Conservative-Liberal Democrat coalition government had commissioned an audit of what the EU does and how it had affected the UK called the Review of the Balance of Competences. Drawn up over the course of two years and based on a wide range of evidence submitted from around Britain, Europe and the world, the final 32 reports (see Table 3.1) covered everything from taxation and transport through to economic policy and the environment. It was the most comprehensive review ever undertaken of the effect of the EU on a member state. It concluded that while in some areas there was room for improvement, none of the 32 reports concluded that powers held by the EU needed to be repatriated to the UK. This was not a conclusion welcomed by Eurosceptics, who quickly claimed the reports were a whitewash.

The review did not provide Cameron much by way of ideas as to what to renegotiate given he had promised to curb the EU's growing powers by repatriating powers to the UK. The reports were quietly buried by government, although two groups of people continued to point to them: pro-Europeans and the rest of the EU. To the latter, they were evidence to resist what some elsewhere in the EU increasingly viewed as a renegotiation for the sake of having a renegotiation. This is not to say that

Table 3.1: List of reports in the Review of the Balance of Competences

Report	Date published
Single market	July 2013
Taxation	
Animal health and welfare and food safety	
Health	
Development cooperation and humanitarian aid	
Foreign policy	
Single market: free movement of goods	February 2014
Asylum and non-EU migration	
Trade and investment	
Environment and climate change	
Transport	
Research and development	
Culture, tourism and sport	
Civil judicial cooperation	
Single market: free movement of persons	
Single market: free movement of services	July 2014
Single market: financial services and free movement of capital	
EU budget	
Cohesion	
Social and employment	
Agriculture	
Fisheries	
Competition and consumer policy	
Energy	
Fundamental rights	
Economic and monetary policy	December 2014
Police and criminal justice	
Information rights	
Education, vocational training and youth	
Enlargement	
Voting, consular and statistics	
Subsidiarity and proportionality	

Source: Foreign and Commonwealth Office (2014).

others elsewhere in the EU were entirely happy with how the EU was being run. The problem for the rest of the EU was that any substantial reforms to the Union would more than likely require a new treaty or changes to the existing ones, a move that would trigger referendums in several other EU member states. At the time no other governments wanted to face such votes, with most talking of any large-scale changes not happening for several years at least.

Despite the conclusions of the Review of the Balance of Competences and resistance from elsewhere in the EU, Cameron was able to identify four areas for renegotiation. First, a bigger role for national parliaments in the EU to increase democratic accountability and an exclusion for Britain from the EU's aim of 'an ever closer union'. It is debatable whether a member state can completely opt out of the latter, even though the European Council had in 2014 made clear in a statement that 'the concept of ever-closer union allows for different paths of integration for different countries'. Some Conservative MPs had also demanded that the UK Parliament be given a unilateral veto over new EU laws, something seen as wildly impractical – if only because it would have required a treaty change. For the UK government, rejecting 'ever closer union' and securing a larger role for national parliaments formed part of a wider aim to resist any future transfer of new powers to Brussels.

Second, steps to increase the EU's economic competitiveness such as by opening up the single market in services – an area Britain was particularly strong in – and pushing forward with international trade deals. This was something many governments across the EU supported.

Third, protection for the UK and other non-euro members against the Eurozone behaving as a bloc that ran the EU in a way that unfairly ignored the interests of the UK and the City of London. Some within the Eurozone itself recognised the need to prevent any such discrimination. In the end the EU agreed that non-Eurozone EU member states could retain their own laws for supervising their financial services (and would thus not be forced to change these by a Eurozone caucus) and would also not be obliged to contribute to bailouts inside the Eurozone.

Finally, action on immigration through limits to the freedom for EU citizens to move around Europe by allowing member states to impose restrictions on welfare payments to EU citizens. Restricting numbers, as Cameron had hoped he could convince the EU to allow him to do, was a non-starter as this would infringe the idea of free movement. Instead the focus moved to what in-work benefits EU citizens could claim, including what child benefit could be paid to EU citizens resident in the UK but whose children resided in another member state. Changes to eligibility were eventually agreed, but could only be phased in over a four-year period for new migrants and if there was an exceptional influx of EU migration.

Doubts about the renegotiation

In all four of these areas the EU therefore eventually, albeit with varying degrees of enthusiasm in each area, agreed to changes. However, doubts persisted as to whether the changes were practical, likely to have any immediate effect, or be legally binding without a treaty change. More importantly, there were doubts as to whether it would be enough to sway the UK public or Conservative MPs.

After nine months of negotiations, the deal eventually reached with the rest of the EU in February 2016 had already been condemned by Eurosceptics as weak and not going far enough. As discussed in the next chapter, a large number of Conservative MPs made clear it was insufficient to convince them to back Remain. The press was even stronger in its dismissal of the deal. Opinion polling soon showed it had not delivered the boost the Remain campaign would need to start any referendum campaign on a high. This contrasted with 1975 when Prime Minister Harold Wilson had been able to successfully sell his renegotiation as a success. Cameron's renegotiation was soon forgotten and barely mentioned in the referendum campaign.

The referendum campaign

The official referendum campaign began on 15 April 2016, even if both sides had been preparing for months in advance and arguments about Britain's relations with the EU had been raging much longer. Eventually the Electoral Commission selected two official groups to lead the campaigns: Vote Leave and Britain Stronger in Europe.

Cabinet divisions

Cameron had long faced the same dilemma of cabinet disunity as that faced by Harold Wilson in 1975. His solution was the same: to suspend collective cabinet responsibility, the convention that the cabinet is always united in public. By doing so he allowed ministers to campaign on different sides, something some of them had been prepared to resign over in order to do so. Six of 24 cabinet ministers chose to reject the government's position. Several prominent ministers were already clearly in favour of backing a Leave vote, including Michael Gove, the Lord Chancellor and Chris Grayling, the Leader of the House of Commons. But it was Boris Johnson's decision to back Leave that received the most attention. The former Mayor of London and MP had long been a charismatic media heavyweight with a long history of attacking the EU that dated back to his time as *The Daily Telegraph's* Brussels correspondent in the 1990s. The effect of his decision was to provide Leave with a campaigner of equal stature to the prime minister. Indeed, some felt it was a calculated decision intended to play to Conservative activists who would be more likely to vote for Johnson in any forthcoming leadership race. His decision, like that of other cabinet ministers who backed Leave, created a dilemma for David Cameron, who wanted to avoid any sense of Conservative infighting in order to ease party unity post referendum. For this reason Cameron sought to avoid what were termed 'blue on blue' attacks, whereby Conservative Remain and Leave campaigners would attack one another.

The disunity also sparked tensions over the use of government officials and evidence to back the different campaigns. The official position of the government was to back Remain, which meant David Cameron and his Chancellor of the Exchequer, George Osborne, were able to use HM Treasury and other departments to boost the campaign. This was only until what is known as 'purdah' began on 27 May, which is the four-week period before any vote (such as a general election) when government departments and officials are restricted from publishing anything that may influence the campaign, the aim being to maintain the neutrality of the civil service. Ministers campaigning for Leave felt cheated at being unable to use the same resources before this. These ministers were also angry when at the start of the campaign the government spent £9 million sending a leaflet extolling the merits of the EU to every British household. Cameron argued that as Her Majesty's Government's position was to back Remain then it had a responsibility to communicate this to the British people.

The Remain campaign

The official Remain campaign, Britain Stronger in Europe, adopted a strategy with a clear and concerted line of attack based on the economic costs of Brexit. In doing so it deployed a wide range of sources that included HM Treasury, the International Monetary Fund (IMF), the Bank of England and various international credit rating agencies. A peak was reached when US President Obama on a visit to the UK argued that the UK's membership of the EU was a core part of the wider multilateral order and that by leaving the UK risked weakening this order, isolating itself, and finding itself at the back of the queue for a trade deal with the US. Leave campaigners dubbed all this 'Project Fear' after the name given to the campaign in Scotland that had opposed independence, which had also focused heavily on the possible economic cost. Indeed, it was the winning experience of those opposed to Scottish independence that Cameron and the Remain campaign hoped to replicate in the EU referendum. Other pro-Remain arguments such as the place of the EU in European peace, of its role in bringing Europe together in 'ever closer union' were occasionally made, but the focus was on the benefits of a transactional, business-like partnership rather than a relationship with the rest of the EU that should be embraced for some greater good.

The economic cost was the one issue the Remain campaign could unite around, it being a conglomeration of campaigners from the Conservatives, Labour, Liberal Democrats and others. Pro-European campaign groups do not have an illustrious history in UK politics. They have generally been weak, lacked funding, been divided and often received sporadic, if any, support from prime ministers. While not based around one political party, the leadership of the campaign rested more with the prime minister, but without the full backing of the Conservative Party, which remained officially neutral. However, as Chapter Four explores, the Remain campaign struggled because Labour leader Jeremy Corbyn appeared hesitant in his support for Remain, the Liberal Democrats were still recovering from being almost wiped out at the 2015 general election and other Remain-backing parties such as the Scottish National Party (SNP), Greens or Plaid Cymru were uneasy (as were members of Labour and the Liberal Democrats) at sharing a campaign with David Cameron, whose domestic policies, and some aspects of his European policies, they had strongly opposed.

The Leave campaigns

While there were official Leave and Remain campaign groups, as in any campaign there were numerous groups and individuals campaigning around both of them. Vote Leave, the official Leave campaign, was a cross-party campaign run by Matthew Elliot and Dominic Cummings, with some of its most prominent political supporters being Conservative politicians such as Boris Johnson and Michael Gove, Labour MP Giesela Stuart and UKIP's sole MP, Douglas Carswell. It was connected to a number of groups including Labour Leave and Business for Britain.

These groups formed part of a much wider network of Eurosceptic groups, which reflected the long history of British Eurosceptics better organising themselves than pro-European groups, such as 'Grassroots Out' and 'The Leave Alliance'. The most prominent alternative Leave group was that of Leave.EU, a group connected to UKIP and funded by Aaron Banks, a millionaire businessman who had also been the leading funder of UKIP, and Richard Tice, a property entrepreneur. Leave.EU lost to Vote Leave in the decision by the Electoral Commission over who should be the official Leave campaign. This caused tensions between the two groups, but it also allowed a series of messages to be communicated to different groups of voters instead of one single message (and mainly about economics) as the Remain campaign often tried to put out.

Vote Leave initially focused on the economic and sovereignty arguments, not least the ability of a non-EU UK to negotiate its own trade deals and more freely adapt to a changing global economy. This leaned more towards a libertarian, global outlook. They were also keen to highlight the extent to which the UK was being drawn into a political union as opposed to an economic one; something they argued a Remain vote would embolden and commit Britain to despite the claims of Remain campaigners that the UK could opt out of such moves. Quickly, however, Vote Leave also moved into the immigration territory, focusing some of its campaign on free movement and the possibility of countries such as Turkey joining the EU. This, to some extent, aligned with the message of Leave.EU. Reflecting its UKIP connections, Leave.EU played heavily on immigration and a message that Britain should 'take back control' of both its laws and borders. This drew on identity politics, especially the idea the UK was being transformed – through multiculturalism, gay rights, globalisation and liberalism – in ways many UKIP supporters were deeply uneasy with.

Immigration was the predominant issue in the debate

In the lead-up to the UK–EU renegotiation Cameron had set out to achieve a more radical set of reforms on immigration, ideally being able to limit the numbers entering the UK from the rest of the EU, over which the UK had less control than it did on those entering from outside the EU. Back in 2010, Cameron had said he wanted to see net immigration to the UK drop below 100,000 a year, a figure his governments had repeatedly failed to deliver on, as shown in Figure 3.1. His commitment was a result of growing public unease at levels of migration to the UK, most notably since Central and Eastern European countries had been admitted to the EU in 2004.

Figure 3.1: Net migration to the UK by nationality

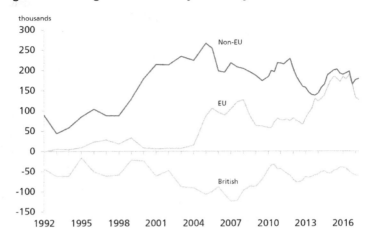

Source: Hawkins (2017, 13) licensed under the Open Parliament Licence v3.0.

The Leave campaigns were able to draw on people's concerns about immigration with regard to security, identity, welfare, cost, border control and, thanks to Cameron's failure to deliver the 100,000 target, the repeated failures of government. Cameron's failure to secure a radical change to the UK's immigration policy vis-à-vis the EU, with only small technical changes achieved, reinforced a message from Eurosceptics that the EU could not be changed. As such Cameron and the renegotiation had failed to address what polling showed was the main concern of voters as the campaign began. It merely reinforced an image of an EU that would not change and a UK government beholden to it and unable to deliver what the people wanted.

A post-truth political campaign

All political campaigns entail lies, half-truths and misleading statements. The EU referendum was certainly no different, although unlike in a general election there is no set date for another vote at which those who lied can be held accountable by the electorate. Both sides made claims that were much disputed. The claim by George Osborne that Britain was doomed for recession that would lead to him having to call a 'punishment budget' if it voted for Leave was a good example of how the Remain campaign made a series of claims based on questionable predictions.

The Leave campaign also put forward a large number of questionable points, offered a range of verifiably fact-free claims and ones that were intended to distort. They were able to make promises and claims which (since they were not and not about to be the government) they could neither guarantee nor be held to account for. Most notorious was the claim, as shown down the side of the Vote Leave campaign's bus that '[w]e send the EU £350 million a week, let's fund our NHS [National Health Service] instead'. This claim was regularly debunked, with the UK Statistics Authority saying it was misleading and the Institute for Fiscal Studies saying it was 'absurd'. Nigel Farage admitted the day after the vote that the figure, which had been used by Vote Leave and not by Leave.EU, of which Farage had been a part, was a mistake and the money for the NHS would more than likely not materialise. As wrong as the claim was, it succeeded in shifting the campaign onto two things the general public can easily understand: money and the NHS. Other Leave campaigners also engaged in what is often termed 'post-truth' politics where facts are ignored and emotion and impulse reign. Nigel Farage himself was accused of stoking racist feelings with some of Leave.EU's anti-immigration posters.

At the same time, questions must be asked as to why such a political climate had emerged. The Leave campaigns were able to often play on the lack of credibility British politicians and the wider elite had acquired in recent years. Cameron himself, as discussed earlier, seemed insincere when he moved from saying he was prepared to vote Leave if he failed to secure the renegotiation he wanted to arguing that a Remain vote was vital for the security of Britain and her allies. The financial crisis had also caught so many unawares, including those in government and the wider elite. The British military, despite gallant efforts by those serving in it, had struggled and in some cases failed in Iraq and Afghanistan. Michael Gove was much attacked for his claim that 'people in this country have had enough of experts', but looking back on the previous few years it was difficult not to conclude that Britain's experts had not delivered their best. In the period since the vote a series of allegations of Russian interference, of spending irregularities and others have also raised questions about the result (Bradshaw 2017). UK politics reached a new low when, only a few days before the referendum, a far-right extremist screaming "This is for Britain" shot dead Jo Cox, a Labour MP and Remain campaigner.

Further readings

Aaron Banks's *The Bad Boys of Brexit* (Biteback, 2016), one of UKIP's leading funders, does not hold back in his account of the Brexit campaign.

Owen Bennett's *The Brexit Club* (Biteback, 2016) takes a close look into the victorious but often deeply fractious Leave campaigns.

Business for Britain, *Change or Go: How Britain Would Gain Influence and Prosper Outside an Unreformed EU* (Business for Britain, 2015). A weighty and comprehensive report published by one of the leading Leave-supporting organisations a year before the referendum.

Matt Goodwin and Caitlin Milazzo, *Britain, the European Union and the Referendum: What Drives Euroscepticism?* (Chatham House, December 2015). An analysis from 2015 of the driving forces behind Euroscepticism that would eventually push Leave to victory.

Daniel Hannan, *Why Vote Leave* (Head of Zeus, 2016). Aligns more closely with the more outward-looking, libertarian side to the Leave campaign.

Adam Hug, *Renegotiation, Reform and Referendum: Does Britain have a European Future?* (Foreign policy Centre, February 2014). A good overview of many of the debates in the lead-up to the renegotiation and referendum.

Harry Mount, *Summer Madness: How Brexit Split the Tories, Destroyed Labour and Divided the Country* (Biteback, 2017). Another account published soon after the vote.

Craig Oliver, *Unleashing Demons: The Inside Story of Brexit* (Hodder and Stoughton, 2016). Cameron's Communications Director and a key player in the Remain campaign published an excellent insider account.

Tim Oliver, 'To Be or Not To Be in Europe: Is That the Question?' *International Affairs*, 91(1), January 2015. Looks at the nature of the question Cameron set out in his Bloomberg speech and questions whether a referendum was the best means with which to answer it.

Tim Shipman's *All Out War: The full story of how Brexit sank Britain's political class* (William Collins, 2016). Remains the best account of both the Remain and Leave campaigns.

FOUR

The referendum result

Introduction

There has been a great deal of analysis into how the British people voted in the referendum of 23 June 2016. This chapter sets out some of the main points that can be put forward about how the British people voted. In particular, it highlights some of the key differences – in terms of identity, education, outlook, occupation and location – of Remain and Leave voters. Having identified how the British people voted, the chapter then looks at the various reasons given for why the British people voted as they did. It identifies eight main reasons why the Leave campaign prevailed. The chapter ends with a brief discussion of what happened next by outlining a series of Brexit processes – in the UK, Europe and internationally – that began to unfold and which are unpacked in the following chapters.

How Britain voted

On Thursday 23 June 2016 British voters (who had not already voted by post) were faced with the ballot paper reproduced in Figure 4.1.

The result that emerged in the early hours of Friday morning and which was confirmed after several days of counting and recounting showed 17,410,742 had voted Leave while 16,141,241 had voted Remain. This was a victory for Leave of 51.9 per cent to 48.1 per cent. The difference was 1,269,501 votes, or just 3.9 per cent of those who voted. This was on a turnout of 72.2 per cent, which means the vote was decided by the votes of 2.7 per cent of the overall electorate (Electoral Commission 2016).

Figure 4.1: Referendum ballot paper

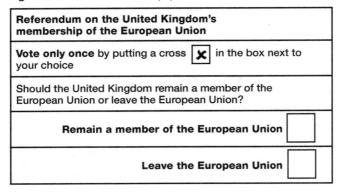

The results and subsequent polling analysis by psephologists and pollsters highlighted a range of patterns and links that show how people voted and give some indicators as to why. Below are some of the most commonly noted ones, drawn from a number of different sources that collected data on the day of the referendum or in periods before or immediately after it.

Clear geographical differences

When looking at the UK's constituent nations and regions along with House of Commons constituencies, an immediate contrast appears (Hennig and Dorling 2016). Remain voting areas included Scotland (62 per cent for Remain), Northern Ireland (55.8 per cent for Remain), London (59.9 per cent Remain) and some areas such as Manchester (60.4 per cent for Remain), and Liverpool (58.2 per cent for Remain). Leave-voting areas could be found across England (53.4 per cent for Leave) and Wales (52.5 per cent for Leave) and in some cities such as Birmingham (50.4 per cent for Leave). Gibraltar, the only UK overseas territory to be part of the EU, voted overwhelmingly in favour of Remain (96 per cent for Remain).

Figure 4.2: Leave and Remain by constituency

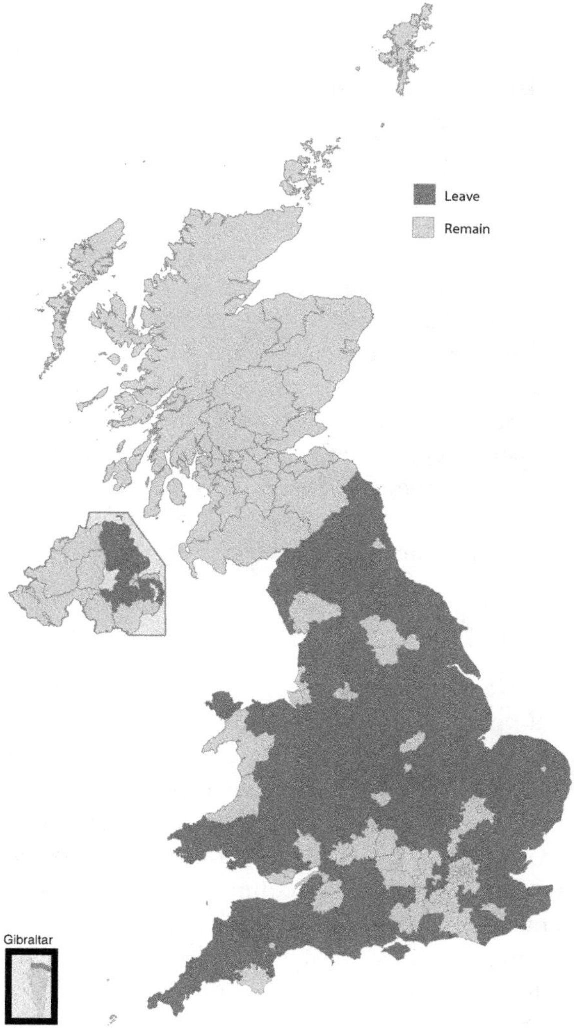

Source: Mirrorme22 et al (2016).

Many constituents voted differently from their MPs

Four hundred and seventy nine MPs (about 74 per cent of the House of Commons) publicly pledged their support to Remain (BBC 2016b). Thanks to the work of Chris Hanretty (2016 and 2017a), it is clear that a large number of MPs now found themselves representing constituencies where a majority of their constituents had voted differently from them. Examples include former Labour leader, Ed Miliband, MP for Doncaster North, where 72 per cent of those who voted probably backed Leave. Another would be David Lidington, then Minister of State for Europe and Conservative MP for Aylesbury, where 52 per cent probably backed Leave. A smaller number of MPs who had supported Leave also found themselves representing seats where a majority of their constituents had voted for Remain. Examples include Gisela Stuart, Labour MP for Birmingham Edgbaston, where probably around 43 per cent voted Leave, and Zac Goldsmith, Conservative MP for Richmond, where 28 per cent probably voted Leave (all figures taken from Hanretty (2017b)). As discussed in Chapter Five, this caused problems for these MPs when they faced votes in Parliament on implementing Brexit: did they follow their personal position or what a majority of their constituents had voted for?

A lot of change between 1975 and 2016

In the 1975 referendum, the British people were asked: 'Do you think the UK should stay in the European Community (Common Market)?' The overall result was a clear win for Yes, which secured 67.2 per cent of the support of those who voted. Voters in Scotland and Northern Ireland were the least enthusiastic, although majorities of 58.4 per cent and 52.1 per cent in each still voted Yes (compared to 62 per cent and 55.8 per cent who voted Remain in 2016). In 1975, it was voters in England who most strongly backed Yes, with 68.7 per cent voting to stay in the European Community. By 2016, it was the English who were the strongest supporters of Leave, with 53.4 per cent of them backing an exit from the EU.

The figure for England hides some large changes within the different areas of England. It is not possible to make exact comparisons of how English regions voted in 1975 and 2016 because the 1975 vote was counted in 47 counting areas that do not align perfectly with the 2016 regions (Butler and Kitzinger

1976). However, it is possible to highlight the degree of change by focusing on some specific areas.

In 1975 the counting area that voted most strongly in favour of Yes was North Yorkshire, where 76.2 per cent voted Yes, with 23.7 per cent voting No. In 2016, using votes drawn from counting areas in the Yorkshire and the Humber region and the North East region, it is possible to recreate (albeit not absolutely accurately) the 1975 North Yorkshire counting area. In 2016 only 44 per cent of voters in this area voted Remain, with Leave winning 56 per cent of the vote. Similar changes can be seen across large swathes of England, including in Greater London. In 2016, 59.9 per cent of Londoners backed Remain. That compares with the 66.7 per cent of Londoners who in 1975 backed Yes.

The results point to significant change across the UK in attitudes towards the EU, and especially so in England. That said, as Clements (2017) has shown, the 1975 and 2016 referendum results also shared similarities, such as strong support for Yes/ Remain among those with higher socio-economic status.

Table 4.1: Referendum results in 1975 and 2016

	1975: Do you think the UK should stay in the European Community (Common Market)?		2016: Should the UK remain a member of the EU or leave the EU?	
	YES	NO	REMAIN	LEAVE
UK	67.2	32.8	48.1	51.9
England	68.7	31.3	46.6	53.4
Northern Ireland	52.1	47.9	55.8	44.2
Scotland	58.4	41.6	62.0	38.0
Wales	64.8	35.2	47.5	52.5
Turnout (UK)	63.9%		72.2%	

Sources: Audickas, Hawkins and Cracknell (2017, 81–82); BBC (2016a); Butler and Kitzinger (1976).

The referendum was decided in England

The map of the UK shown in Figure 4.2 reveals some of the areas of support for Remain and Leave, for example majorities of those who voted in Scottish constituencies did so for Remain. However, it does not show the levels of support in terms of the actual numbers of Britons who voted in the different areas of the UK. England is just under 54 per cent of the UK landmass, but home to 84 per cent of the UK's population. As Figure 4.3 therefore shows, England was always going to be the centre of the vote. Figure 4.3, which lists the English regions by the total size of their electorate, also better illustrates the size of the vote in London, something Figure 4.2 does not convey.

Figure 4.3: Total votes cast in each UK region

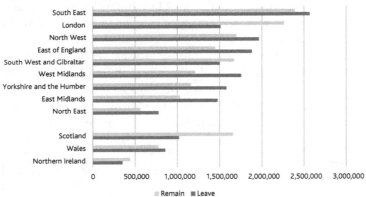

Source: BBC (2016a).

There were clear social and age differences in how people voted

While no clear differences were registered between men and women, with both voting 48 to 52 per cent, there were clear differences between age groups and class. Voters under the age of 34 were more likely to vote Remain and older groups likely to vote Leave. Leave support grew with age, the crossover point being in the late 40s.

In terms of social class, AB, who are professionals and higher or intermediate managerial such as lawyers, doctors, academics and head teachers (about 22 per cent of the population) were the only social group to vote Remain. All other groups registered support for Leave, with C2 (skilled manual positions) and D/E (semi or unskilled labourers and the unemployed) being the most likely to vote Leave (these two groups making up about 47 per cent of the population). The remaining 31 per cent of British voters, who can be classified as C1 (supervisory, clerical, administration and junior management) split in a similar way to the overall national vote.

Figure 4.4: Demographic breakdown of voters

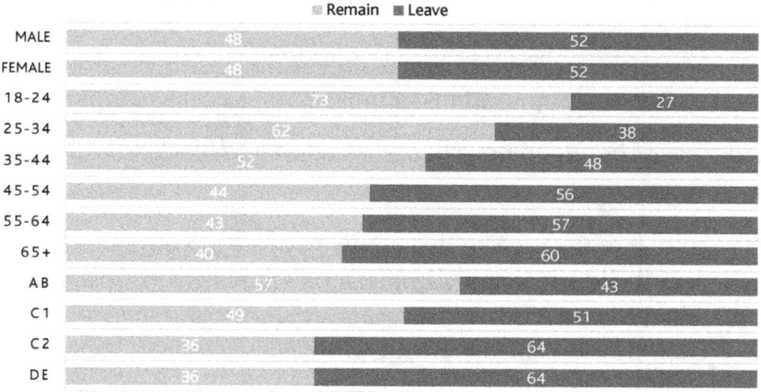

Source: Ashcroft and Culwick (2016).

Educational background was a strong indicator of voting intention

Educational background has emerged as one of the key background factors to explaining how Britons cast their votes. A Briton with only GCSEs or lower (the General Certificate in Secondary Education being the outcome of the final set of exams sat by students at 16 years of age in England, Wales and Northern Ireland) the more likely they were to vote Leave. The more a Briton was qualified – not least if a graduate of a university – the more likely they were to vote Remain. That older voters backed Leave also reflects that they were born before the era of mass qualifications in education. Leave votes were higher in areas where the number of educational qualifications was low, while those with high numbers of graduates saw low levels of support for Leave. This also translated into stronger support among those in professional occupations and those with higher levels of median hourly pay.

Figure 4.5: Educational levels of remain and leave voters

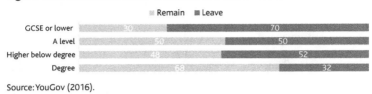

Source: YouGov (2016).

Alignment between newspaper position and readers' voting intention

The power of the press to shape how people vote might be much less than it once was, but a link can be seen between readership and editorial lines on how to vote. The *Guardian*, *Financial Times* and *Daily Mirror* backed Remain, with *The Times* and *The Sunday Times* split in favour of Leave and Remain. The *Daily Express*, *Daily Mail*, *The Sun* and the *Daily Telegraph* all backed Leave. As noted earlier, the UK press is largely on the Right and has grown increasingly Eurosceptic since 1975 when all of the major newspapers backed a vote to remain in the then EEC.

Figure 4.6: Leave vote by newspaper read most often

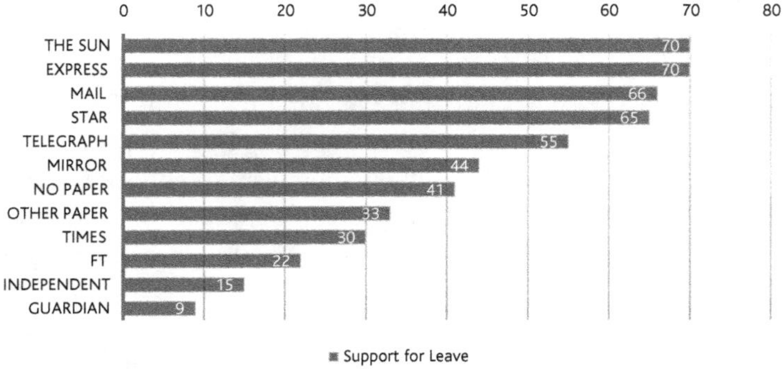

Source: Swales (2016).

Large numbers of people voted differently from the position of the party they voted for in the 2015 election

As Figure 4.7 shows, the figure for Conservative voters shows the degree to which Cameron failed to carry the majority support of his own party and its voters. All of the other parties (except UKIP) also saw large numbers of their voters vote for Leave despite the parties themselves backing Remain. As discussed further below, the number of Labour voters who backed Leave has led to accusations that Labour leader Jeremy Corbyn failed to do enough to win over Labour voters. At the same time, a similar percentage of SNP voters also backed Leave despite SNP leader and Scottish First Minister Nicola Sturgeon being forthright in her support for Scotland and the UK remaining in the EU. Just under a third of Liberal Democrat voters and a quarter of Green voters backed Leave despite those parties' clear and long-standing commitments to Britain's membership of the EU.

Figure 4.7: Voting preference and 2015 general election vote

Source: Ashcroft and Culwick (2016).

Voters who identified as English voted strongly for Leave

A range of authors have noted links between English nationalism and Euroscepticism (Barnett 2017). What has driven this is discussed in later chapters. As Lord Ashcroft's polling revealed (shown in Figure 4.8), 79 per cent of respondents who identified themselves as English voted Leave. Those who identified more as British were more likely to vote Remain.

Figure 4.8: Votes according to strength of English and British identity

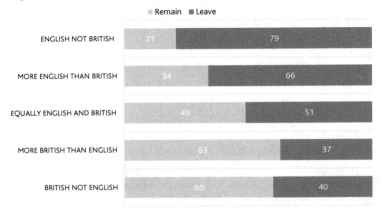

Source: Ashcroft (2016).

Remain and Leave voters are divided by values

Clear attitudinal differences can be identified between Remain and Leave voters. Large numbers of Leave voters held negative views of multiculturalism, social liberalism, feminism, environmentalism, globalisation and immigration. Remain voters on the other hand viewed these more positively (Ashcroft and Culwick 2016). As Erik Kaufmann (2016) has shown, it is not geographical location or social class that is the best indicator of whether a person votes for Leave or Remain, but their attitude to such things as the death penalty. Irrespective of income, the likelihood somebody votes Leave increases from 20 per cent for those opposed to the death penalty to 70 per cent for those who support it. In short, poor and rich people who are opposed to capital punishment more than likely voted Remain, while poor and rich people who support capital punishment more than likely voted Leave. Similar findings can be seen in attitudes to whipping criminals. As Kaufmann points out, this highlights the importance of authoritarian–libertarian or order–openness axes in UK politics.

Views and experiences of immigration were important dividing lines

In line with many other pollsters, Lord Ashcroft's polling (see Figure 4.9) showed that 79 per cent of those who viewed immigration as a force for good voted Remain, while a similar percentage – 80 per cent – of those who viewed it as a force for ill voted Leave. Given the prominent place of immigration in the campaign it might seem strange that, as shown in Figure 4.11, some Leave voters did not necessarily live in areas that had seen large levels of immigration. However, in those areas that had seen sudden and large increases in immigration there was a strong vote for Leave. Support for Remain in areas that had high levels of immigration can be explained by their longer experience of immigration: for example, many of the districts in Figure 4.10 are located in London, a global city. Fifteen of the 20 areas with the lowest levels of EU migration backed Leave, while 18 of the 20 with the highest levels of migration backed Remain (Goodwin and Heath 2016).

Figure 4.9: Positive and negative views of immigration. Measured by response to the question: 'Do you think of each of the following as being a force for good, a force for ill, or a mixed-blessing?'

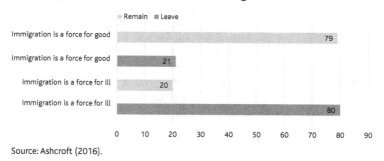

Source: Ashcroft (2016).

Figure 4.10: The 10 districts with the lowest Leave votes and the percentage of non-UK residents in each

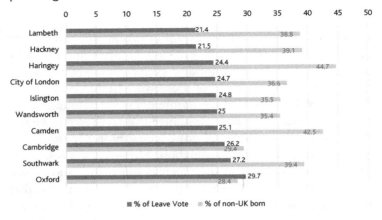

Source: Lawton and Ackrill (2016).

Figure 4.11: The 10 districts with the highest Leave votes and the percentage of non-UK residents in each

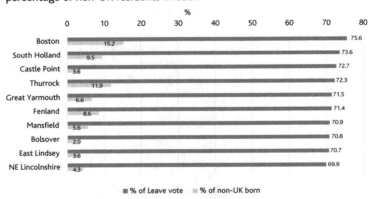

Source: Lawton and Ackrill (2016).

Summaries of the average Leave and Remain voter

Based on the above, the average Leave voter left school before the age of 17, was above the age of 44, had few if any educational qualifications, worked in a less-secure, low-income job, lived in an area that had not seen high levels of immigration, identified themselves strongly as English and held an authoritarian-leaning political outlook. Polling by Lord Ashcroft (Ashcroft and Culwick 2016) showed their main concerns were taking back control, especially of immigration and borders; that remaining would leave Britain vulnerable to the EU's decisions and future; and that by leaving the UK would benefit economically though new trade links. By contrast the average Remain voter was under the age of 44, had more educational qualifications, worked in a secure and above-average-paid job, identified themselves as British and more liberal in their outlook. As Ashcroft's polling revealed, their first concern was the economic cost of leaving, but they also felt the UK had the best deal already, worried leaving would isolate the UK, and felt some – but by no means strong – commitment to the EU and its ideals.

Why Britain voted Leave

As discussed in the next chapter, why Britain voted Leave and, more urgently from a practical point of view, what that should mean in terms of the exit deal and new relationship to be sought with the EU, became the defining debate in British politics after the vote. Numerous arguments and theories have been put forward to explain why the British people voted as they did. This section outlines nine commonly cited reasons why the British people backed Leave.

Cameron's renegotiation failed to convince

As discussed in Chapter Three, Cameron had, with some difficulty, managed to secure a deal over the UK's relationship from the rest of the EU. This contained a series of commitments by the rest of the EU on matters such as competition, the role of national parliaments, acceptance the UK would not be bound by 'ever closer union', and changes to what welfare benefits EU citizens in the UK could claim. While not insubstantial, they failed to live up to the scale of the renegotiation he had promised to seek in his Bloomberg speech and during the 2015 election. It failed to convince three groups.

The first group whose support it failed to secure was Cameron's own parliamentary party. Conservative backbench MPs and ministers had been restless throughout the renegotiation, many doubting either Cameron's commitment to seeking a genuine renegotiation and/or the EU's willingness to grant one. Jacob Rees-Mogg MP, a strong advocate of Britain's withdrawal, described a draft of the renegotiation as 'thin gruel', claiming, once the final deal was made clear, that 'the thin gruel has been further watered down'. In the end 138 (42 per cent) of the 330 Conservative MPs backed Leave.

The second group was the Conservative-backing media, who were even less forgiving than some members of the Conservative Party. *The Sun* claimed the deal 'stinks' and the *Daily Mail* branded it 'a joke'. It was an early sign of how critical the Conservative-leaning press would be of the Prime Minister and the Remain campaign.

The final group it failed to connect with were the public and Conservative voters, who were unconvinced by it. As seen above, a majority of Conservative voters backed Leave, in no small part because their faith in Cameron as a leader was not as strong as it had been in the 2015 election.

The renegotiation also hobbled the Remain campaign. Campaigning could not get under way until the negotiations were complete. While this might have reflected Cameron's belief that the renegotiation was crucial to winning the final vote, it also meant it was time wasted that he could have spent at home campaigning or building a stronger coalition for the Remain campaign. The renegotiation also exposed tensions within the Remain camp. Parties such as Labour and the Liberal Democrats were uneasy at backing a deal that appeared to pander to anti-immigration feelings or the needs of the City.

Finally, in focusing on the renegotiation Cameron may have overlooked the UK's ability to unilaterally deliver a series of changes that could have had an effect on the campaign. As covered in Chapter Two, Britain has been a quiet European that has a positive history of enforcing EU laws. A willingness to challenge or ignore EU laws, guidelines or conventions could have seen Britain unilaterally make a series of changes to its benefit system and such symbolic but highly emotive issues as the colour of UK passports (which in 1988 Britain had, despite not being legally required to, changed from blue to red, something much lamented by some Eurosceptics). By the time this became clear the campaign was already under way and the renegotiation had quickly been forgotten, playing no prominent role in the campaign.

The Leave campaign had stronger messengers

Cameron's struggle to sell the renegotiation reflected weaknesses surrounding him and other Remain campaigners compared to those on the Leave side (Grant 2016). As the campaign approached, polling showed Cameron was a leading asset for Remain (Clarke, Goodwin and Whiteley 2017). The potential for him to play a leading role had been seen in the 2011 AV referendum. Having remained largely silent in the early phases of that campaign, his decision to publicly campaign against the change was seen as a pivotal moment that swung the vote.

By 2016 his reputation was no longer what it had been in 2011. He might have unexpectedly delivered a victory in the 2015 general election, but to many voters – especially non-Conservative ones – he and the Chancellor of the Exchequer, George Osborne, were strongly associated with a status quo of austerity and government cuts. Austerity, in particular, had hit many people across the UK and, as discussed further below, a common complaint during the referendum was that too many people had been left behind economically and ignored by those in UK politics. Cameron's reputation had been further damaged by revelations only a few months before the referendum when the leaked 'Panama Papers' revealed that he had profited from his late father's offshore investment fund, which had never paid taxes in the UK. It reinforced an appearance that he and other members of a metropolitan pro-EU elite were distant and privileged.

Other Remain campaigners, such as former Liberal Democrat leader Nick Clegg were electorally tarnished or, in the form of Labour leader Jeremy Corbyn, lacked the enthusiasm shown by leading Leave campaigners or were portrayed poorly in the press. Where Remain was able to count on popular and vocal campaigners they were mostly in the UK's countries and regions, such as Nicola Sturgeon, the First Minister of Scotland, and Sadiq Khan, the Mayor of London.

By contrast, the Leave campaigns were able to count on a mix of messengers at the UK level, who, while not without their own weaknesses, did have two advantages. First, Boris Johnson's decision to back Leave was a key moment in boosting the Leave campaign. Without him, the official Leave campaign would have lacked a strong, charismatic figurehead who could – and did – outshine Cameron. Second, when Johnson was combined with several other members of the Cabinet, such as Michael Gove and Priti Patel, the Leave campaign was able to not only deploy senior politicians, but also, in the form of Conservative ministers, give the appearance of a government in waiting, albeit one which had the advantage that when pushed it was able to disclaim any actual responsibilities about delivering on its promises.

The Leave campaign was better organised and run

As in any campaign, neither side ran campaigns that were without a series of weaknesses and mistakes, but in the EU referendum it was the Leave campaign that proved more professional and focused on achieving its aim. The official Remain campaign, Britain in Europe, was not able to draw on as large a range of activists and groups compared to the Leave campaigns, which were able to draw on a long history of Eurosceptic groups and networks. A concentration of decision making in Downing Street weakened its ability to respond, not least to attacks from Conservative Leave campaigners. Jeremy Corbyn's hesitations about backing the EU, of which he had long been a Left-wing critic, weakened Labour's contribution to the Remain campaign. He was also a leader regularly portrayed in the media as weak and ineffective.

By contrast, one of the main advantages of the Leave campaigns lay in their many factions. Competition between Vote Leave, the official Leave campaign, and Leave. EU meant they were able to perform a flanking manoeuvre on the Remain campaign, with different messages targeted at different groups of voters. Vote Leave, with Boris Johnson and Labour's Gisela Stuart MP, delivered a Leave message that reached beyond the voters UKIP was able to appeal to. As Clarke, Goodwin and Whiteley (2017) noted, Vote Leave's message lacked many of the negatives associated with Farage and UKIP that repelled a wide range of voters. At the same time, Leave.EU, with Nigel Farage at the forefront, was able to secure the support of such voters thanks to its focus on immigration and a more English nationalist slant. UKIP had been an important development in the Eurosceptic campaign. In the 1975 referendum there had been no organised Eurosceptic party around which a series of networks and campaigning could be built.

This awkward setup for the Leave campaigns was not without its tensions. Dominic Cummings, one of the leaders of Vote Leave, went so far as to argue that Farage's lack of appeal to many swing voters may have cost Leave some votes. Vote Leave was also able to draw on the experiences of campaigners such as Matthew Elliot and Cummings, who had played leading roles in the 'No to AV' referendum campaign in 2011. As Charles Grant (2016) argued, their ruthless campaigning – such as over the claim Britain sends the EU £350 million a week – 'exploited the fact that in political advertising, unlike commercial advertising, there are no penalties for untruths'.

Economic arguments proved insufficient to win the vote

The decision by Cameron and Britain Stronger in Europe to focus on the economic costs and uncertainties of Brexit was effective in the sense that, as Clarke, Goodwin and Whiteley (2017) have shown, even a large proportion of Leave voters felt there would be an economic cost from leaving. However, their campaign overly focused on this message, leading to widespread doubts as to the reliability of the figures put forward and giving their campaign a feeling of pessimism and lack of faith in the UK.

While an extensive number of businesses did warn of the potential costs, the degree of support was much less compared to the overwhelming support given by the business community in the 1975 vote. A number of firms were uneasy at taking sides, fearing a backlash from some shareholders. Memories of the 2008 financial crisis meant banks and large firms in the City were unlikely to receive a warm hearing from the British people. Small and medium-sized enterprises, which make up the majority of the British business community, were also divided, with many such firms lacking the clear direct links with the rest of the EU that large multinational firms had.

The economic argument also overlooked that the economic situation was already bleak for many Leave voters in deprived areas of the UK. This was something Professor Anand Menon (2016) of King's College London discovered when during a talk in Newcastle he asked his audience to imagine the potential hit to the UK's GDP from Brexit. "That's your bloody GDP. Not ours," replied a member of the audience. Remain also struggled to counter the two economic messages from the various Leave campaigns, which on the one side offered a political economy of neoliberalism, globalisation and a love of free markets while the other looked more to protectionism, nationalisation and restricted mobility for labour and capital.

Remain had no answer to arguments about immigration

Polls had shown for some time that immigration had overtaken the economy as the number-one concern of most voters (Clarke, Goodwin and Whiteley 2017). This was problematic for the Remain campaign because attitudes to immigration and free movement had become strongly associated with Euroscepticism (Evans and Menon 2017). This was a stark contrast to the 1975 vote, when immigration had barely been an issue. In the face of this the Remain campaign found it almost impossible to counter the Leave campaigns' argument that the only way for the UK to control immigration was to leave the EU. As discussed in the previous chapter, David Cameron had in 2012 committed to bringing net migration to the UK down to under 100,000 a year, a figure the UK never came close to achieving during his time in office because of large number of migrants from the rest of the EU and from outside it (see Figure 3.1). Cameron's failure to deliver on this commitment became a recurring theme of UK politics and the referendum. Remain campaign arguments that the economic data pointed to net gains for the UK from immigration had little traction when the various Leave campaigns were able to connect immigration to a whole set of fears about security, identity politics (not least English nationalism) and economic uncertainty, especially stagnant wages. Labour especially had a problem focusing on immigration, with Labour MPs uneasy at facing constituents in economically struggling areas that were angry over the issue. At the same time a large number of Labour MPs represented seats in areas such as London where immigration was not such a contentious issue. Balancing this and his own Euroscepticism may explain Labour leader Jeremy Corbyn's less than enthusiastic campaigning.

The media campaign was won by Leave

The British printed press had for a long time been heavily Eurosceptic, with some focusing on immigration in ways that fed some of the Leave campaigns' messages about losing control and membership of the EU being a threat to Britain's security and identity. It therefore came as no surprise that many newspapers on the political Right dismissed Cameron's renegotiation and campaigned for Britain to leave the EU. It did, however, come as a surprise to Cameron and his advisers, who, as Conservatives, had rarely faced the full campaigning might of Britain's Right-leaning press. This had normally been directed at other parties during election campaigns (C. Oliver 2016).

As required by British law, the broadcast media was more impartial during the campaign. But in doing so broadcasters such as the BBC risked the ire of either side. Remain campaigners complained that in seeking to be impartial the BBC always offered a space and equal time to the opposite argument, irrespective of how accurate it was. There were no such limits online, where despite the pro-European stance of many younger voters, the campaign in online and social media was dominated by the Leave campaigns. This reflected how across the Western world populist and Right-wing parties had been ahead at organising themselves online.

The EU was a very difficult sell

In 1975 the EEC had been experiencing sustained growth and appeared to be the future for the UK. The image of the EU in

2016 was very different, faced as it was by a series of large and small ongoing crises. It had been wracked by a Eurozone crisis that had brought hardship to southern states such as Greece. The Union had struggled to cope with a refugee and migration crisis that had led to a breakdown of part of Schengen. It had responded slowly to Russia's occupation of Crimea. Euroscepticism was on the rise across the EU, with parties such as Marine Le Pen's National Front making progress in France. Compared to a stagnant EU with an ageing and declining population, emerging economies such as China or Brazil appeared to be the future of the world economy. Majorities of both Leave and Remain voters held negative views of the EU, many feeling uneasy or angry about it (Clarke, Goodwin and Whiteley 2017).

Such views had grown not only in the UK, but also across Europe, where support for the EU had been in decline for some time, although in the UK the level of support was always much lower. What did not help in the UK was a low level of knowledge about the EU. Polling had long shown the British were among the least knowledgeable when it came to EU matters (Hix 2015a).

It was against this backdrop that a range of British politicians, who had rarely said anything positive about the EU, now tried to sell the idea of it being something of which it was worth remaining a member. In facing a tough campaign, Cameron himself was reaping what he had sown. It seemed strange for him to argue in the campaign that the UK's membership of the EU was of vital national interest that connected to the security of Europe when a few weeks before he had been ready to campaign for Leave had he not secured the renegotiation he had wanted. This inconsistency appeared patronising. For this reason many elsewhere in the EU steered clear of getting involved in the debate, although this did not stop US President Obama. His comment that a Britain outside the EU would be at the 'back of the queue' for a trade deal with the US reinforced the Remain message but provoked rather than calmed support for Leave.

The electoral franchise benefited Leave

In the run-up to the referendum there was much discussion about the right to vote in the referendum for 16- and 17-year-olds, EU nationals resident in the UK, and British citizens who had lived abroad for longer than 15 years. The UK government decided not to pursue changes that would have extended voting to any of these groups, in large part out of a fear it would provoke backbench Conservative MPs and lead to allegations that the vote was being rigged. The decision was therefore made to base eligibility to vote in the referendum on the criteria used for a UK general election. This excluded EU nationals while allowing the citizens from a total of 54 Commonwealth states – such as Australians, Nigerians and Indians – living in the UK a vote. As a result the only EU nationals allowed to vote were Cypriots, Maltese and Irish.

Whether or not the vote would have been different had these groups been allowed to vote is much debated. Even a 100 per cent turnout among 16- and 17-year-olds would have been insufficient in terms of numbers to swing the vote to Remain. But as Cameron's advisers realised too late in the campaign, efforts to extend the vote to these groups, especially 16- and 17-year-olds, would have shifted debate so that discussion would have been about what the vote would mean for young people, a move that would advantage Remain (C. Oliver 2016). Older voters were more likely to turn out or vote by post, something Leave were far more successful at encouraging and organising than Remain. Inaccurate polling may also have played a part, with some Remain voters feeling a Leave vote was unlikely and so lacking any sense of urgency to vote.

The campaign connected to matters not directly about EU–UK relations

As discussed earlier, referendums can often turn into votes on other matters. The EU referendum was no different in this respect. As Evans and Menon (2017) argue, the EU has not always been a very salient issue in UK politics, but became so in recent years because it was linked by UK voters with other issues, especially immigration. In calling for a vote, Cameron had argued that it was time to settle the 'European question' in British politics. Instead the referendum debate ranged over matters as diverse as the future of European integration and arguments about sovereignty through to the claims about the future of the NHS and elitism in British politics.

The vote certainly captured a large degree of anti-European sentiment among the British, but it was also driven by a mix of anti-politics and anti-austerity feelings, along with hostility to ill-defined targets such as a distant and elitist London, or the challenges (and for some, the opportunities) of globalisation. As noted above, the vote connected to strong opinions and concerns about immigration from the EU and from elsewhere such as by asylum seekers and economic migrants from North Africa and the Middle East. The referendum also took place against a backdrop of the financial crisis and the parliamentary expenses scandal of 2009, both of which cast a shadow over the credibility of the political class and wider elites, not least in the business community. The Leave campaign was able to connect the campaign to such issues, with the '£350 million a week' claim linking to concerns about the NHS (which is cherished to such a degree that it is sometimes described as the closest the British have to a national religion).

The vote also highlighted differences between Remain and Leave voters over attitudes to the death penalty, multiculturalism, social liberalism, environmentalism and feminism. As such the Leave vote can be explained not by socio-economic factors but by socio-cultural ones (Kaufmann 2016). As touched on earlier, surveys had also repeatedly shown that the British people's knowledge of the EU is relatively lower than elsewhere in the EU. As Menon and Fowler (2016, R5) argued:

> Low levels of EU knowledge are not, of course, an explanation for low levels of support for membership (whatever some committed 'Remain' supporters might claim). However, they left the electorate – and even, arguably, much of the media – ill-prepared to assess the claims made by either side as the referendum approached.

What happened next

The most immediate and obvious consequence of Britain's vote to leave was David Cameron's resignation as prime minister within only a few hours of the result being confirmed. His resignation was the first development in a series of processes that are explored in the following chapters. As discussed in the introduction, Brexit is not a single event or process but a series of time-limited and open-ended multi-level processes that touch on and are shaped by a wide range of interests, ideas, institutions and individuals. To understand them and track them as they progress, these processes need to be broken down into groups, the main issues at stake identified, and a note taken of who the key participants are that will shape them. As set out earlier in Table 1.1, the processes can be divided into three groups.

The first group of processes are those unfolding within the UK as it comes to terms with the vote. These are explored in the next chapter. The most important surround the 'Brexit narrative': what 'Leave' means in terms of why the British people voted Leave and what destination that should lead to. This is being argued about within UK government, both between officials tasked with delivering this and ministers arguing about it within cabinet. The government's definition of Brexit will be subject to parliamentary approval, with the process of how this is to happen being a key issue. According to parliamentary sovereignty there is no higher power in the UK than Parliament, raising questions as to the extent to which Parliament is bound by the referendum result. How Parliament responds will in large part be shaped by how the political parties come to terms with Brexit. Debate will also be taking place across the different parts of the UK as to what the vote means for the Union, in particular for the three areas that voted Remain: London, Northern Ireland and Scotland. Northern Ireland, especially, presents some unique challenges for dealing with the outcome of the vote. Finally, there are two other broad sets of processes by which the Brexit vote is being handled in the UK. First, in terms of the outcome for UK society, not least for what it could mean for British identity and immigration policies. Second, what the vote will mean for the UK's economy and economic model.

The second set of processes will take place at the European level and can be divided into two sub-groups. The first sub-group covers the negotiations over the UK's exit and new relationship with the EU. There are three processes of negotiation here: over the exit, a transition, and a new relationship. A final process here surrounds the way in which the rest of the EU agrees to whatever overall deal is offered to the UK, a process that could be quite complex. The second sub-group of processes involves the remaining EU as it comes to terms with being a Union without the UK. Internally, the remaining EU will witness a shift in the balance of power brought about by the departure of one of its largest member states. That could see changes to the EU's economic direction, political goals, unity and in a host of specific policy areas, including the EU's budget. Brexit will not only change the EU but also the EU's place in Europe given a large European country will now be outside the EU. This could have implications for the EU's relations with such organisations as the EEA and EFTA. Finally, there is the short-term challenge of continuing with the EU's daily business as a Union of 28 member states, but where one of those states is set to leave but in the meantime retains the same rights (excepting in some areas connected to the negotiations over its exit) as all other member states.

The final group of processes are those which will see the UK and EU come to terms with the wider international implications of Brexit. Britain will need to work through such issues as what Brexit means for its international strategy, its relations with allies such as the US, trade links, and position at the World Trade Organization (WTO). Both the UK and the EU have expressed hopes to continue some form of cooperation on foreign, security and defence matters, with working out how to do this being one of the key negotiations to be undertaken. This will depend in part on how the EU itself moves forward in its international standing and attempts at cooperation on foreign, security and defence matters. This will be shaped by how other powers, such as Russia and China, respond to the EU post Brexit. It will also be shaped by whether Brexit is a sign of a changing Western world and attitudes within it towards globalisation.

Further readings

Michael Ashcroft and Kevin Culwick, *Well, You Did Ask ... Why the UK Voted to Leave the EU* (Biteback, 2016). Lord Ashcroft, businessman, Conservative peer and prolific pollster, was quick to collect and publish some of the earliest polling on the referendum.

British Journal of Politics and International Relations (BJPIR) published a special issue (Vol. 19(3)) on Brexit in August 2017. Contributions cover a wide range of topics including analysis of why Britain voted as it did.

Cato the Younger, *Guilty Men: Brexit Edition* (Biteback, 2017). A powerful polemic, it is based on a 1940 book of the same title that condemned the British decision makers guilty of the policy of appeasing Hitler. This Brexit edition is aimed squarely at those in Britain and Europe who, Cato the Younger argues, led Britain into making its biggest foreign policy mistake since the 1930s.

Harold Clarke, Matthew Goodwin and Paul Whiteley, *Brexit: Why Britain Voted to Leave the European Union* (CUP, 2017). A very detailed analysis of the referendum. Required reading for anyone interested in how and why Britain voted as it did.

Sir John Curtice, 'Why Leave Won the UK's EU Referendum'. *Journal of Common Market Studies* 55(S1) September 2017. Britain's leading psephologist offers his analysis of the Leave victory.

Jason Farrell and Paul Goldsmith, *How to Lose A Referendum: The Definitive Story of Why the UK Voted for Brexit* (Biteback, 2017). In setting out 18 reasons for Leave's victory they delve into both the history of UK–EU relations and more recent developments in the campaign.

Andrew Glencross, *Why the UK Voted for Brexit* (Palgrave, 2016) provides a short academic analysis of the referendum divided into four sections covering the history of Euroscepticism, the renegotiation, the campaign and the future handling of Brexit. It focuses on the nature of direct democracy in the UK and the nature of Euroscepticism.

Denis MacShane, *Brexit: How Britain Left Europe* (IBTauris, 2016). The former Labour minister was quick to update his pre-referendum book *Brexit: How Britain will leave Europe*. In 2017 he also published *Brexit, No Exit: Why (in the End) Britain Won't Leave Europe.*

Political Quarterly issue of July–September 2016 (Vol. 87(3)) contains some of the earliest post-referendum analysis published in an academic journal.

Kirby Swales, *Understanding the Leave Vote* (NatCen, 2016). Published six months after the vote, this report provides a comprehensive overview of the Leave campaigns' success at appealing to a broad-based coalition of voters.

FIVE

Britain after the referendum

Introduction

Brexit has triggered a series of processes in the UK, summarised in Table 5.1, that are not only about handling the UK's exit from the EU. They are also about defining what sort of country the UK wants to be. The first and arguably most important process in the way the UK is handling Brexit surrounds defining the 'Brexit narrative'. British politics since June 2016 has been largely about defining why the British people voted as they did and what they voted for when 51.9 per cent of them who voted backed Leave. Theresa May, who succeeded David Cameron as prime minister, has often tried to define the narrative, but as the chapter shows, this has been far from straightforward. If May has struggled to define the Brexit narrative then that is in part because she has struggled to find unity within her own government over what Brexit should mean. This has seen arguments and negotiations between ministers and with officials who are tasked with putting Brexit into action in an extremely wide range of policy areas. Whatever May and her government want Brexit to mean will depend on what Parliament approves, with a great deal of media and public attention placed on the processes by which this will happen and on whether these processes will involve proper scrutiny. That will depend on how the UK's political parties respond, with each of them facing their own particular problems and opportunities in coming to terms with Brexit. The chapter then turns to negotiations and developments outside of Westminster, starting with the way in which Brexit is unfolding in the different parts of the UK. Here focus is mainly given to the situation in Northern Ireland, Scotland and London, and the question of where it leaves England. Finally, the chapter turns to two other broad sets of processes by which the Brexit vote is being handled in the UK: first, in terms of the outcome for UK society, not least for what it could mean for British identity and immigration policies; and second, what the vote will mean for the UK's economy and economic model.

The Brexit narrative

Sir Winston Churchill is believed to have said that 'history if written by the victors'. If that is so, then the referendum presents a problem. The Leave option was victorious but given differences and divisions between and within the Leave campaigns and, as

Table 5.1: Britain's Brexit processes

Processes	Key participants	Issues
Brexit narrative	The prime minister, the UK's political parties, media, academia, the public	What the vote by the UK's population meant. 'Brexit means Brexit' means ...?
UK government	The prime minister, ministers and officials	Developing and implementing a strategy for Brexit, managing the administrative challenge
Parliament and the judiciary	Ministers, MPs, the Lords, the courts, the British people through elections	Scrutinising and approving the Brexit process, its aims and outcomes
Party politics	Conservatives, Labour, UKIP, Liberal Democrats, SNP, DUP	Positioning the parties to manage Brexit and fit with their ideological outlooks
The Union	UK government, Scottish government and Parliament, Northern Ireland government and Assembly, Welsh Assembly and government, and London and local government in England	The role of devolved and local administrations in Brexit; the place (and identities) of Scotland, London, Wales, England and Northern Ireland in the UK
UK society	UK government, political parties, civil society, the Home Office	Managing divisions from the referendum, stimulating debate about Brexit, the place of immigration in the UK and developing a new immigration system
The economy	UK government, HM Treasury, Bank of England, WTO, business community	Choices over the UK's political economy, winners and losers from Brexit

discussed later, within the political parties and government that will have to implement Brexit, who the victors are and what they want remains the most contested issue in UK politics. It has bedevilled Theresa May's time as prime minister. 'Brexit means Brexit' she proclaimed not long after becoming the new Conservative leader and prime minister. That might sound self-explanatory, but it is meaningless unless Brexit itself is defined. The referendum had produced a result for leaving the EU without specifying an end destination. While several themes were clear in the Leave victory – the cost of UK membership, taking back control of laws, and restricting immigration – there are a range of possible destinations to delivering on these themes. What May herself thought she meant by 'Brexit means Brexit' has at times been unclear given that during the referendum campaign she quietly aligned herself with the Remain campaign. And there have not just been doubts about what May thinks Brexit should mean. Brexit has lacked a clear narrative, making the fight to define that narrative the defining issue of UK politics.

Theresa May's Brexit narrative

In January 2017 Theresa May set out her ideas as to what Brexit should mean (May 2017). She defined 12 aims for the UK in the then forthcoming negotiations:

1. provide certainty about the process of leaving the EU;
2. control of our own laws;
3. strengthen the Union between the four nations of the UK;
4. maintain the Common Travel Area with Ireland;
5. Brexit must mean control of the number of people who come to Britain from Europe;
6. rights for EU nationals in Britain and British nationals in the EU;
7. protect workers' rights;
8. free trade with European markets through a free trade agreement;
9. new trade agreements with other countries;
10. the best place for science and innovation;

11. cooperation in the fight against crime and terrorism;
12. a smooth, orderly Brexit.

For May, it was immigration, sovereignty and Britain's place in the world that were the primary drivers behind the victory for Leave (Hammond and Oliver 2017). Controlling immigration from elsewhere in the EU, ending the jurisdiction of the CJEU so Britain would control its own laws, and opting for a free trade agreement with European markets so it could then pursue trade agreements with others were three of the most important aims she set out. This also formed part of a wider narrative in which she seemed determined to sideline the City, focus on areas of the UK that had been left behind (thus her aim to protect workers' rights) and therefore pursue a strategy of rebalancing the economy.

May's narrative about Brexit has been challenged from several quarters, and not just from opposition political parties and Remain-leaning campaigners and journalists. As raised in Chapter Four, there were not only diverse and sometimes divergent views expressed by people voting to exit the EU, but the various Leave campaigns themselves were often unclear as to what Leave would mean. This uncertainty was something the Remain campaigns targeted throughout the campaign. Some Leave voters had focused on the costs and constraints of EU membership other than immigration and sovereignty, including the issue of the much-disputed claim that the UK pays £350 million a week to the EU. Others backed a more libertarian and globalist outlook of a UK that post Brexit would pursue ties with countries outside of Europe. Some voters also used the referendum as a way of registering their anger about domestic matters such as austerity policies and growing inequality. The vote for Leave therefore encapsulated a range of hopes and concerns and with no clear consensus about any specific vision of Brexit. When in 2017 May called a general election, she did so in part in the hope she could secure a mandate for her definition of Brexit. The result of a hung parliament only confused things further.

HM Government and Brexit

Brexit has presented the UK's government with an unprecedented peacetime challenge in terms of political unity, administration and delivery.

Collective responsibility

Theresa May's premiership has struggled because of Conservative divisions over Europe, something many of her predecessors also faced. In appointing her first cabinet she tried to bring some balance to these tensions by appointing leading pro-Leave campaigners such as Boris Johnson, Liam Fox and David Davis to senior posts. But this has not been enough to cope with a series of divisions within the cabinet and Conservative party over the direction of Brexit. Her leadership has been overshadowed by doubts from the start. She won the leadership race without a vote. Other candidates either withdrew or destroyed each other, as happened with the campaigns of Michael Gove and Boris Johnson. Her leadership style also rankled, not least her centralisation of decision making in 10 Downing Street around her two closest advisors, Nick Timothy and Fiona Hill.

Her surprise decision to call a general election, in part on the advice of some of her closest advisers, caught many in her cabinet by surprise. Her weak campaigning skills and a dire campaign left her even more vulnerable with post-election cabinet responsibility strained to the limit. The Foreign Secretary, Boris Johnson, especially challenged her positions over Brexit. HM Treasury, under Philip Hammond, also appeared to pursue a soft Brexit policy that challenged the prime minister and prominent Leave ministers. In calling the general election she had claimed an increased majority in the House of Commons would strengthen her position in negotiations with the EU. More than anything it was intended to strengthen her position in the UK so she could define the aforementioned Brexit narrative. Her failure in the election means questions persist about her mandate: she did not campaign for Leave, did not win a vote for the leadership, and lost her party's majority in a general election she called. Cabinet ministers have openly manoeuvred for a leadership race they feel could happen at any time.

Her vulnerabilities are a good example of how the place of a prime minister within the UK's core executive (the system of departments, committees and networks that sit at the heart of the British state and which attempt to coordinate it) is a fragile one which at best can be one of 'prime ministerial predominance' (Heffernan 2003): 'Predominance enables the Prime Minister to lead, but not command, the executive, to direct, not control, its policy development, and to manage, but not wholly dominate the legislature.' In facing Brexit, May has struggled to lead the executive, been overwhelmed in directing policy, and following the 2017 general election cannot be sure she can manage the legislature. That it was revealed in the autumn of 2017 that there had been no full cabinet discussion of what new final relationship the UK would seek with the EU was a good demonstration of how weak and vulnerable her position was.

The administrative challenge

If May has struggled to define a Brexit narrative and policy then that is in part because the UK government overall has faced the biggest set of administrative, legal, negotiating and constitutional tasks since 1945. Planning had to begin from a standing start on 24 June 2016, because David Cameron had explicitly forbidden the civil service from undertaking any advance planning for a Leave vote on the grounds that Brexit was not the policy of HM government. Organising the UK government for Brexit has been a formidable task that has included the establishment of two new departments – the Department for Exiting the EU (DExEU) and the Department for International Trade (DIT) (Rutter and McCrae 2016). Across government – at national, regional and local level – departments have had to commit resources to staffing and preparing for Brexit. Some have more work to do than others, for example the Home Office will need to undertake some form of registration of the 3 million EU citizens resident in the UK.

The number of tasks to undertake overall to prepare and deal with Brexit is a long one. As the 32 volumes of the Review of Balance of Competences points to (see Table 3.1), the stretch of UK–EU links is extensive and all could require some administrative changes or checks to see what will and will not need changing. An extensive range of reports, inquiries and debates have come out of the UK's various parliaments and assemblies on the topic of Brexit. So prodigious have these outputs been that the House of Commons Library began producing reports listing them (House of Commons Library 2018b). Denis MacShane's (2017, 24–41) list of 'Brexits' itself tells of the long administrative to-do list that these reports cover: political Brexit, single market Brexit, customs union Brexit, foreign and security policy Brexit, frontier with France Brexit, free movement Brexit, expat Brexit, geo-political Brexit, policing and security Brexit, environmental and global warming Brexit, human rights Brexit, social Europe Brexit, farming and fisheries Brexit, university, scientific and student Brexit, SatNav Brexit, Euratom Brexit, insurance and savings Brexit, ratings agencies Brexit, lawyers/professionals Brexit, European Communities Act Brexit, Gibrexit (the status of Gibraltar), flying Brexit (legal agreements over flight to and from the UK), and cooperation Brexit.

The scale of the task means the UK government has had to set out some broad strategies. In the summer of 2017, the UK government published a series of position papers outlining its plans for Brexit (see Table 5.2).

Table 5.2: UK government position papers on Brexit

Continuity in the availability of goods	Privileges and immunities
Confidentiality and access to documents	Safeguarding the position of EU and UK nationals
The situation with Northern Ireland and Ireland	Security, law enforcement and criminal justice
Ongoing EU judicial and administrative proceedings	Foreign policy, defence and development
Nuclear materials and safeguards	Collaboration on science and innovation
Exchange and protection of personal data	Enforcement and dispute resolution
Cross-border civil judicial cooperation	Future customs arrangements

The reports were welcomed as progress, not least by EU negotiators. However, two things had become clear. First, Brexit was consuming the time and attention of UK government and politics. Brexit had become so important and the main focus of government work that in December 2017 the four members of the board of the UK government's cross-party Social Mobility Commission resigned, citing a lack of progress on the issue because ministers were too focused on Brexit. Second, despite all this focus, it did not pass unnoticed that at the time of the publication of the above reports, which was six months after the UK government had triggered Article 50, the UK government was still trying to outline the ends, ways and means to its Brexit strategy.

The search for strategy

A strategy is a combination of ends (the goals sought), ways (the plans and ideas on how to reach the ends) and means (the resources and capabilities available to pursue the strategy), which is designed with an assessment of risk (does the strategy add up or are the ends too ambitious because the ways and means are too limited?) and an assessment of the opponent (what do they seek, what ways and means do they have available, and how might this influence the pursuit of your strategic ends?). The UK government's strategy for Brexit has been a good example of strategic overstretch (T. Oliver 2017a). The desired ends have often been unclear, with UK decision makers often appearing unsure of what transition deal they want with the EU let alone what new relationship they want to eventually agree with the EU. It has not just been the Conservative government that has struggled here. Other parties have also tried to avoid the choices facing the UK.

The inability of British decision makers to know what they want and whether they can get it led to calls for the EU to take the initiative by explaining to the UK what its options are. No clear ends means the ways to achieve them are also confused. It makes sense, as Theresa May did on becoming prime minister, to task the UK government to prepare for a range of outcomes to the negotiations, including a no-deal scenario. But such planning only started in June 2016 because of David Cameron's refusal to contemplate a Leave vote. Since then Britain's negotiators and civil servants have sometimes appeared to struggle to face the scale of work facing them. This has not stopped British ministers from promising to achieve great things. They ignored the fact that they often appeared to lack the ways – not least the time – to settle Brexit in the two-year time frame provided by Article 50.

With no clear ends and confused ways, it should come as no surprise that Britain has struggled to prepare, configure or effectively deploy the means it has available. As noted in previous sections, Britain needs to put in place a range of changes, with some of the more immediate including legal arrangements, trade agreements, IT and structural facilities (for example new port facilities), employing new personnel and setting up new bodies to replace EU ones. None of this is impossible and work has begun, but from the start there have been widespread doubts that they can be in place for the end of the Article 50 two-year time frame. Britain's assessment of the risks involved in Brexit has therefore been lacking.

In triggering Article 50 when she did, May made time an ally of the EU by increasing the risk of Britain not having the time to secure the exit it wanted. The British government forgot what the ancient Chinese general Sun Tzu argued in the 5th century BC: 'The victorious strategist only seeks battle after the victory has been won, whereas he who is destined to defeat first fights and afterwards looks for victory.' Having jumped headlong into Article 50 exit negotiations, the British government soon realised that it lacked the ways and means that would ensure victory. This can in part be explained by a repeated failure to analyse and understand the positions of the rest of the EU, which is the main 'opponent' here. Frustration at this failure was one factor behind the resignation in January 2017 of Sir Ivor Rogers, the UK's Permanent Representative to the EU. Despite repeated statements from the rest of the EU that the UK faces trade-offs in exiting, some British politicians have stated that Britain can get what it wants or walk away. How Brexit fits into a changing EU has rarely been discussed in the UK despite that being one of the most important contexts in which Brexit is unfolding and being shaped.

Parliament, the judiciary and Brexit

Parliament's role

The idea of parliamentary sovereignty is that there is no higher power in the UK than the Westminster Parliament. Whether Parliament was therefore bound by the referendum result has been a key debate about how to move Brexit forward. A majority of MPs in the 2015–17 Parliament had backed the Remain campaign. Yet a majority of voters in 421 of 574 English and Welsh constituencies are estimated to have voted Leave (Hanretty 2016). This presented a dilemma for those Remain-backing MPs with constituencies that voted Leave: do they back Leave or follow their own beliefs and back Remain?

The 2017 general election means these numbers changed, but MPs sill face a series of questions over what sort of Brexit to authorise and how to hold to account the UK government as it negotiates Brexit. There is also the issue of the House of Lords, where no political party has a majority and which could therefore delay or modify the legislation necessary to implement Brexit. The role of Parliament will therefore be considerable and controversial in some areas.

Parliament's role will also be overshadowed by a common complaint against the UK's legislative system: that it is nothing more than an 'elected dictatorship' where the executive almost always gets its way. This may not be the 'taking back control' that some voted for if it allows the UK government to change a wide range of laws and gain new powers without adequate scrutiny. While there are a large number of parliamentary checks on the executive, many of which are often informal and hidden from public view (Russell and Gover 2017), Brexit has once again highlighted the centralisation (and desire to centralise) and high degree of power exercised by the UK government compared to many others in the democratic world.

Parliament's Brexit workload

The challenge of holding the UK government to account over Brexit can be seen in the three sets of tasks Parliament faces. First, both houses will scrutinise the ongoing Brexit negotiations and preparation through debates, written and oral questions and the work of select committees. This can be effective, but government can also claim a need for secrecy in the negotiations as a reason to withhold information. The willingness of the UK government to hand over information is an issue over which Parliament has faced a long battle (House of Commons Public Administration Committee 2008) and was clearly on display when it came to Brexit when Parliament had to fight to see the government's impact assessments on Brexit.

Second, it must authorise the necessary Brexit legislation such as the EU Withdrawal Bill (once known as the 'Great Repeal Bill'). The EU Withdrawal Bill repeals the 1972 European Communities Act through which the UK Parliament voted to join the then EEC and which gave EU law precedence over UK law. The EU Withdrawal Bill copies into UK law all existing EU laws so as to ensure continuity between the UK and EU markets after Brexit, which is important for trading purposes. Government and Parliament will then be able to amend, repeal and change those laws as and when necessary. This will not be a simple task. Not only is the scale of legislation quite daunting (estimates are that 186 Acts of Parliament, 12,000 regulations, and 7,900 statutory instruments are connected to EU law), but parts of it will need amending quite quickly because it will no longer work, for example because specific laws refer to EU institutions and regulators of which the UK would no longer be a member. To quickly correct the laws, the UK government has proposed using what are known as Henry VIII powers. These powers allow a government to change laws already passed by Parliament with little or no further parliamentary scrutiny. This has led to concerns that the government will abuse these powers.

Finally Parliament will play a central role in authorising the final deal. In the face of legal challenges over whether the UK government had the right to trigger Article 50 without a vote in Parliament (discussed further below) the government stated that Parliament would get a vote over the final deal. But what this vote might entail remains open to debate. If Parliament was presented with a take it or leave it vote and rejected a UK–EU deal negotiated by the government, would that mean the UK opts for a no-deal hard Brexit scenario? Would it mean the UK government is compelled to attempt further negotiations? Would it mean the UK would not leave at all? Would it mean a second referendum? Would it mean another general election?

The 2017 general election

On calling the surprise 2017 election, Theresa May claimed that a large mandate for her would strengthen her government's negotiating position in Brussels. Instead, the outcome of a hung parliament and a minority Conservative government supported by an arrangement with the Democratic Unionist Party (DUP) has strengthened Parliament's role in Brexit for three reasons.

First, simple arithmetic means May lacks a large majority with which to vote through the necessary laws and changes to implement Brexit. While she has been able to count on several pro-Leave Labour MPs and the DUP, this does still leave her government facing some difficult votes (and difficulties in Northern Ireland, about which more below). It also means she is more beholden to her own backbenchers, many of whom were left feeling dismayed at her leadership during the campaign.

Second, Leave supporters can now point to the fact that both the Conservative and Labour Parties campaigned on 2017 general election manifesto commitments of implementing Brexit, committing a large majority of the House of Commons to such a policy. At the same time, Remain supporters point to the surge in Remain voters backing the Labour Party, which has not committed to the same sort of Brexit as the Conservatives. During the campaign, Labour fudged the choice of a hard or soft Brexit, leaving its policy on this open to change.

Third, the failure of the Conservative Party to secure a majority in the House of Commons means some members of the House of Lords (largely Labour and Liberal Democrat peers) do not feel they are bound by the Salisbury Convention, which is an unwritten rule that the unelected chamber will not oppose government legislation drawn from the party's election manifesto. Because no party has a majority in the House of Lords, the government could struggle to get some legislation through. The limited time available may also prohibit the use of such measures as the Parliament Acts, which the House of Commons can use to assert its primacy over the Lords but where a one-year time frame is required.

The role of the judiciary

Uncertainty about Parliament's role in Brexit and the wider legality of the process of implementing Brexit led to a series of legal challenges that eventually reached the UK's Supreme Court. Most famously, a unanimous decision by three judges of the High Court to uphold a legal challenge led by campaigner Gina Miller, on the grounds that the government did not have the power to invoke Article 50 without the consent of Parliament, led to front-page headlines that the judges were 'Enemies of the people' (*Daily Mail*) and 'The Judges Versus the People' (*The Daily Telegraph*).

The UK government argued it had the power to invoke Article 50 as the matter of UK membership of the EU is a foreign policy matter and therefore comes under the remit of the Royal Prerogative powers (powers held by the Crown but exercised by HM Government) which do not require parliamentary consent. The Supreme Court upheld the High Court's ruling in a decision on 25 January 2017. It made clear the UK government required an Act of Parliament to invoke Article 50 because it meant the government would need to overturn existing laws – mainly the European Communities Act 1972 – something it could not do without the permission of Parliament.

The press attacks on the judiciary led to accusations that sections of the media were overreacting, attacking an independent judiciary, and ignoring the need for the law to be clarified and the rule of law to be upheld. It also led to calls, including from the then head of the Supreme Court, Lord Neuberger, for the government and Parliament to be absolutely clear about what the judiciary should do in future when faced with a lack of clarity over UK and EU law, not least over rulings of the CJEU. The government has said that existing CJEU rulings will be incorporated into UK law, but this leaves doubts about whether UK courts should continue to pay heed to CJEU rulings post Brexit. This is something the UK government has said that UK courts will be able to consider. Without a clearer legal framework on which to work, Lord Neuberger warned that this could lead to the judiciary being blamed for misinterpretations and political decisions.

Can a second referendum be called?

Even before the referendum took place some have wondered if a second vote might be necessary, or, in the event of a Remain victory, likely at some point given Eurosceptics would more than likely continue their campaign. Several reasons have been put forward for another vote following the Leave result (Bellamy 2018). There have been questions about the legitimacy of the 23 June vote, such as over the fairness of the campaign, that the vote was on a range of matters and not specifically on UK–EU relations, and that it lacked a 'supermajority'. Some countries require that for certain matters, for example constitutional reforms, a supermajority – for example two thirds or 60 per cent – is required to prevent a major decision being taken on the basis of only a slim majority of support. Supporters of a second referendum also point to the 2016 referendum being the second time the UK has voted on its EU membership, the first being in 1975. If the 1975 vote could be revisited then why not that of 2016? More specifically, there have been calls for the British people to be given the chance to vote on the deal the UK is offered for exiting the EU.

There are several problems facing the idea of a second referendum (Menon 2018). As Bellamy (2018) points out, there is the problem of the increasingly limited time frame in which to legally organise such a vote before the UK formally leaves in March 2019. As discussed further in Chapter Six, there are also a series of questions about the legitimacy of voting again, whether the background factors that drove the Leave vote have actually changed, and – often largely overlooked – whether the UK would be allowed to reverse the triggering of Article 50. Finally, there is the issue of what question would be put to the British people. If the question were 'Do you accept the withdrawal agreement' would a rejection mean the British people want the UK to leave the EU without an agreement or stay in the EU?

Party politics and Brexit

Each of the UK's main parties, and especially their leaders, has struggled to cope with the referendum result.

The Conservatives

As covered in Chapter One, the Conservative Party's unity has long been tested by divisions connected to Britain's membership of the EU. The renegotiation and referendum were called in no small part as a way for Cameron to deal with such tensions. Given this history it is doubtful if even a vote for Remain would have provided the party unity he sought. Nor in voting for Leave has the party been spared divisions. As the governing party its tensions have played out in the UK–EU negotiations, leaving EU decision makers exasperated that the UK's position and approach can change depending on the internal dynamics of the Conservative Party.

Theresa May has proved incapable of bringing order to the party. Having won the leadership race thanks to all the other candidates falling by the wayside, she set out an agenda that pushed to a more traditional Right wing in British politics. This included the pursuit of a 'hard Brexit' and an attempt to appeal to large numbers of Leave voters, who, as discussed in Chapter Four, had been motivated by a mix of socio-economic and socio-cultural concerns. In her 2016 Conservative Party conference speech she famously argued that 'if you believe you're a citizen of the world, you're a citizen of nowhere'. Her ambitious speech, in which she both extolled the role of the state and attacked global elites, was a mix of 19th-century Conservative politics in the mould of Joseph Chamberlain but also populist appeals reminiscent of UKIP.

Her ideas, however, did not translate into the votes she needed in the 2017 election. The party succeeded in drawing in a large number of UKIP and Leave voters and managed to increase its share of the vote from the 2015 general election. However, a large percentage of Leave voters also stayed with Labour and a large number of liberal-leaning (and especially younger) Remain voters moved to Labour and in some areas the Liberal

Democrats. The result of a hung parliament reignited challenges to her leadership, reopened party divisions over Europe and left the party unsure of how to get through the next five years without a crisis.

The Labour Party

Conservative divisions over Europe have distracted attention from Labour's own problems with the issue. Accusations of Jeremy Corbyn's somewhat apathetic efforts in the EU referendum campaign led to an immediate leadership challenge. While Corbyn saw off the challenge, his leadership continued to suffer from infighting among the Labour parliamentary party, media attacks, opinion polling that showed the party struggling to attract voters, and local election results in May 2017 (only a month before the general election) that saw the party perform poorly. Many Labour MPs faced difficulties in voting through Brexit legislation because most of them had voted Remain. At the constituency level the situation was more polarised: Labour MPs held both the top 20 Leave-voting constituencies and the top 20 Remain-voting constituencies.

The 2017 election result changed the narrative on Corbyn's leadership and Labour's prospects. While Labour lost the election, it did much better than many – especially pollsters – had predicted. Its success was helped by problems in the other parties: a weak campaign from the Conservatives; the invisibility of the Liberal Democrats; a decline in support for the SNP; and UKIP's collapse. It was also able to stand as the party of change, and attract Remain voters while not losing Leave voters thanks to it fudging the issue of what sort of Brexit it sought. Instead the party focused on domestic matters and less on Brexit.

Corbyn emerged a strengthened and popular leader, but one still facing problems about how to approach the issue of Brexit. His own Euroscepticism is based on a view of the EU as a liberal, free-market organisation that limits how the British state can intervene. Labour therefore faces choices over what type of Brexit they want (and might have to implement should they enter government during negotiations or any transition period) and how they wish to use parliamentary votes on Brexit and any possible by-elections to harass the Conservative party and in turn shape the current negotiations.

The Liberal Democrats

Despite putting in a strong result in the by-election triggered by David Cameron's decision to leave the House of Commons and not long afterwards winning Conservative MP Zac Goldsmith's seat in Richmond (a constituency that voted heavily for Remain), the Liberal Democrats have failed to benefit from the Brexit vote, although they did see a surge in new members. As the most pro-Remain UK-level party, their failure can be attributed to a range of factors, not least Labour better positioning itself to attract Remain and Leave voters, and the continued damage to their image from their decision to enter into coalition with the Conservatives in 2010. Their large number of members of the House of Lords gives them a pivotal position in votes over Brexit legislation in the upper house. Meanwhile, they wait in the wings of British politics, hoping to eventually benefit from the Conservative and Labour Parties' own tensions over Brexit.

UKIP

The referendum result was in no small part the result of the efforts by UKIP, a party whose growth in support played a role in pushing both the Conservatives and Labour into their support for a referendum. The vote to leave the EU, a succession of leaders, and poor publicity has left it a party in search of both unity and a cause. It lacks MPs, has lost many councillors and after 2019 will (like every other party listed here) not have any MEPs. Does this mean UKIP are doomed? This depends on how powerful a force populism remains in UK and European politics. UKIP's appeal was always about more than just the EU. As covered in earlier chapters, the vote to leave the EU was fuelled by a range of concerns. Whether UKIP or any other party can achieve a national-level electoral breakthrough as UKIP did when it came top in the 2014 European Parliament elections will be limited by the lack of a proportional electoral system for UK-level elections. Nevertheless, UKIP's growth was applying political pressure before 2014 thanks to the fallout from the financial crisis, concerns about immigration, and disenchantment with the British political elite. UKIP members also shared similarities in attitudes to many average UK voters (Clarke, Goodwin and Whiteley 2017). Should Brexit be handled badly then UKIP, or an outgrowth of the party, could benefit from the fallout.

The Union and Brexit

As set out in Chapter Four, there were notable differences in the referendum result between the various nations and regions of the UK. Scotland, Northern Ireland and Greater London voted Remain, while Wales and non-London England voted Leave. Brexit therefore poses a test to the constitutional, legal, political and social frameworks that hold the union together.

A United Kingdom?

Implementing Brexit requires the UK government to make decisions on behalf of the whole UK. In some policy areas it may be legally required to consult with devolved bodies. In some instances, it may make sense politically to do this. Legally, the Supreme Court ruled that the UK government did not have to consult the devolved administrations over triggering Article 50. It decided that the Sewell Convention, which states that if Westminster is introducing legislation on issues that have been devolved, it 'normally' has to seek the consent of devolved parliaments, is not a law and not within the jurisdiction of the court. This was a setback to the Scottish and Welsh First Ministers, Nicola Sturgeon and Carwyn Jones, who from their different political standpoints of the SNP and Labour respectively had both said that they could not support Brexit without membership of or full access to the single market. In response, the UK government has held meetings through the Joint Ministerial Committee, which is a forum for discussion between the UK government and the devolved administrations. Representatives of the devolved bodies have also sought meetings with EU decision makers and negotiators. But the power to negotiate Brexit has remained firmly in the hands of the UK government.

Since joining the EEC in 1973 the UK's constitutional setup has seen significant changes. Devolution, in particular, has happened within a framework of UK membership of the EU. This has meant that UK ministers have dealt with devolved powers, such as over agriculture, at the EU level. This has often been handled in consultation (albeit to varying degrees) with devolved governments. In returning powers from Brussels to the UK, devolved bodies have expressed concerns that the UK government may refuse to devolve them. The UK government argues the UK's own single market has been shaped in many areas by being part of the EU's single market, and that ensuring a UK-wide level playing field will require it to exercise some of the powers returned from Brussels. To critics, this is merely another power grab, typical of an overly centralised system of government. As explored when discussing the role of Parliament in Brexit, parliamentary sovereignty can often mean executive sovereignty, which would be boosted by the repatriation of powers from the EU. Leaving the EU will not change this unless there are reforms to the parliamentary system, the royal prerogatives, the quasi-federal nature of devolution, and the UK's uncodified constitution.

Scotland

Nicola Sturgeon asserted that the UK's vote for Leave could trigger a second Scottish independence referendum. While she ruled out such a vote in 2017, a draft Bill for a second Scottish independence plebiscite was published for consultation in October 2016. She and many other supporters of Scottish independence pointed to how one of the leading arguments of the anti-independence campaign in 2014 had been that a vote to leave the UK would endanger Scotland's place in the EU. However, the 2017 general election result dampened Scottish nationalist hopes of another referendum. The SNP's losses were by far the biggest of any party in the election. While it would have been difficult for them to improve on their 2015 performance when they won all but three of Scotland's seats, the prospect of another vote after two referendums and several elections was not one voters in Scotland seemed to relish. The party also struggled in the face of a Labour party led by Jeremy Corbyn and the Scottish Conservatives led by Ruth Davidson. The 62 per cent vote to remain in the EU, while still the highest of any region in the UK, was also not as overwhelming as some had expected, revealing something of a lack of enthusiasm in some areas of Scotland for the EU.

Exiting the UK and rejoining the EU would also present a myriad of political, economic, social, constitutional and legal questions. The rest of the UK is Scotland's main economic market by a long way. Seeking to break from this in favour of rejoining the EU could entail several costs. There is no guarantee that Scottish membership of the EU would be the same as that which it enjoyed as part of the UK, which has included a budget rebate, opt-outs from the Euro, Schengen and some areas of justice and home affairs cooperation. If the UK and EU fail to agree on a new relationship then in the most extreme circumstances, that could, as with the UK–Irish border in Northern Ireland, require a hard border between the remaining UK and an independent Scotland. Nevertheless, the possibility of Scotland holding another referendum should not be discounted. The SNP remains the main party in Scotland and supporters of independence foresee problems arising from Brexit helping to fuel demands in Scotland for another independence vote.

Northern Ireland

Northern Ireland has long had a unique place within the UK. The partition of Ireland in 1921 left Northern Ireland as a constituent part of the UK, with its own devolved government at Stormont, a unique party-political setup and a religiously defined politics not found elsewhere in the UK. From 1923 this included Northern Ireland as an integral part of the UK-Ireland common travel area, established because the UK did not want to have to police a porous border between the Republic of Ireland–and Northern Ireland. The violence, sectarianism and economic problems that have long defined Northern Ireland's politics have also left it a place apart, as has the Northern Irish peace process, which has managed these tensions since the 1990s.

Its unique politics means it can often be overlooked in political debates in Great Britain (England, Wales and Scotland).

Its position with regard to Brexit has therefore raised some sensitive and difficult dilemmas (Hayward 2017). The people of Northern Ireland voted 56 per cent to 44 per cent for Remain, leaving it, along with Scotland and London, at odds with a majority of the UK. The 2017 election result added to this, with the Conservative government dependent on the votes of the DUP. As discussed in Chapter Six, the status of the Northern Ireland border is one of the central issues to be settled as part of the Article 50 exit deal. The border question is about more than trade. It connects to questions of identity that have been at the heart of Northern Ireland's political tensions. A collapse of the peace process is not something to be overlooked given how difficult the political situation is following the collapse in January 2017 of the power-sharing arrangement that ran devolved government in Northern Ireland. Elections that followed left Sinn Fein only one seat short of overtaking the DUP. The situation is further complicated by the Good Friday Agreement, which forms the basis for the peace process, being an international treaty with the Irish Republic that requires the UK to consult with the Irish government over any changes.

London

London's vote to remain in the EU highlighted a gap between the capital city and the two countries – the UK and England – it dominates. While not all of London gains from it being a global city, London as a whole has appeared to win from the UK's membership of the EU. The Mayor of London, Sadiq Khan, in particular, repeatedly made clear his concerns about the implications of Brexit for the metropolis, a city that from 12 per cent of the UK's population generates about 23 per cent of the UK's GDP. If London suffers a hit from Brexit, then the UK will feel the knock-on effect in terms of less money to be redistributed by the UK government to poorer areas of the UK. Despite this, the financial services industry in the City of London appeared at first to struggle to make much headway in shaping Brexit, in part because its usual connections in HM Treasury did not give it much traction with a prime minister determined to ignore the City's interests (James and Quaglia 2017).

The referendum also highlighted concerns of a London 'bubble', inside which live the UK's political, media, business, legal, cultural and diplomatic elites. That bubble, defined by a globalised, multicultural, metropolitan elite (which Theresa May was also targeting with her 'citizens of nowhere' conference speech) was a frequent target for UKIP. While London lacks the constitutional standing that devolved governments in Scotland, Wales and Northern Ireland have, its informal political power remains substantial. That was seen in the 2017 general election when large numbers of Conservative MPs in London lost their seats as the capital's Remain voters moved to Labour. Managing the growing disparities in wealth, outlook and politics between the capital city and the rest of the UK looks set to be one of the defining issues of UK politics (T. Oliver 2017c).

England

For several years UK political debate has touched on but rarely confronted the growing issue of English nationalism, identity and questions pertaining to the constitutional place of England within the UK. The referendum result, with non-London England voting for Leave, did provoke debate about the English question, although a willingness to confront this or do much about it remains limited (Barnett 2017). As touched on in Chapter Four, polling showed that a voter in England who identified as English was more likely to be Eurosceptic and vote Leave than one who identified as British. That does not explain all Euroscepticism or the vote to leave. A majority of Welsh voters backed Leave, as did 38 per cent of Scots, 40.1 per cent of Londoners and 44.2 per cent of people in Northern Ireland. The connection between English nationalism and Euroscepticism is also not automatic. It is difficult to explain the vote as the result of a move from British to English identity as such moves can take a long time.

Nevertheless, English nationalism has become something of a hallmark for angry, disillusioned sections of English society that feel left behind in the modern world and modern Britain. When unease at immigration is mixed in it creates a combination that some British politicians have been loath to go near. Instead they have been more comfortable with being 'British', fearing English nationalism as racist, one that causes tensions with Scotland and as an outlook of the working class and football supporters and hooligans. One of the problems facing any attempt to address this is the lack of political institutions and networks elsewhere in England outside of London.

British society and Brexit

The referendum result appeared to leave British society divided, divisions that the country's political elite has tried to overcome. It has also raised difficult questions about the place of immigrants in Britain and what immigration system Britain plans to adopt post Brexit.

Brexit Britain's divisions

As discussed in Chapter Four, there is no one type of Leave or Remain voter. However, patterns could be seen that point to differences between: those who feel they are winners and losers in British, European and global society; those with qualifications and those without; young Remain voters and older people who voted Leave; people with liberal and multicultural outlooks on one side and those with more authoritarian and nationalist outlooks on the other; those who identify as British, Scottish or Londoner, who were more likely to vote Remain than those who identify strongly as English who backed Leave; and those with faith in the UK's institutions and direction compared to those who doubt them and believe the status quo is against them.

These divisions are not just socio-economic but socio-cultural. They highlight the growing place in Britain of identity politics with 'us' verses 'them' a growing feature of political debate, which is reinforced by the echo chambers of social media. It is important to remember, however, that the referendum did not cause these divisions, but it brought them more into the open, crystallising them and in some areas exacerbating them. Nor does it mean these divisions are extremes that can never be bridged. It is helpful to think of there being gradations between them, with large numbers of people holding opinions or having backgrounds that are somewhere in between either end of the above dichotomies (Richards and Heath 2017).

As mentioned above, how Parliament and the political parties have responded to Brexit matters because it will be for them to make key choices about how Brexit unfolds constitutionally, diplomatically, economically and socially. However, the debate is much more widespread. The referendum and its result have made debates about Brexit a mainstream topic of life for many in their families, communities, businesses and civil society. The topic has worked its way into British culture, from books shortlisted for the Man Booker Prize through to artwork and theatre. This reflects how the debates about defining the Brexit narrative have not just been about what type of Brexit the British people voted for in terms of a new relationship with the EU, but in terms of what sort of country Britain wants to be.

As May's aforementioned 2016 Conservative party conference speech pointed to, she tried to pitch her party towards those who had voted Leave. Her speech and policies also reflected a desire to reach out to those who felt they had been left behind and overlooked by an elite governing from the comfort of a global metropolis. Rebalancing the UK away from the domination of London and addressing growing inequality are not new ideas. However, as negotiations have begun and moved forward over Brexit, the country has appeared to remain divided with no unity over what Brexit should mean, although large numbers feel continued free movement as happened in the past would not deliver on the result (Carl 2017).

The 2017 general election result showed May's own efforts had alienated large swathes of Remain voters who moved to backing the Labour party, despite that party's own tensions over what Brexit should mean. The election, despite being overshadowed by the EU referendum, failed to bring any unity. While Brexit has become a mainstream topic of British life, attempts to stimulate detailed policy-focused debates about Brexit among the British people, such as UCL's Citizen's Assembly on Brexit (Renwick 2017), have been few and far between. As a result, formal attempts to assess what the British people want from Brexit – in terms of type of exit and what this means for the country, communities and families – have been limited, with most such debate, as always in British politics, centred in and around Westminster and other areas of central London such as the City. It also raises the possibility of some people feeling betrayed if Brexit is seen as delivered in ways that are at odds with what the people voted for, does not deliver social and economic change, or is managed in such an incompetent way that it fuels doubts in society about Britain's political institutions and elites.

Brexit and immigration

Immigration's place as one of the defining issues of the referendum means there are many questions about what Brexit means for immigrants in the UK and what new immigration system the UK might adopt. As the next chapter covers in more detail, settling the status of EU citizens in the UK (and UK citizens elsewhere in the EU) has been one of three priorities for reaching agreement over a UK–EU exit agreement. Since the vote there have been reports of growing numbers of hate crime and attacks directed at immigrants. Polling has also shown that immigrants from both the EU/EEA and from around the world have felt less welcome and wanted by British society. The number of immigrants to the UK has also declined (Travis 2017). This can be explained by a number of factors such as the Brexit vote putting people off immigrating to the UK, the uncertain future that now hangs over anyone who migrates to the UK, the decline in the value of the pound sterling, making Britain a less attractive place to work, and migration levels from some Eastern European countries having reached a high-water mark.

There are several systems the UK could develop for its immigration policy post Brexit (Portes 2016). First, non-visa requirements, as apply to citizens of a number of other countries entering the UK for a short period, could be applied to EEA nationals. This may entail some form of pre-entry system, similar to the US Electronic System for Travel Authorisation (ESTA) system. This, however, does not directly link to immigration because this system is for short visits (for example holidays or business trips) and not for work or long-term residency. It would mean that some form of increased control would apply to EEA nationals entering the UK because as a current EU member state outside of Schengen the UK already has border controls for EEA nationals where their passports are checked, but only a tiny number are denied entry, something that also happens with non-EEA nationals attempting to enter the UK on a visa-waiver programme.

Second, and more importantly, will be the design of a system for immigration to the UK, that is for people who intend to stay for more than three months and to work in the UK. Debate has often raised the prospect of an 'Australian-style points based system'. Such debate can often overlook the fact that the UK already operates a points-based system (based on criteria connected to skill needs, salaries, limits on numbers and so forth) for non-EEA immigration. The issue then is whether the criteria would be changed if it were now to be extended to all EEA/EU nationals (with the exception of Irish nationals, assuming the UK-Ireland common travel area is maintained) and how liberal or restrictive the system would be. The design of the system is therefore dependent on what end it is intended to deliver. It could be aimed at keeping numbers low to restrict population growth and limit the changes immigration can have on the social composition of the UK.

Instead of meeting political needs the immigration system could be configured to meet economic needs. The two are not necessarily compatible. The UK economy has increasingly relied on large numbers of immigrants who are more likely to work and pay tax and less likely to use public services as they are younger, educated and healthier. As a result, as Portes (2016) notes: 'Non-UK workers make up just over 17 per cent – more than 1 in 6 – of those in work.' As with so much of Brexit, there are trade-offs in the choices to be made. There will be an inevitable increase in regulatory and administrative burdens for some employers and for government. There could be a decrease in the flow of both skilled and unskilled labour. A more restrictive system could encourage illegal working.

Finally, as Portes (2016, R17) argues, the approach of building a system that can respond to the needs of the UK economy overlooks the inherent restrictions in such a system. 'The view that we can devise an immigration system that allows in those, and only those "immigrants that have the skills we need" implicitly assumes both the feasibility and the desirability of a centrally planned labour market.' As discussed further below, this connects to a debate about what Brexit could mean for the UK's economic model.

The British economy and Brexit

Debate about Britain's relationship with the EU has often been about the economic benefits it brings. While, as discussed earlier, the EU has never been solely about economic integration and the referendum result saw large numbers of Britons put aside such economic concerns, discussion about the EU's role in Britain's economy remains at the heart of debate about Brexit. But how important is the EU to the UK's economy? How might that change because of Brexit? Finally, just as Brexit raises questions about what type of society the British people want their country to have and what role it should play in the world (which is explored further in Chapter Seven) so too does it raise questions about what type of economy Britain should have.

Brexit Britain's economy

Britain is one of the world's largest economies, albeit in a world where the three largest economies – the US, China and the EU – dwarf the UK and everyone else. Britain is ranked as one of the world's most open economies. It has long attracted large amounts of inward investment, relied on immigration to supply both high-skilled, high-income labour and low-skilled, low-income labour, and has relied increasingly on services as opposed to manufacturing. In 2013 the service sector accounted for 79 per cent of the UK's economy, with manufacturing at 14 per cent, construction around 6 per cent, and agriculture around 1 per cent (James and Quaglia 2017, 8). In terms of trade, the EU is collectively the UK's single largest trading partner as seen in Table 5.3.

Table 5.3: UK's trade with its main trading partners, 2011 and 2013–15

Partner	Block A goods and services, 2011				Block B goods only, average 2013–15			
	Exports ($bn)	Export share %	Imports ($bn)	Import share %	Exports ($bn)	Export share %	Imports ($bn)	Import share %
EU28	347.1	47.0	389.4	49.9	226.7	45.1	350.9	53.8
US	109.4	14.8	88.5	11.4	64.2	12.9	57.1	8.8
China	26.2	3.5	58.4	7.5	23.9	4.8	61.6	9.4
India	19.0	2.6	24.8	3.2	6.7	1.3	9.9	1.5
Canada	18.4	2.5	13.3	1.7	6.5	1.3	13.1	2.0
Australia	16.7	2.3	7.7	1.9	5.8	1.2	3.2	0.5
Japan	16.4	2.2	17.1	2.2	6.9	1.4	10.6	1.6
Russia	15.1	2.0	14.1	1.8	5.4	1.1	9.1	1.4
Switzerland	13.7	1.9	8.7	1.1	46.0	9.0	10.4	1.6
Norway	10.5	1.4	46.1	5.9	5.3	1.1	24.1	3.7
Rest of world	146.2	19.8	111.8	14.3	105.6	21.0	102.9	15.8
Total	738.7	100.0	779.9	100.0	503.1	100.0	652.9	100.0

Source: Holmes, Rollo and Winters (2016, R23).

As Holmes, Rollo and Winters (2016, R23) explain:

> The table shows the predominance of the EU as a market and a supplier, accounting for approximately half of both goods and services imports and exports. Next comes the USA, but with about a quarter to a third or the volume of trade with the EU, followed by China which supplies far more imports than it takes exports and India of which the opposite is true. Australia and Canada both figure in the goods and services list but barely for goods alone, because they are more important in services than in goods. In goods alone, exports to Switzerland are dominated by gold and imports from Russia and Norway by oil.

As Holmes, Rollo and Winters go on to point out, to compensate for a 1 per cent reduction in exports to the EU, exports to the US would have to increase by nearly 4 per cent. Generating extra growth will also be hindered by the difficulty of freeing trade in services, an area where the UK is a leading exporter, but where trade liberalisation remains a leading challenge in international trade negotiations. Does this mean the UK needs the EU more than the EU needs the UK? Almost certainly given that 45 per cent of UK exports go to the EU but on average 6.7 per cent of other EU countries' exports go to the UK (Holmes, Rollo and Winters 2016, R25). About 54 per cent of the UK's imports in goods come from the EU. Disruption to trade with the UK would certainly bring some costs for the EU, but there would be a far greater cost for the UK in terms of lost exports and disrupted imports.

The economic effect of Brexit

Estimating how Brexit might change the UK's economy is not simple for four reasons (Oxford Review of Economic Policy 2017). First, this is an unprecedented event. Most analysis of changes in trade works on the assumption of integration and the slow removal of barriers, not the other way and certainly not suddenly. Second, the scale and complexity of what to model makes it an incredibly difficult challenge. Brexit entails changes in almost every area of economic activity and to varying degrees. The models used have to be based on certain assumptions to generate predictions of changes in trade, consumption, welfare and production. Third, the time frames involved are not short. The effects of Brexit could take decades to become clear. Forecasting that far ahead is always challenging. Finally, and related to the previous point, the number of variables – such as in relation to the UK's exit deal, the specifics of a new relationship, developments in the wider global economy, or 'black swan' (an unexpected event that has a major effect) events – complicate things further. Simulating changes Brexit could bring – to trade, foreign direct investment, immigration, taxes and much more – is therefore extremely difficult.

What can be said is that case studies have shown that Britain has gained substantial economic benefits from being a member of the EU because it has improved Britain's productivity through breaking down tariff and non-regulatory barriers to trade in Europe (Crafts 2016). Economic models have largely shown that breaking from this would involve an economic loss. A study by Dhingra et al used a simulation that involved 35 countries, 31 sectors, and intermediate inputs to produce optimistic and pessimistic scenarios (Dhingra, Huang, et al 2017). Their optimistic estimate sees Brexit leading to a 1.3 per cent decline for UK households while their pessimistic one estimates a 2.7 per cent decline. Other case studies that focus on financial services have pointed to a decline in revenue in this sector of between 12 and 18 per cent and employment by 7 and 8 per cent (Djankov 2017).

By contrast, those who support Brexit have argued that it will allow the UK to deregulate and more effectively compete in the world. The think tank Open Europe, for example, identified 57 pieces of EU legislation that the UK government estimated had higher costs than benefits, with an overall cost of 0.9 per cent of UK GDP. Critics pointed out that half of this came from two regulations on reducing carbon dioxide emissions and limiting working hours. Nevertheless, they point to some costs for the UK that it may wish to abandon outside the EU.

The overall picture of how many expected the UK economy to be changed, however, is clear. As part of a review of the economic and financial costs and benefits of the UK's EU membership, taken just before the EU referendum, the House of Commons Treasury Select Committee plotted the estimates of the long-term impact of leaving the EU on UK GDP, as shown in Figure 5.1.

In its conclusions the Committee noted that '[t]he key question is how far these negative effects are offset by: the scope for increased openness to trade with the rest of the world; productivity gains from deregulation; and lower contributions to the EU budget'. This all depends on the deal the UK secures with the EU on leaving and the free trade deals and economic relations it could then seek with others.

A great deal of what happens will depend on whether Britain will be a closed, protectionist economy or an open, liberal and global economy. This has been one of the questions at the heart of the debate about Brexit. There are several sides to this. First, what economic models exist for the UK going forward? There are three models. On the one hand is a deregulated, open, liberal economy sometimes described as 'Singapore on steroids'.

Figure 5.1: Estimates of the long-term impact of leaving the EU

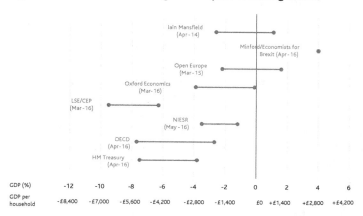

Source: House of Commons Treasury Select Committee (2016).

This would focus on deregulation and free trade (including in some scenarios the UK unilaterally scrapping all tariffs on goods entering the UK) and would see the UK turn away from Europe and pursue relations with emerging economies. This model would also point to the growing importance of international regulatory bodies, with Brexit allowing the UK to engage with them directly and so bypass the EU, which acts as a middleman. There is a status quo model, which would see the UK continue close relations with the EU through some form of relationship that replicates as far as possible the UK's existing membership such as through mutual recognition or some form of close regulatory alignment. Here, as explored further in Chapter six, the question is what the UK might have to pay – either financially and/or in terms of accepting EU laws and regulations – to gain such access. Finally, there is a protectionist, inward looking model, which would seek significant limits on the free movement of goods, capital, services and people in and out of the UK with both the EU and global markets. In such a scenario, the UK state would run a largely interventionist economic model.

Who wins and loses?

How Brexit plays out in costs and losses for certain individuals and groups and wins and benefits for others depends on a range of factors, not least what type of agreement the UK and EU reach over the UK's exit and new UK–EU relationship. Increased competition from a hard Brexit, seeking new trade agreements, and deregulation could deliver a longer-term change to the UK economy that leaves it more resilient to an increasingly competitive global economy. At the same time, several studies have shown that areas across England where majorities of people voted to leave the EU are those most likely to feel negative economic effects because their economies are more closely connected to the rest of the EU than areas such as London that voted for Remain (Springford 2016). This would add to existing political pressures on the UK government to take action to compensate or alleviate any losses in such areas.

This is not to argue Remain areas will not be hit. London could see significant losses. But it has a globalised and diversified economy that is less dependent on the EU than other parts of the UK. This was shown by how London and the South East of England were hit hardest by the 2008 financial crisis, but recovered more quickly and strongly than other areas of the UK (Dhingra, Machin and Overman 2017).

An approach is therefore needed that assesses the economic impact in a broad and encompassing way. Menon (2017) set out four economic tests to assess the effect of Brexit; these tests can be used to assess Brexit's economic effect as it emerges. First, will Brexit improve the UK's economy, prosperity and public finances? Second, will it lead to a fairer society with more opportunities across the UK or will it benefit only a select few and certain areas? Third, will it preserve and extend an economy and society that is open? Fourth, will it enhance the democratic control the British people have over their own lives and the future of the UK?

Further readings

Anthony Barnett, *The Lure of Greatness: England's Brexit and America's Trump* (Unbound, 2017). A veteran campaigner for a more democratic Britain, Barnett identifies a range of causes of Brexit and especially those connected to the place of non-London England within the UK.

Nick Clegg, *How to Stop Brexit (and Make Britain Great Again)* (Vintage, 2017). The former Liberal Democrat leader and deputy prime minister takes aim at some of the myths of Brexit and sets out how it can be reversed.

Ian Dunt, *Brexit: What the Hell Happens Now?* (Canbury Press, 2016). Published soon after the vote, it gives an easily digested – but Remain-leaning – account of what may unfold. An updated edition is due out in 2018.

Gary Gibbon, *Breaking Point: The UK Referendum on the EU and Its Aftermath* (University of Chicago Press, 2017). The *Channel 4 News* political editor's short pamphlet not only looks into what drove Brexit, but also provides some analysis of what it could mean for the UK and the remaining EU.

Stephen Green, *Brexit and the British* (University of Chicago Press, 2017). Another pamphlet that delves into the divisions in British society to find answers to why Britain voted as it did.

Liam Halligan and Gerald Lyons, *Clean Brexit: Why Leaving the EU Still Makes Sense – Building a Post-Brexit Economy for All* (Biteback, 2017). Offers a positive case for Brexit that addresses many of the concerns raised in the debate since the vote to leave.

Daniel Hannan, *What Next: How to Get the Best from Brexit* (Head of Zeus, 2016). The Conservative MEP and longstanding Eurosceptic offers a Leaver's analysis of where Britain and UK–EU relations can go next, with a focus on the nature of UK democracy.

Gerry Hassan and Russell Gunson (eds), *Scotland and the UK After Brexit. A Guide to the future*. (Luath Press, 2017). An edited volume covering a wide range of issues about what Brexit means for the future of Scotland, especially in terms of its relations with the UK and the EU.

Janice Morphet, *Beyond Brexit: How to Assess the UK's Future* (Policy Press, 2017). A detailed and academic analysis that looks at the implications of Brexit across a wide range of institutions and policy areas.

Robert Peston, *WTF* (Hodder & Stoughton, 2017). One of Britain's best-known political and business journalists, Peston offers a much-lauded account of what has happened over the past few years to Britain's politics, economy and society, and offers some ideas on how to fix things.

SIX

Europe and Brexit

Introduction

This chapter looks at the second set of negotiations and processes outlined at the end of Chapter Four, which are taking place at the European level. They are summarised below in Table 6.1. They can be divided into two groups: those between the UK and the EU, and those within the remaining EU. UK–EU negotiators need to reach agreement over three deals: an exit deal, a deal over a transition arrangement, and a new post-Brexit EU–UK relationship. This chapter examines what options exist for each and sets out what the two sides have said they want. It also examines the way in which the remaining EU approaches the negotiations, especially in terms of how the 27 member states and EU institutions maintain their unity in the face of the UK. What Britain can expect from the EU in terms of an overall deal depends on what happens to the remaining EU, which is the focus of the second group of processes. The chapter examines arguments about how the balance of power within the remaining EU will shift, what this could mean for the unity and direction of the EU, and in turn what that might mean for Brexit. It could also, as the chapter then examines, have implications for the relationship between the EU and the rest of non-EU Europe, especially organisations such as the EEA and EFTA. Finally, there is the challenge of continuing with the EU's daily business as a union of 28 member states, where one of those states is set to leave but in the meantime retains the same rights (excepting in some areas connected to the negotiations over its exit) as all the other member states.

Table 6.1: Europe's Brexit processes

Negotiations	Participants	Issues
UK–EU: Article 50 and an exit deal	European Parliament, European Commission, UK, EU 27 governments	The divorce: exit agreement for the UK covering mainly UK budget contributions, Northern Ireland border, the status of UK and EU citizens.
Brexit transition	European Parliament, European Commission, UK, EU 27 governments	The moving out: possible transition arrangements for the UK out of the EU. Or is it an implementation period or an extension to the negotiations?
New relationship	European Parliament, European Commission, UK, EU 27 governments	The new relationship: agreement between the UK and EU over a new relationship.
Brexit and the 27 other EU member states	EU 27 governments and their domestic political structures, European Parliament, European Commission, CJEU	Facing a Britishless EU: remaining EU member states need to reach agreement over what to offer the UK and over what time frame, with countries potentially ratifying any agreement individually.
Rebalancing the EU	EU 27, European Parliament, Commission, the CJEU	The future of the EU: the new balance of power within the post-Brexit EU, the Eurozone's place in the EU, and European integration, disintegration or muddling through.
EU in Europe	EU, Norway, Switzerland, Iceland, Lichtenstein, Turkey, Ukraine, non-EU Balkan countries, UK	EU in Europe: ideas about the future of the EU's relations with non-EU European countries, EU–EEA/EFTA relations, and European geopolitics.
EU's daily business	EU as a union of 28 member states until the UK exit becomes formally effective	Continuity: how to let the UK and the rest of the EU continue normal non-Brexit business until the UK withdraws.

Phase 1: exit negotiations

British and EU negotiating teams have been led by David Davis and Michel Barnier. Davis, who has twice run for the leadership of the Conservative Party, was a prominent Leave campaigner and not a member of David Cameron's cabinet. Barnier, a former French foreign minister and European Commissioner, was portrayed in the British press as anti-British because of his reportedly negative views on Anglo-Saxon economics. Despite Davis's and the UK negotiating team's hopes that negotiations over an exit deal and new relationship would happen in parallel, the UK and EU agreed to negotiations unfolding in three phrases. The first phase covers such issues as a budgetary settlement, the status of UK citizens in the EU and UK citizens in the EU, and cross-border issues, especially that of the UK-Irish border. In

December 2017, the European Council agreed that 'sufficient progress' had been made and so negotiations moved on to the second phrase, which will cover a transition arrangement. If a deal over phase 2 is successfully agreed, and one was provisionally agreed in March 2018, then phase 3 negotiations begin over a new relationship between the UK and the EU, which will mainly focus on trade but where other aspects of the relationship (such as security relations) will be agreed.

If negotiations move according to the time frame agreed then it is hoped an overall deal will be ready to be put to the British Parliament and European Parliament at the end of 2018. That would allow time for the Article 50 deal to be signed before 29 March 2019. Agreeing to a new relationship might take longer, and while it is possible – under Article 50(3) – to extend the two-year time frame, this would mean the UK remains a member state during any extension. A transition deal is therefore considered more likely.

The overall structure of the negotiations is unique, given only overseas territories such as Greenland have ever withdrawn from the EU. Can it therefore be compared with anything? Charles Grant of the Centre for European Reform offers a useful analogy of the process of accession by which a country joins the EU, albeit in reverse. As he told *The Guardian*:

> Departing the EU has turned out to be very much like accession. It's called a negotiation, but that is a way of trying to be polite. The truth is if you want to join, you join on their terms. You can quibble about the details but the broad lines are decided by the EU and dressed up as a negotiation. Similarly, when you leave the EU, once you declare your red lines, then the range of opportunities for the future relationship are very limited. (Roberts 2017)

Article 50

In its statement following the UK's referendum result, the remaining EU member states made clear that formal negotiations would only begin when the UK triggered Article 50. The article, largely unknown and overlooked until the UK held a referendum, was first proposed as part of the European Constitution, which later became the Lisbon Treaty, ratified in 2009. Before its inclusion, the EU treaties contained no provision for a member state to withdraw, although this is possible under international law as the EU is an international organisation from which its member states have the right to withdraw at anytime. The article was included in the EU's treaties so as to provide some structure to what would be an unprecedented experience. This meant the article was untested, viewed as an unopened Pandora's box and therefore seen also as a deterrent to attempting withdrawal rather than something designed to facilitate it (T. Oliver 2013). The wording, set out in box 6.1, leaves several issues unclear.

Box 6.1 Article 50 TEU

1. Any Member State may decide to withdraw from the Union in accordance with its own constitutional requirements.

2. A Member State which decides to withdraw shall notify the European Council of its intention. In the light of the guidelines provided by the European Council, the Union shall negotiate and conclude an agreement with that State, setting out the arrangements for its withdrawal, taking account of the framework for its future relationship with the Union. That agreement shall be negotiated in accordance with Article 218(3) of the Treaty on the Functioning of the European Union. It shall be concluded on behalf of the Union by the Council, acting by a qualified majority, after obtaining the consent of the European Parliament.

3. The Treaties shall cease to apply to the State in question from the date of entry into force of the withdrawal agreement or, failing that, two years after the notification referred to in paragraph 2, unless the European Council, in agreement with the Member State concerned, unanimously decides to extend this period.

4. For the purposes of paragraphs 2 and 3, the member of the European Council or of the Council representing the withdrawing Member State shall not participate in the discussions of the European Council or Council or in decisions concerning it.

A qualified majority shall be defined in accordance with Article 238(3) (b) of the Treaty on the Functioning of the European Union.

5. If a State which has withdrawn from the Union asks to rejoin, its request shall be subject to the procedure referred to in Article 49.

The article refers to 'arrangements for [the member state's] withdrawal, taking account of the framework for its future relationship with the Union'. That is two sets of deals: one on withdrawal, arranged through the process set out in Article 50, the other on a future relationship to be agreed under Article 218(3). But it is only for the withdrawal deal that Article 50 sets down a time frame for negotiations, which is two years.

There have long been widespread doubts that it is possible to negotiate and ratify both deals in two years. This meant that triggering Article 50 would make time an ally of the EU because it would be largely the UK that needed a deal, meaning it would be in a race against time to agree one. As a result, the British government would lose control of the negotiating process, which would then be in the hands of the EU. At the same time, the two-year time frame ensures a departing member state cannot be held hostage by the EU through an open-ended process. The EU was also bound to negotiate under the provisions of Article 50 because otherwise it would be in breach of its own treaty, something the CJEU could have been asked to intervene to prevent. The UK government had hoped that the EU would negotiate Brexit before Article 50 was triggered, but the EU was adamant that this would not happen.

In the end, Prime Minister May gave in to pressure from her backbenchers and ministers, who felt any significant delay in triggering Article 50 would be a betrayal of the referendum result. When she triggered Article 50 on Wednesday 29 March 2017 she started the two-year countdown to Britain's formal exit from the EU at midnight (Central European Time) on 29 March 2019. The Article 50 negotiations, which began as Phase 1 of the Brexit negotiations, have been about shared assets, liabilities, and responsibilities such as towards UK citizens living elsewhere in the EU and EU citizens living in the UK.

The budget

How much Britain owes to the EU, and whether it owes anything at all, has been one of the most contentious issues in the Article 50 negotiations. Figures ranging from €20 billion to €100 billion have been raised, with some arguing the UK owes nothing or in some cases is owed money because of its share of EU assets. Such speculation is the result of legal uncertainties about what the UK does and does not owe, precise amounts being difficult to calculate because of changing exchange rates, differences over the choice of financial years on which to calculate an estimate, and because arguments over any budget – EU or national – can often be difficult, poisonous and divisive.

Questions about money are also something the general public can easily relate to. In the UK's case the '£350 million a week' claim made by Vote Leave overshadows the calculations for the UK's exit. Despite that figure being frequently debunked, the claim that Britain would receive a financial windfall from leaving the EU now contrasts with Britain being asked to pay billions to the EU for several more years. The figures themselves also highlight a difference in perspective between what governments spend and what the public perceives as fair or proportional. While a figure such as £30 billion is a lot of money (not least at a time when the UK state continues to impose tough austerity measures), it is just under 4 per cent of overall UK government spending, which in 2016–17 totalled £772 billion, and a smaller amount when spread over several years. This approach can also be used to argue that the cost of making up for a hole in the EU's budget from Brexit is equally small on the EU side, not least when spread out over 27 member states. Yet just as in the UK, the publics and parliaments of other EU member states are deeply uneasy at paying more into the EU to replace one of the EU budget's largest contributors.

What might the UK owe money for and what might it be owed in return? First, the UK has committed to spending money on EU projects (such as research or transport infrastructure) that will not be complete until after the UK leaves. Second, the EU budget is set in a seven-year framework, with the existing one running from 2014 to 2020. As shown in Figure 6.1, Britain is one of the largest contributors and in committing to this budget is, from the EU's perspective, liable for paying its seven years of contributions. The legality of this is much disputed by the UK government. The House of Lords European Committee also concluded that legally the UK will not owe anything on exiting the EU without a deal because EU law, and therefore the agreements over the budget, would no longer apply; although it notes this would cause considerable tensions in wider UK–EU relations (House of Lords European Committee 2017). Third, there are longer-term commitments such as pensions for UK staff and MEPs. The UK could attempt to buy itself out of this commitment. Finally, the UK may be owed money because of its share of the EU's assets (the EU's buildings and investments in such things as the EU Investment Bank) and any calculation needs to also take into account what money the UK would have received up to 2020 in the form of EU projects in the UK. Whatever Britain is asked to pay has to be contrasted with the potential costs for the UK of a 'chaotic' or 'no deal' Brexit. This is one factor the UK government has had to consider. At the same time, the stability and predictability of the EU's own budget is a highly important matter for the remaining EU, which explains why it moved to ensure the question of the budget was solved in phase 1 of the negotiations.

Finding a way forward led to suggestions that the UK 'pay for access' as part of a transition deal. David Davis said that the UK government would consider making a continuing EU financial contribution to 'get the best possible access for goods and services to the European market'. It means that as in so much of the Brexit negotiations the UK faces trade-offs that connect to other parts of the Brexit negotiations. In the December 2017 deal over the end of the phase 1 negotiations, a formula was agreed without specifying an exact amount the UK is to pay. Estimates put the figure at around £40 billion.

Figure 6.1: Contributions to the EU budget (share of total after all rebates, percentage, 2016)

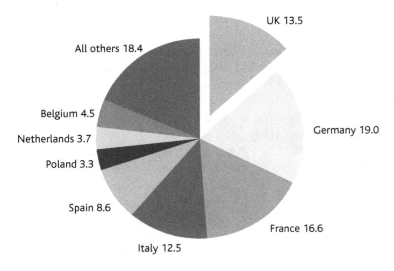

Source: HM Treasury (2017, 12).

Northern Ireland

Anglo-Irish relations have been transformed over the past few decades. Centuries of antagonism and conflict have been replaced with partnership inside the EU and a peace process in Northern Ireland. Brexit has cast a shadow over both, especially the latter. Common membership of the EU, which both countries joined on the same day in 1973, has been an important background feature to improved UK-Irish relations and especially the Northern Ireland peace process. Negotiators have faced the challenge of finding solutions to several sets of problems.

Political relations in Northern Ireland remain difficult. Northern Ireland voted to remain in the EU, but there were clear divides along sectarian lines in both voting and party positions. The main unionist party, the DUP, campaigned for Leave while the main nationalist party, Sinn Fein, supported Remain. The Northern Ireland Executive, which operates under a consociational power-sharing arrangement where both unionists and nationalists are represented, has since the referendum collapsed due to the failure of an energy scheme. Elections to the Northern Ireland Assembly and the UK Parliament saw the gap between the DUP and Sinn Fein close, but there was still no clear end in sight to the strained relations that led to the collapse of the power-sharing executive. If no new government is formed then London can impose direct rule. The situation has been further complicated by the UK's general election result, leaving the minority Conservative government dependent on the DUP for votes to keep it in power. The potential for a collapse in relations between the two sides in Northern Ireland is not to be casually overlooked. The spectre of a return to violence is something many fear.

Brexit raises broad questions about the freedom of movement between Ireland and Northern Ireland (and the rest of the UK), the identity and rights of Northern Ireland's citizens, and the economic needs of a region that faces significant problems. The British government, the Irish government and the EU have all been clear that Northern Ireland is a major concern for the Brexit negotiations. It is around the future of the Republic of Ireland–Northern Ireland border that many wider issues of Republic of Ireland–Northern Ireland–UK cooperation have come to hang. Because of the UK-Irish Common Travel Area the border has always been an open one, which today sees an estimated 110 million crossings a year. All sides say they wish to avoid a 'hard border', but how to do this is unclear. On leaving the EU the border will be not only the UK-Irish border but also the UK–EU border. If Brexit is a 'hard Brexit' then the UK leaves the EEA and the EU's customs union with the result that a hard border would be needed by both the UK and the EU/Ireland to check the movement of people and goods. Otherwise the border would become an opening through which people and goods could move between the two in ways that are unmonitored. A border would cause political tensions among the nationalist community, who are committed to free movement around the island of Ireland.

In the deal reached in December 2017, the UK agreed that in order to avoid a hard border, unless Northern Ireland's institutions decide to align separately with the EU, then the rest of the UK would maintain alignment with 'those rules of the Internal Market and the Customs Union which, now or in the future, support North-South cooperation, the all-island economy and the protection of the 1998 Agreement'. Essentially, the UK conceded that if no new relationship deal were agreed then in order to guarantee the regulatory alignments required by the 1998 Good Friday Agreement – and thus avoid a hard border between the Irish Republic and Northern Ireland and so maintain the Northern Ireland peace process – the UK would 'propose specific solutions to address the unique circumstances of the island of Ireland'. If solutions cannot be agreed then the UK will maintain the aforementioned requirement for full alignment with the rules of the Internal Market and Customs Union. The UK, Ireland and the EU disagree as to what this might mean. Michel Barnier has said that alignment would be with the 'full internal market'. In the EU's view the UK's baseline now amounts to partial de facto single market and customs union membership, a view meeting with the approval of the Remainers in the UK cabinet. Advocates of a hard Brexit, in contrast, would limit alignment to areas necessary for the operation of the Good Friday Agreement such as the cross-border supply of water. A broad interpretation would severely restrict the UK's ability to forge an independent UK trade policy with non-EU countries and markets. The deal allows the Northern Ireland institutions to accept regulatory divergence between Northern Ireland and Great Britain. This would allow an internal UK border with the consent of Stormont. Should Northern Ireland not adopt such an approach then the UK is bound, as set out in paragraph 49, to apply that amount of regulatory alignment necessary to preserve the integration of the all-Ireland economy. This also opens the possibility of other parts of the UK – including Scotland, and, perhaps, London – pushing for the right to diverge or align, although neither the UK government nor the EU has hinted at being prepared to countenance this.

The problems over the situation of the border between the Irish Republic and Northern Ireland is a reminder of how the biggest challenge has been the UK government's – and more specifically the cabinet and Conservative parliamentary party's – inability to agree what they want the new UK–EU relationship to be. This is clear in the deal's fudge over the future status of Northern Ireland and the extent of the UK's eventual alignment with the rules of the single market and customs union. It is therefore important to note the line used in the report, and one often heard in EU negotiations: 'that nothing is agreed until everything is agreed'. As the first of a three-part process, it will be in the deals over a transition and then a new relationship when the UK and EU will have to confront the fudge over the Northern Ireland border.

Citizens' rights

Freedom of movement has long been an integral part of the EU and has been one of the reasons why today there are an estimated 3.2 million EU citizens living in the UK and 1.2 million Britons living elsewhere in the EU. Concerns about immigration were also one of the reasons why, as discussed in Chapter Four, many British people voted to leave the EU. Brexit means the rights of those 4.4 million people will now need to be renegotiated. Both the UK and the EU have made the need for guarantees over the status of their citizens a key requirement. Negotiations focused on how to guarantee these citizens their rights, such as those covering residence, employment, pensions, welfare, education and health care. The EU has sought to preserve a status quo for EU citizens in the UK, something the UK has been opposed to as this could entail a role for the CJEU in protecting these citizens' rights.

The UK also faces a considerable administrative and political task of registering 3.2 million EU citizens. The Home Office will need to register EU citizens and confirm how long they have been resident so as to ensure they are entitled to remain beyond Brexit. As members of the EU, the right to reside in the UK has been automatic for other EU citizens. They have not been required to register, although they could have done so voluntarily. The UK has not kept any detailed track of people entering from the rest of the EU, and on the Northern Ireland border people can come and go freely as part of the UK-Irish Common Travel Area. The process by which EU nationals will now have to prove they have resided in the UK could therefore be a complex one, dependent on them providing proof which can then be checked by the Home Office. The existing system has already led to a large number of mistakes, often highlighted in the media in the UK and elsewhere in Europe. Simplifying the procedure in order to process the large numbers will be required, otherwise a nightmare of an administrative backlog will soon emerge.

Whatever system is adopted, there will inevitably be complex cases such as over the rights of non-resident spouses or parents with UK-born children who might not qualify for residence while their children do. Some people will inevitably be rejected and will appeal to the courts, with some – mainly poorer, mentally ill or sick individuals – struggling to do so. Such problems are seen in every immigration system, but for the UK, Brexit poses a sudden large increase of demand on the system that could last several years and leave legal cases going on for much longer. It also places the burden on the individuals, possibly on businesses who employ them. This issue, like those surrounding Northern Ireland, would be simplified if the UK were to remain in the EEA and guarantee continued freedom of movement. That is unlikely if the UK insists on ending free movement and the jurisdiction of the CJEU. However, the role of the latter in protecting citizens' rights is something the EU has put forward. If the rights of UK and EU citizens were set down in a withdrawal agreement then it would be for the CJEU to interpret this for UK courts and courts in other EU member states. This stems in part from a lack of trust in the UK, and especially the Home Office's abilities to treat EU citizens fairly. Allowing the CJEU a role would also ensure uniform application of their rights across the rest of the EU.

Finally, the 1.2 million Britons – sometimes referred to as 'Brexpats' – living elsewhere in the EU should not be overlooked. They are a diverse and growing group of people who vary according to country, with large numbers of pensioners in Spain compared to younger and highly educated workers in Germany (Benton 2017). They therefore present an equally diverse range of problems associated with defining in each of the remaining 27 member states their legal status, labour rights and access to welfare.

In December 2017, as part of the agreement over the end of the phase 1 negotiations, the UK and EU agreed that EU citizens in the UK on the date of Britain's withdrawal will have the right to stay in the UK, with the CJEU playing a role for eight years in settling any disputes. UK citizens resident in the EU will also be guaranteed their existing rights. As mentioned above, this will form part of the overall deal to be ratified at the end of the negotiations by the UK and the remaining EU.

Figure 6.2: Numbers of EU citizens in the UK and UK citizens in other EU member states

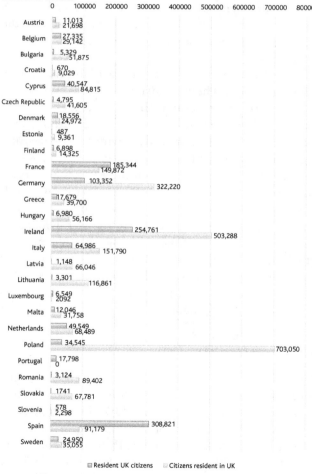

Source: United Nations Department of Economic and Social Affairs (2015).

A chaotic 'no deal' Brexit

One possible Brexit scenario would see UK–EU negotiations collapse or run out of time with the UK leaving the EU without an exit deal or a deal over a new relationship. This is known as a 'no deal' or 'chaotic' Brexit. If negotiations broke down then the UK, as it or any other member state is allowed to do under international law, could unilaterally decide to end its membership of the EU before March 2019. Alternatively, it could wait out the time remaining in the two-year time frame of Article 50 and use this time to prepare itself for Brexit. The outcome of such a breakdown would more than likely be acrimony on both the UK and EU sides, causing wider tensions, including on defence and security matters.

It would also leave the UK in an extremely uncertain legal and economic position. There are many questions and doubts about what will happen as soon as the EU's treaties and laws cease to apply, not least the regulations and laws governing trade (including UK participation in trade deals with other states) and such things as the movement of aircraft between the UK and the EU and all other states with which the EU has air service agreements. Tariffs would immediately apply to any goods exported into the EU, which would bring unwanted costs. EU citizens in the UK and UK citizens in the EU would find themselves facing a myriad of legal and political problems over defining their status. It might be thought that both sides would prefer to avoid such a scenario, but Theresa May has said that 'no deal is better than a bad deal', meaning she is prepared to contemplate such a development.

Can the UK reverse Brexit?

The opposite to a 'chaotic' or 'no deal' Brexit would be for the UK to remain in the EU. Whether and how this could happen depends on the domestic politics of the UK, the technicalities of Article 50 and the response of the EU. Domestically, as discussed in the previous chapter, the UK Parliament could vote to remain in the EU, either by voting to rescind Article 50 or by rejecting any exit deal eventually put to them and instead voting in favour of remaining rather than exiting without a deal. Parliamentary sovereignty allows parliament to vote at any time to remain without the need for another referendum. However, as touched on in the previous chapter, a second referendum that voted in favour of remaining would also be one way to secure the domestic authority to attempt a reversal of Brexit.

Holding a second referendum would give rise to accusations that those who lost the first referendum have been 'sore losers'. It is likely the EU would also be accused of facilitating a second vote to get the answer it wants, something it has been accused of doing in the past when the citizens of a country have voted against an EU treaty only to be asked to vote again, albeit following some minor changes. Finally, as Menon and Fowler (2016, R9) argue:

> The same background factors as underpinned the referendum result remain in place – the lack of popular affinity for the EU, low levels of public knowledge, the lack of practised and effective public arguments for integration, splits within the two main UK parties and divisions and disaffection in the country at large that undercut support for internationalized economic liberalism and the elites who advocate it.

If attitudes change and the UK decides in future to rejoin then it will have to do so through Article 49 of the Treaty of the European Union and therefore follow the same procedures any other new member state has faced, including the need to meet membership requirements set down by the existing member states and EU institutions.

Whatever the British people or Parliament think, whether Brexit can be reversed is not something the UK can unilaterally decide on as the decision also rests with the remaining members of the EU. Article 50 does not set out how it might be reversed once triggered, although one of its drafters, former UK diplomat Lord Kerr, has argued that it can be reversed (Weaver 2017). The only body capable of deciding the legality of such a move would be the CJEU, whose role is to interpret and enforce the EU's treaties. Much would also hang on how to interpret the Vienna Convention on the Law of Treaties, which includes articles on how states withdraw from treaties. Politically, the other member states may want the UK to remain, but this would more than likely require unanimous agreement and be met with much frustration and anger at the UK's behaviour at triggering Article 50 in the first place. In such a situation the rest of the EU could demand that Britain pay a price. Without this, Article 50 could end up being seen as a negotiation tool whereby a member state can repeatedly start and stop the two-year time frame until they get a favourable negotiating position. It was for this reason that a time limit was included.

Phase 2: Brexit transition

It has long been clear that Article 50's two-year time frame is inadequate for settling both a deal over an exit and the full contents of a new relationship. Article 50 does include the possibility of the UK and the rest of the EU agreeing to an extension of the two-year period, but that extension would require the UK to remain a member state. There has therefore been much discussion about the need for some form of arrangement to bridge the end of the two years and the formal start of a new relationship. Negotiating what this might entail is, however, far from simple. Not only do some question whether a transition is needed, but it is also unclear as to whether it should be called a 'transition', an 'extension' to the negotiations, an 'interim period', or a period of 'phased implementation'. As is explored further below, each of these carries different meanings. Whatever it turns out to be, the bigger question to be asked is what new relationship it is to be a bridge to.

Reasons for and against a transition period

There are two main reasons put forward for a transition period and two sets of reasons put forward by those who oppose it. First, as noted, the two-year period is widely considered inadequate for concluding all the negotiations. By providing a period of continued close relations after March 2019 the UK and EU would avoid a 'no deal' or 'chaotic' Brexit. At the beginning of the negotiations the EU itself was open to the possibility of such a transition period. Both sides may need extra time to put administrative, legal and physical plans in place, such as extra facilities at the ports of Dover and Calais. It also allows time for negotiations with third countries that may be affected by Brexit, such as those with trade deals with the EU. That said, the British government has been unclear as to whether it sees a transition period as allowing it more time to prepare and implement Brexit or to fully negotiate what it means.

Second, the prospect of a transition period allows the UK's Conservative government a degree of obfuscation. On the one side it allows the government to declare that the UK has left the EU in March 2019 even if in reality many aspects of the UK's relations with the EU remain the same. Those opposed to such a transition deal argue it would be a betrayal of those who voted for Brexit. Nigel Farage accused the UK government of 'backsliding' over Brexit in its willingness to consider a transition. He and other Eurosceptics see a transition as a way of watering down Brexit or delaying it in the hope of reversing it. The UK could also be turned into a 'vassal state' because it would no longer have any say over how the EU is run but could remain bound by its laws and the jurisdiction of the CJEU and be required to allow continued free movement. Opponents of a transition period also argue it prolongs uncertainty and plays into the EU's hands. Instead, they argue the UK should opt for a 'clean Brexit' whereby it cuts all ties in March 2019, something others term a 'no deal' Brexit.

The contents of a transition deal

A transition deal could see the UK and EU enter into one of several arrangements. First, it could be a phased transition period in which the UK withdraws – or changes its relationship – in stages, such as over customs, immigration, justice and home affairs. The UK government has argued this would also allow the UK the time to strike its own trade deals with third countries. Second, an 'off the shelf' model could be used such as the UK remaining a member of the EEA in a way similar to that of Norway. This would be the simplest option in terms of similarity with existing arrangements. It would, however, see the UK largely remain in the EU and bound by its rules. Third, should the UK seek to maintain as close a relationship as its existing one then for the EU this would have to fit with the EU's negotiating guidelines set down in April 2017: 'Any such transitional arrangements must be clearly defined, limited in time, and subject to effective enforcement mechanisms. Should a time-limited prolongation of Union acquis be considered, this would require existing Union regulatory, budgetary, supervisory, judiciary and enforcement instruments and structures to apply.'

In keeping with the EU's negotiating mantra that 'nothing is agreed until everything is agreed', what a transition deal might entail can only be settled once it is agreed what new relationship the UK and EU are transitioning to, the subject of the third phase of negotiations. In a sense, arguing what should be in a transition deal is, as the saying goes, putting the cart before the horse. Arguing about a transition as opposed to the final UK–EU relationship has therefore been described as a 'phoney war' (Menon and Portes 2017). Michel Barnier said that he is open to the idea of an implementation phase. However, he also declared that 'until we know what the intentions of a request from the UK are, what they would like and what they are prepared to accept with this new partnership, it's going to be difficult to talk about a transitional period'.

It would also make for a difficult process for approving a transition deal. If the transition were part of the Article 50 deal then that would be simpler as it would only require a QMV in the Council after securing the agreement of the European Parliament. Any other route may require unanimity and face challenges within the member states. In the UK the EU Withdrawal Bill is designed to end such things as the jurisdiction of the CJEU, which might need to continue during a transition period. However, the Bill grants the government the powers to implement the withdrawal agreement, which could lead the government to allow the CJEU and EU laws to continue applying to the UK. Securing the necessary votes for this may also be difficult given the numbers in the House of Commons.

Phase 3: a new relationship

The conundrum of 'Brexit means Brexit' will only be answered once the new UK–EU relationship becomes clear. A great deal of debate has focused on the possible major changes to the UK–EU trading relationship. As Holmes, Rollo and Winters (2016, R22) point out, among the things that need to be negotiated are:

- extracting the UK's WTO schedules from the EU's schedules and resetting relations with the non-EU members of the multilateral trading system;
- negotiating a new trading relationship with the remaining 27 members of the EU;
- designing and agreeing the UK's future trade relations with least developed countries and other developing countries covered by the EU's Generalised System of Preferences; and
- agreeing trade deals with other countries, including those with which the UK already has deals via the EU, those with which the EU has agreed but not ratified a deal, those with which the EU is currently negotiating and other potential trade partners.

The issue of the UK's new trade deals outside of Europe is explored in Chapter Seven. Here the focus is on the options for a new UK–EU relationship and some of the WTO negotiations that will need to be undertaken. Debate about the new relationship has largely focused on the economics, a reflection of the referendum debate itself, which often portrayed the UK–EU relationship as primarily an economic relationship. As Table 5.3 showed, the UK has a large trading relationship with the rest of the EU, with the EU accounting for approximately half of the UK's goods and services imports and exports. However, as covered in the next chapter, the focus on trade can overlook the political and security sides to the UK–EU relationship. Below are set out some of the most frequently debated new relationships, ranging from the softest – EEA membership – through to the hardest – WTO relations.

UK–EU options

Having EU cake and eating it

The ideal Brexit deal for the UK would be one that allows it to retain the parts of EU membership it likes while jettisoning those parts it dislikes. This can sometimes be referred to as 'cherry picking'. It would see the UK retain complete access to the EU's single market in the areas it likes (free movement of goods, services and capital), dropping the commitment to free movement of people, leaving such things as the Common Agricultural Policy and Common Fisheries Policy, ending the jurisdiction of the CJEU, ceasing payments to the EU, being allowed to negotiate its own trade deals, and having some form of working relationship with the EU that allows it a voice in the EU's decision making, especially on foreign and security matters.

Such a relationship would defy the old saying that you 'can't have your cake and eat it' or have more than is reasonable. Boris Johnson disagreed, arguing that on UK–EU relations, '[m]y policy on cake is pro having it and pro eating it'. The EU would never allow such a deal. The EU's single market is the most ambitious form of trade cooperation in the world. It allows for the free movement of goods, services, capital and people with no tariffs, quotas or taxes on trade. Because of different national regulations and standards, the EU is a regulatory union that provides and enforces regulatory convergence to create a level playing field. The market (and the EU's efforts to police and coordinate it) are far from perfect, but it offers greater freedoms than in any other form of trade deal. It also has some costs, such as compliance with EU laws, membership of the customs union (thus restricting the right to negotiate separate trade deals) and payments into a central pot to fund pan-European projects. By allowing Britain a deal where it gets to drop the costs but retain the benefits, the EU would create a form of relationship with the EU with more benefits than the remaining members gain from membership.

Norway/EEA

Continued membership of the single market is widely considered the softest of the plausible 'soft Brexits' (Fossum and Graver 2018). This can happen for non-EU states through membership of the EEA. The EEA consists of both EU member states and some members of EFTA who have decided to participate, which are Norway, Iceland and Liechtenstein. These three accept the four freedoms (with all three also having joined Schengen) and are committed to adopting EU law, which is enforced, albeit indirectly, through a Brussels-based supranational EFTA Surveillance Authority and adjudicated on by the EFTA Court based in Luxembourg, which follows the rulings of the CJEU. Members are exempt from some EU policies, such as the EU's agricultural policies. The members also contribute towards the EU's funding for less-developed areas of the EU.

Switzerland/EFTA

Compared to most other non-EEA countries, Switzerland has extensive access to the EU's single market, albeit much less than being inside it or that enjoyed by Norway, Iceland or Liechtenstein. Switzerland is therefore under no obligation to accept new EU legislation, but given its location and dependence on the single market, it often develops its laws with the EU in mind. To facilitate access to the single market, the EU and Switzerland have drawn up a number of bilateral agreements covering a range of areas, but they are not comprehensive and as yet do not include an agreement on financial services. Switzerland is also under no obligation to accept further EU legislation implemented after these agreements come into force, unlike in the case of Norway, Iceland and Liechtenstein.

From the perspective of the EU, Switzerland has cherry-picked agreements and, unlike Norway, Iceland and Liechtenstein, lacks supranational oversight of the agreements, meaning disputes can go unresolved. The arrangement was never intended to be a long-term model and has created growing frustrations on both sides. It is therefore unlikely to be a relationship the EU would willingly agree to with the UK, because the size of the relationship would be far more complex and present much bigger problems.

Canadian-style free trade agreement

A number of trade deals that the EU has negotiated or has been negotiating with countries around the world have been put forward as possible models for a new UK–EU relationship. The recently agreed EU–Canada Economic and Trade Agreement (CETA) has often been mentioned, as has the Transatlantic Trade and Investment Partnership (TTIP) the EU and US have been negotiating. Compared to membership of the single market, trade agreements such as that with Canada do not guarantee the same degree of free movement of goods and services, especially the latter. This is important for the UK given the large size of its service sector and the large service exports the UK produces. Compared to other free trade agreements (FTA), negotiations over TTIP have focused on access to services, but this has made it very controversial as this has meant discussing access to areas such as health services (something discussed further in Chapter Seven). An FTA would mean there is no free movement and the UK would be exempt from the jurisdiction of the CJEU, although there would be institutions to arbitrate over disputes (such as TTIP's controversial Investor–State Dispute Settlement panels) with UK access to the single market restricted in the event of non-compliance.

Customs union

A customs union is one where the member states apply the same tariffs to all goods from outside the union, but once cleared in one country they can be freely shipped to another. Membership of the EU's customs union includes non-EU states, with Turkey being a member. This restricts the options open to such countries in pursuing their own trade deals. By contrast, Norway, which is in the EEA, is not in the customs union. As a result of this 'rules of origin' apply, whereby tariffs can be applied to goods imported to Norway but then sold on inside the single market. The EEA agreement provides for tariff-free movement for goods produced in the participating member state (which because of multinational supply chains often means at least 60 per cent of the good must have been produced in the state). Rules of origin requirements add an administrative cost but prevent Norway being a backdoor into the single market for goods not produced within it.

Association agreement

The UK and EU could develop an association agreement similar to the Deep and Comprehensive Free Trade Area (DCFTA) the EU negotiated with Ukraine. As Emerson (2016) sets out, this does offer some gains for the UK in the form of some access to the single market, continued membership of such agreements as the Single European Sky (which manages European airspace), participation in scientific and research initiatives, and provisions for cooperation in foreign, security and defence cooperation. However, compared to the EEA, this would not entail the same degree of access to the single market and the UK would more than likely expect more than is set out in the association agreement.

WTO membership

A Brexit without any form of deal would see the UK trade with the EU on WTO terms, widely considered to be the hardest of hard Brexits. Because this would entail non-membership of the single market, a large number of tariffs and non-tariff barriers would exist between the UK and its largest trading partner. As noted above, as Holmes, Rollo and Winters (2016, R22) point out, the UK will also need to extract the UK's WTO schedules (which are the agreements about how one member state of the WTO will treat the trade from another WTO member) from the EU's schedules and reset relations with the non-EU members of the multilateral trading system, especially those with whom the EU has negotiated trading agreements to which the UK has been a party but may not be after Brexit.

No major economy relies solely on WTO terms with which to trade. In addition to WTO terms, countries such as Australia or Japan have negotiated a number of arrangements such as mutual recognition in some areas through to a series of free trade deals with other countries that are an important and integral part of their economy. The US and EU have no free trade agreement with one another but they do have a large number of agreements over matters ranging from air travel to data sharing. If the UK withdrew from the EU without any new relationship with the EU and if in doing so it lost access to the trade deals and other arrangements the EU has with other states, then the UK would (until it signed agreements of its own) become the only major economy in the world to trade solely on WTO terms.

Deep and special partnership

Theresa May has spoken of her desire to see the UK and EU negotiate a 'deep and special partnership'. What this might mean in practice can be about as clear as 'Brexit means Brexit'. A broad outline exists of what the British people voted for, and as discussed in Chapter Five, in early 2017 May set down a list of 12 negotiating principles. What is lacking is a model or clear proposals to turn these outlines and principles into a concrete deal. Indeed, May herself has made clear that Britain cannot accept any 'off the shelf model', such as those mentioned above.

Despite this, there has been an unwillingness by the UK government to confront the limits to the choices on offer, not least acknowledging that trade-offs – either with the EU or for the UK's economy – are inevitable. For this reason, there have been calls for the EU to set out for the UK what its options are. One response is seen in Figure 6.3. The EU's lead negotiator, Michel Barnier, set out for EU leaders his 'Stairway to Brexit', in which the likely new UK–EU relationship is defined largely by what the UK's red lines leave as possible.

Barnier's stairway begins with EU membership, with the steps downward being EEA (Norway, Iceland, Liechtenstein), EFTA (Switzerland), an association agreement (Ukraine), membership of the EU's customs union (Turkey), a trade deal (Canada, South Korea) and, failing all of the above, no deal and trade on WTO terms. Based on the UK's red lines, an FTA akin to something such as that which the EU has with Canada is the UK's desired end point for a new UK–EU relationship. There are two

Figure 6.3: 'Barnier's Stairway to Brexit'

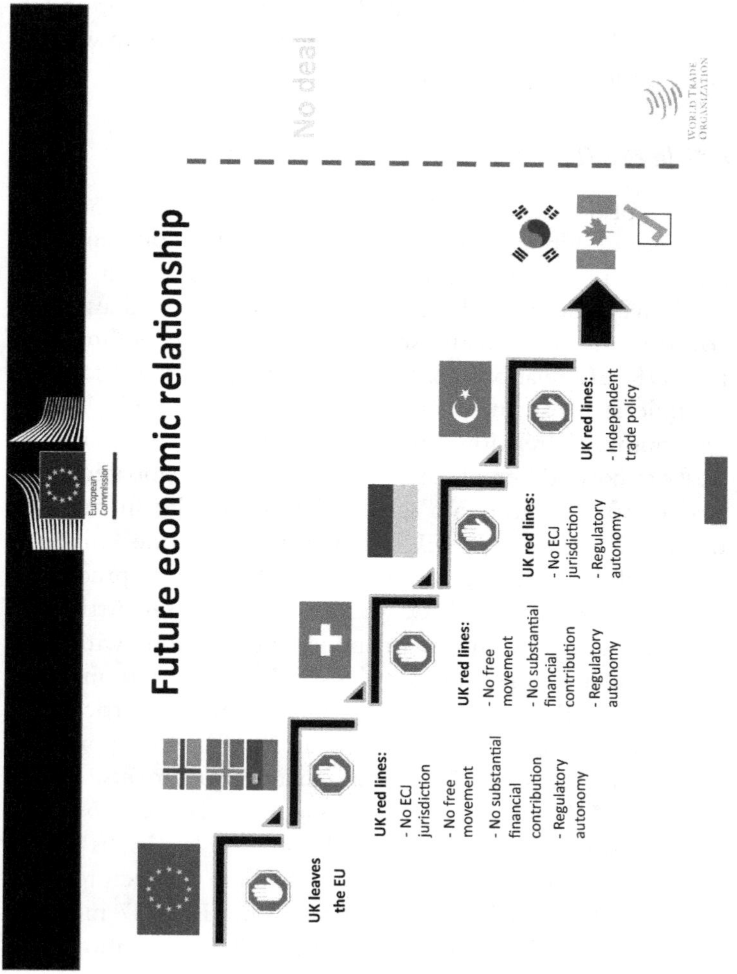

Future economic relationship

European Commission

No deal

WORLD TRADE ORGANIZATION

UK leaves the EU

UK red lines:
- No ECJ jurisdiction
- No free movement
- No substantial financial contribution
- Regulatory autonomy

UK red lines:
- No free movement
- No substantial financial contribution
- Regulatory autonomy

UK red lines:
- No ECJ jurisdiction
- Regulatory autonomy

UK red lines:
- Independent trade policy

problems here. First, as mentioned above, a Canadian-style deal would give weak access for services, meaning the UK would have to either push for agreement in such a difficult area or accept an economic cost to its service trade with the EU. Second, the above focus largely on the trade and regulatory relationship, when, as discussed in the next chapter, the relationship will also be a political and security one.

Article 218 TEU: ratifying a new relationship

An exit deal under Article 50 only agrees to the exit and not a new relationship with the departing member state (or 'framework for its future relations with the Union' as it is phrased in Article 50). Given the limited time, the part of the withdrawal deal covering the new relationship will likely be an outline for a new UK-EU relationship. Discussions to fill in the details will be undertaken during the transition period. For the EU, a new relationship (or relationships if there needs to be more than one treaty to cover different parts of it) will not be negotiated under Article 50 but through a series of other articles in the EU's treaties. That new UK–EU relationship, even one limited to trade, will be largely agreed by the EU through the procedures set out in Article 218 TEU, which is referred to in Article 50. This sets out how the EU conducts negotiations with third countries. It stipulates what roles the European Commission, Council and Parliament will play. A range of other articles will also be involved. Article 207 concerns how the EU approaches FTAs, while Article 217 covers association agreements. As seen above, the UK and EU may seek one or a mixture of both.

All eyes, however, will be largely on Article 218, as set out in box 6.2. Final agreement will require the Council to agree through a QMV where 72 per cent of the EU's 27 members (representing at least 65 per cent of the EU's population) vote in favour. The European Parliament would also be required to give its consent. However, the process becomes far more complex if the agreement includes an area where QMV is not allowed and unanimity is required, as happens over association agreements and in deals that are known as 'mixed agreements'. Unless a trade deal with the UK only touches on those areas for which the EU has competence, it will be a mixed agreement, a very likely development given the comprehensive deal the UK would like. Such trade deals must be ratified by each member state individually according to their constitutional requirements. This means that some of the 21 months of the proposed transition period will need to be set aside for the ratification of a new relationship in each member state. In some this will be a vote in Parliament. In other states it means the UK's new relationship could face approval by a large number of different national and regional parliaments, some putting the figure as high as a total of 37 parliaments (27 national parliaments, five of these also requiring votes in their upper chambers, and five regional parliaments in Belgium). In some cases there could be referendums on the deal. The Canada–EU trade agreement ran into problems in the Parliament of Wallonia, while in April 2016 the EU–Ukraine association agreement was rejected in a non-binding referendum in the Netherlands. In both cases concessions had to be negotiated for both Wallonia and the Netherlands before they would ratify the agreements. Ironically, the UK has been a keen advocate of mixed agreements so as to ensure national control of the EU's relationships. It may now find that process is a particularly difficult one for a third country. The CJEU can also be asked to rule on whether a deal is compatible with the EU's treaties, which has happened over certain aspects of the EU–Singapore and EU–Canada trade deals.

Box 6.2 Article 218 TEU

1. Without prejudice to the specific provisions laid down in Article 207, agreements between the Union and third countries or international organisations shall be negotiated and concluded in accordance with the following procedure.

2. The Council shall authorise the opening of negotiations, adopt negotiating directives, authorise the signing of agreements and conclude them.

3. The Commission, or the High Representative of the Union for Foreign Affairs and Security Policy where the agreement envisaged relates exclusively or principally to the common foreign and security policy,

shall submit recommendations to the Council, which shall adopt a decision authorising the opening of negotiations and, depending on the subject of the agreement envisaged, nominating the Union negotiator or the head of the Union's negotiating team.

4. The Council may address directives to the negotiator and designate a special committee in consultation with which the negotiations must be conducted.

5. The Council, on a proposal by the negotiator, shall adopt a decision authorising the signing of the agreement and, if necessary, its provisional application before entry into force.

6. The Council, on a proposal by the negotiator, shall adopt a decision concluding the agreement.

Except where agreements relate exclusively to the common foreign and security policy, the Council shall adopt the decision concluding the agreement:

(a) after obtaining the consent of the European Parliament in the following cases:

   (i)   association agreements;

   (ii) agreement on Union accession to the European Convention for the Protection of Human Rights and Fundamental Freedoms;

   (iii) agreements establishing a specific institutional framework by organising cooperation procedures;

   (iv) agreements with important budgetary implications for the Union;

   (v) agreements covering fields to which either the ordinary legislative procedure applies, or the special legislative procedure where consent by the European Parliament is required.

The European Parliament and the Council may, in an urgent situation, agree upon a time-limit for consent.

(b) after consulting the European Parliament in other cases. The European Parliament shall deliver its opinion within a time-limit which the Council may set depending on the urgency of the matter. In the absence of an opinion within that time-limit, the Council may act.

7. When concluding an agreement, the Council may, by way of derogation from paragraphs 5, 6 and 9, authorise the negotiator to approve on the Union's behalf modifications to the agreement where it provides

for them to be adopted by a simplified procedure or by a body set up by the agreement. The Council may attach specific conditions to such authorisation.

8. The Council shall act by a qualified majority throughout the procedure.

However, it shall act unanimously when the agreement covers a field for which unanimity is required for the adoption of a Union act as well as for association agreements and the agreements referred to in Article 212 with the States which are candidates for accession. The Council shall also act unanimously for the agreement on accession of the Union to the European Convention for the Protection of Human Rights and Fundamental Freedoms; the decision concluding this agreement shall enter into force after it has been approved by the Member States in accordance with their respective constitutional requirements.

9. The Council, on a proposal from the Commission or the High Representative of the Union for Foreign Affairs and Security Policy, shall adopt a decision suspending application of an agreement and establishing the positions to be adopted on the Union's behalf in a body set up by an agreement, when that body is called upon to adopt acts having legal effects, with the exception of acts supplementing or amending the institutional framework of the agreement.

10. The European Parliament shall be immediately and fully informed at all stages of the procedure.

11. A Member State, the European Parliament, the Council or the Commission may obtain the opinion of the Court of Justice as to whether an agreement envisaged is compatible with the Treaties. Where the opinion of the Court is adverse, the agreement envisaged may not enter into force unless it is amended or the Treaties are revised.

Views from the remaining EU

Too often British debate about Brexit has been about what deal would be best for the UK. As the outgoing French Ambassador to the UK noted in 2017, Britain talks to itself about Brexit. This overlooks that Brexit not only affects others, but will be shaped and decided on by the actions of others, most notably by what new relationship the rest of the EU is prepared to accept with the UK. How the rest of the EU responds can be understood by looking at four issues.

Member state views

Overall, the EU has stressed the unity of the 27 other member states on Brexit and support for the EU rose across the Union in response to Britain's vote to leave (T. Oliver 2018; De Vries 2017). Nevertheless, each country has distinctive interests that inform its own stance. Positions vary according to factors such as domestic election pressures, levels of Eurosceptic support within their populaces, security considerations, trade ties and patterns of migration with the UK. This varied, complex set of positions ranges from the likes of the UK's fellow non-Eurozone member, Sweden, whose political and economic interests have been broadly aligned with UK positions, to countries with more countervailing postures.

Take the example of France, which has long had a complex, contradictory relationship with the UK in the context of EU affairs. One reason Paris took a hard-line stance in the early phases of Brexit negotiations was political pressure from the 2017 French presidential race. The French government perceived that any early, significant concessions to the UK could feed political oxygen to National Front Leader Marine Le Pen, who had promised to change France's EU membership if she won power. Election-year issues aside, the toughness of France's Brexit positioning was reinforced by broader plans to tout Paris as a competing financial centre to London.

France has not been alone in having a complicated Brexit stance. For instance, Spain, home to hundreds of thousands of UK citizens, has a significant trade deficit with the UK, which might, other things being equal, favour softer negotiating positions. However, this picture is complicated by other factors, including Gibraltar's future. Madrid invited the UK government to post-Brexit negotiations on Gibraltar, including proposals for joint sovereignty. Such a solution has been touted by Spain as the only way for Gibraltar to secure continued access to the European single market, which is key for its economy.

To some other member states Brexit matters more than others in economic terms. As Table 6.2 shows, in 2016 all but three EU member states (Denmark, Ireland and Malta) exported more

Table 6.2: Trading links between EU member states and the UK

Country	UK exports to (2016) (GBP)	UK imports from (2016) (GBP)
Austria	£3 billion	£4.6 billion
Belgium	£15.9 billion	£26.2 billion
Bulgaria	£0.7 billion	£0.7 billion
Croatia	£0.3 billion	£0.6 billion
Cyprus	£1.1 billion	£1.3 billion
Czech Rep.	£3.1 billion	£6.1 billion
Denmark	£5.8 billion	£5.4 billion
Estonia	£0.3 billion	£0.3 billion
Finland	£2.7 billion	£2.8 billion
France	£33.8 billion	£37.6 billion
Germany	£49.1 billion	£75.1 billion
Greece	£1.8 billion	£3.5 billion
Hungary	£1.9 billion	£3.5 billion
Ireland	£26.7 billion	£20.8 billion
Italy	£17.3 billion	£22.6 billion
Latvia	£0.4 billion	£0.9 billion
Lithuania	£0.5 billion	£1.0 billion
Luxembourg	£2.6 billion	£2.6 billion
Malta	£1.1 billion	£1.0 billion
Netherlands	£31.0 billion	£42.4 billion
Poland	£5.9 billion	£11.5 billion
Portugal	£2.3 billion	£5.3 billion
Romania	£1.8 billion	£2.6 billion
Slovakia	£0.8 billion	£2.9 billion
Slovenia	£0.4 billion	£0.5 billion
Spain	£14.6 billion	£28.0 billion
Sweden	£6.3 billion	£4.6 billion

Source: Office for National Statistics (2018).

to the UK than they imported. As Figure 6.2 showed, for some member states, such as the Baltic states, a leading issue is the status of the large numbers of their citizens resident in the UK. For some member states Brexit is a question of budget (both net contributors, who could pay more, and net recipients, who could receive less), security (not least countries in Eastern Europe but also those with strong commitments to NATO or bilateral defence links with the UK such as France or Denmark) and the advantages and disadvantages from Britain's withdrawal from the EU's balance of power (of which more below).

The argument sometimes used in the UK that 'the EU needs us more than we need the EU' is based on the fact – as shown in Table 6.2 – that the UK imports more from the rest of the EU than it exports. Therefore, exporters elsewhere in the EU, not least those with large supply chains such as car manufacturers, should be keen to ensure the EU secures a deal with the UK that protects this. The potential cost from disrupted trade to the rest of the EU does not pass unnoticed. However, this varies from state to state and the EU's overall trade with the UK is a smaller proportion of the EU's GDP than it is for the UK.

EU institutional views

Deals over the UK's exit, transition arrangements and new relationship will need the approval of the European Parliament and, potentially, the CJEU. It is often forgotten that in the early 1990s the CJEU struck down some early arrangements for an EEA–EU relationship, ruling that they breached the EU's treaties. For these institutions the changing nature of the EU will be a factor never far from their outlooks. The European Parliament, for example, has been determined to ensure that the larger member states do not control the process of Brexit by which they would assert an intergovernmental character to the Union as opposed to the supranational one the Parliament forms part of. By contrast, there were concerns that the Commission might take advantage of its position in leading the negotiations and providing the necessary expertise as a way to assert its power. The EU's own negotiating guidelines were therefore clear that the

Council and the European Parliament were not to be excluded from the negotiations by the Commission.

Unity in the face of Brexit

How united is the remaining EU in the face of Brexit and how united will it remain? These are two questions that overhang the longer-term nature of Brexit. As touched on earlier, the EU succeeded in maintaining a united front in the early phases of the Article 50 negotiations. It is important, however, to remember, that Brexit is forever and not just for the two years set out in Article 50. Whether unity can be sustained over a much longer time frame is debatable given the EU struggles to maintain unity in its relations with the US, Russia, Turkey, Israel and many other countries. Each member state will in some way be calculating Brexit in terms of bilateral links with the UK and their multilateral links with one another within a Union that will be changed by Brexit. The UK is and will remain one of the EU's largest, if not largest, trading partner. While it currently struggles to shape the rest of the EU's approach to Brexit, it could in future be more successful at doing so. By leaving the EU the UK will move from a decision maker that sits in the decision-making chambers in Brussels to a decision shaper that works to shape EU policies and laws from the outside, but it has the potential from experience, interests and networks to be a formidable actor on this front.

EU calculations

Shortly after the UK triggered Article 50 the EU published and adopted unanimously its own negotiating guidelines, which not only set out some of the arrangements by which the EU would negotiate with the UK, but also set down some principles such as that acceptance of the EU's four freedoms is key to accessing the single market and that there is a balance between rights and obligations. Professor Kalypso Nicolaidis (Nicolaidis 2017) has set out three formulas to explain the EU's choices over a new EU–UK relationship. They highlight how the deal the UK wants (Duk) fits with what the EU feels it can give and the structural limits it faces given the existing relationships it already has with non-EU states.

Equation 1: $\underline{Vm > Duk > Vnfm}$

The value of the UK deal (Duk) cannot be greater than the value of EU membership (Vm), but it could be greater than value of non-former member (Vnfm) states' relationships with the EU such as Norway, Switzerland, Turkey, and FTAs such as the one with Canada. The first part is something EU decision makers have repeatedly made clear in the face of comments that the UK can have its cake and eat it. It would be absurd for the EU to offer a deal to the UK that is better than the deal its existing members have. At the same time the UK, as a former member and one of Europe's largest countries and a leading power, cannot be treated worse or perhaps even the same as Norway, Switzerland or Canada. That said, as Nicolaidis points out, the UK should tread carefully. If UK negotiators are arrogant, demanding and dismissive then the rest of the EU may wonder why the UK should be treated better than these other countries, with whom the EU has a more respectful and positive working relationship, not least those in the EEA who respect the EU's rules without having much input into them. In such a situation the formula could become

$$Vm > Vnfm > Duk$$

Equation 2: $\underline{Duk = FI - CP}$

The UK's deal (Duk) would allow the UK to opt in to certain areas of the EU's membership subject to Flexible Integration (FI) but this would not be allowed to include Cherry Picking (CP). This would fit with the EU's increasingly flexible integration (sometimes also referred to as 'differentiated integration'), where some members integrate more in some areas while others do not. If EU laws and policies apply to some member states differently then this opens up the possibility of extending this to non-members in the EEA or in whatever relationship the UK secures. This does not mean, however, that the UK can expect to simply opt in to the bits of the EU it likes. Some in the UK may see such participation as a backdoor to membership, something others in the EU may also resent as it may weaken the degree to which overall integration can move forward. Here a great deal hangs on how the rest of the EU decides to move forward, something discussed further below.

Equation 3: $\underline{\text{Duk} = \text{Min (U+B)} + \text{Max (M)}}$

Here the focus is on the approach the UK takes in negotiating the new deal (Duk), which must minimise Unilateralism (U) and Bilateralism (B) while maximising Multilateralism (M). British unilateralism would come in the form of threats to deregulate and undercut the EU. Bilateralism would be aimed at divide and rule in the EU by courting some states while threatening others. As Nicolaidis argues, this is important for an EU that likes to define itself by its multilateralism as opposed to a transactional approach focused on national interests.

Adjusting the EU

The withdrawal of one of the largest member states will lead to a series of changes to the EU's institutions, policies and balance of power. In some areas these adjustments will see the EU rebalanced in accordance with existing setups and distributions of power, while in others that rebalancing could lead to significant shifts in the direction of the EU.

Adjusting the EU's institutions

On leaving the EU the UK's budget contribution, seat allocation in the European Parliament, share of votes in the European Council, and staffing quotas will need to be redistributed. This has already led to proposals as to how to restructure the number of MEPs, with suggestions focusing on three proposals that would see: the 73 British MEPs' seats abolished so as to reduce the size of the Parliament; the seats distributed among the remaining 27 member states according to the formulas already used to allocate the number of MEPs per member state; or the creation of 73 EU-wide MEPs for whom all EU citizens will be able to vote in European Parliament elections. As touched on earlier in this chapter, the budget issue raises awkward questions for the rest of the EU given the size of the UK's net contribution. It does, however, provide the EU with the opportunity to try to phase out other smaller rebates such as those for Germany, Austria and Denmark. Suggestions that English could lose its status as an official EU language after Brexit ran into the immediate problem of its use by the Irish and Maltese, and the fact that it is often the working language of the EU. Finally, a reallocation of votes under QMV will need to be agreed, a change which could see the EU's balance of power shift.

The EU's balance of power

Britain's withdrawal will lead to five shifts in the EU's balance of power. First, in relations between the Eurozone and the non-Eurozone members. As the largest non-Eurozone state, Britain was at the forefront of efforts to ensure the Eurozone did not form a caucus within the EU, something that was raised during the UK's renegotiation. While Eurozone members have agreed steps to prevent this, the UK's departure reduces the number of non-Eurozone members to eight out of 27, with the Eurozone's proportion of the EU's GDP increasing from 72 per cent to 86 per cent.

Second, it will affect relations between Germany and France. Britain and France have sometimes aligned to balance against Germany on some issues while on others Britain and Germany have aligned to balance France. Britain's part in this trilateralism has varied, with Germany and France often balancing Britain and its scepticism. Nevertheless, Britain's withdrawal leaves Germany and France in search of new partners for when they need to balance against each other, which overall creates the possibility for not only Franco-German unity but also splits between French and German groups in the Council of the EU.

This plays a part in the third area, which is that smaller member states may lose out to the larger states. Under current QMV arrangements a proposal put to the Council can be blocked if it is opposed by at least four member states with a total of 35 per cent or more of the EU's population. This has meant that Britain (12.79 per cent), France (13.05 per cent) and Germany (16.06 per cent) would often work individually with smaller member states to form a blocking minority.

Fourth, Britain's departure means the disappearance of one of the main bodies of votes around which some in the EU aligned on economic, political, social and security issues. States such as Italy, Spain and Poland may now try to fill this gap, as might regional groupings such as the Benelux, Nordics or Visegrád groups. It raises the possibility for new leadership, alliances and groupings. It will also raise the prospect of a rebalancing of votes towards smaller member states so as to avoid the aforementioned Franco-German hegemony or splits. Such calculations will be at the forefront of the thinking of any decision makers in governments worried by the loss of a large Western European state that strongly supports a liberal, free-trading, Atlanticist outlook.

Fifth, the EU is losing a member state that has been more willing to say no than others have been. As discussed in Chapter Two, Britain's willingness to oppose proposals has been one reason why it has been seen as 'an awkward partner'. Yet that willingness was one other states sometimes hid their own scepticism behind. Member states will now have to be more open about opposing or leading in opposition to EU policies.

One final point to take into account regarding the above is that how important Britain has been depends on whether Britain's role in the EU has been declining given the country's often distant relationship, sometimes verging on indifference and isolation, with the EU in recent years and crises (Krotz and Maher 2016). This self-marginalisation means other member states have already adapted their alliances, groupings and positions, the result being that Britain's departure could be more of a soft landing than an abrupt change.

EU integration or disintegration

Whether Brexit will lead to the EU's further integration, disintegration or something in between such as a multi-speed Europe or differentiated integration has been a key concern for the rest of the EU since the British vote. There has only been limited discussion of theories and ideas of European disintegration (Webber 2014; Rosamond 2016). For Brexit to trigger European disintegration, it would require the UK to be the first in a domino effect that sees other member states move towards departure because of their publics' frustrations at such problems as those in the Eurozone and Schengen, or because of the loss of sovereignty. Much hangs on whether or not the UK is an attractive enough model to follow, which will depend on how well it does compared to the rest of the EU. On the other hand, Brexit can be seen as an opportunity for the EU to strengthen its unity by removing an awkward partner and allowing the remaining EU member states and EU institutions the chance to work together in the face of the departing member state.

As discussed above, the EU has prioritised maintaining its unity and in the earlier phases of negotiations was successful at doing so. This unity may not necessarily lead the whole of the EU to integrate further, but instead move forward with some form of differentiated integration where some members integrate more quickly in some areas compared to others. Whatever happens, a key member state, not least with regard to any pressures to disintegrate, will be Germany. As Douglas Webber (2014) argues, the EU has never faced a 'crisis made in Germany', which is the EU's principal driver and paymaster and therefore an indispensable nation. What such a crisis might be is not something Webber is clear on, but if Brexit were to combine with another crisis in the Eurozone or Schengen to cause something such as an unprecedented breakdown in EU solidarity, then it could strike deep into the EU's heart, leading both Germany and other members to question their commitment. This might seem an extreme scenario, not least given how united the EU was in the first phase of the Brexit negotiations compared to the UK's more shambolic performance. It is important to remember, however, that Brexit is a not a short-term process. The effect of

Brexit on EU unity or disunity is something that will play out over several years if not decades.

The EU in Europe

The growth of the EU to become Europe's predominant political, economic and social organisation is reflected in how often it can be the EU that is referred to when people talk of 'Europe'. However, Europe is more than the EU, although defining where Europe starts and ends is a complex debate in itself. Britain's own decision to leave the EU is the latest development in its long-running debate as to whether it is 'European' (Garton-Ash 2001). Brexit means a large European country will no longer be a member of the continent's predominant organisation. Where does this leave the EU and the UK vis-à-vis the rest of Europe?

First, Brexit raises questions about the EU's relationship with non-EU European countries, namely Norway, Switzerland, Iceland, Ukraine, Turkey, Liechtenstein and non-EU states in the Balkans. Each has developed relations with the EU that, most obviously in the case of Norway, Iceland, Liechtenstein and Switzerland, but also to a lesser extent Turkey and Ukraine, were intended as a means to the end of eventual EU membership or at least closer relations with the EU. Brexit does not throw these automatically into reverse, with eventual membership remaining an option. It does, however, open up new possibilities for relations. In the cases of Norway, Iceland, Liechtenstein and Switzerland, it has been pointed out that any deal that entails UK membership of the EEA will require their input and, potentially, permission. Both the EEA and EFTA have been shaped to meet the needs of the existing members. Adapting these organisations to cope with the non-EU membership of the UK would change them considerably.

Second, Brexit has triggered some discussion as to whether there are now opportunities for a radical overhaul of Europe's institutional architecture, with one such proposal calling for a 'continental partnership' (Pisani-Ferry et al 2017). Such ambitious plans have faced considerable suspicion, but they do point to opportunities for radical change. Such reforms may be needed not only to deal with the changes that the UK exiting the EU brings to European geopolitics, but also to deal with wider trends of which Brexit is only one. Europe has long felt the pull of different world powers (being divided during the Cold War between the US and USSR), and today Europe itself shows signs of becoming multipolar, with Turkey and Russia as two clear European poles but with other global poles such as the US and China also drawing the attention of different parts of Europe (Krastev and Leonard 2010). Brexit adds another non-EU pole in Western Europe. If population projections hold (and they are notoriously difficult to predict), by mid-century it will be Russia, Turkey and the UK that will – in that order – be the three most populous European states. Population levels, of course, do not automatically equate to power. Nevertheless, the EU and its member states look set to increasingly find themselves in a geopolitical arena in which competing powers – the UK included – attempt to shape its unity and direction.

EU daily business

The final set of processes in which Brexit will play out is in how it will affect the EU's daily business of meetings and events. Until the UK officially withdraws from the EU – as a result of an exit deal that is agreed and implemented, the two-year time frame of Article 50 expiring, or the UK unilaterally withdrawing – the UK remains a member of the EU with all the same rights and powers as any other member state. The only exception is that its representatives are not allowed to partake in discussions and votes among the remaining 27 member states about how to handle Brexit negotiations.

This means that UK representatives could cast votes that shape policy to be implemented post Brexit and will be privy to internal negotiations and documents pertaining to such matters. UK citizens and companies and the UK government will also have the right to petition the CJEU on affairs pertaining to EU matters. In turn the UK remains bound by EU law until it officially leaves.

The UK's continued membership up to the point that it leaves has led to some discussion as to whether UK ministers can threaten to disrupt EU business as a means of leveraging a better exit deal. The UK government could pursue such a course of action, although this risks antagonising rather than facilitating negotiations with a Union already frustrated by Britain's vote to leave and the UK government's continual problems with negotiating a UK exit.

Conclusion

'Soft Brexit', 'Hard Brexit', 'Chaotic Brexit'... the list of Brexits can seem a long one. At the end of the book is a 'Brexicon', which is a glossary listing some of the most common forms of Brexit and other Brexit-related terms. It has not been helped by the word Brexit – a portmanteau, created by fusing together two words – spawning a host of other portmanteau such as 'Bregret', 'Brexiteers', 'Brexedous', 'Brexperts' and many, many more (T. Oliver 2016a). To summarise:

Phase 1: Article 50 deal

A successful deal (and one was provisionally agreed in December 2017) would see agreement between the UK and EU on the status of UK and EU nationals in the EU and UK, over the UK's budgetary contributions, and an arrangement to manage the border between Northern Ireland and the Republic of Ireland. This would eventually be agreed by the EU's member states through a vote in the European Council, after securing the agreement of the European Parliament. The UK would ratify the deal through a vote in Parliament. Failure to agree this deal or the collapse of all negotiations could lead to the UK unilaterally leaving (what can be termed a 'Premature Brexit') or leaving at the end of the two years (also known as a 'timed-out Brexit'). Either of these would lead to what is called a 'chaotic Brexit' or 'no deal Brexit'. This would entail Britain facing what is also called a 'hard Brexit' whereby it relies on WTO rules for its trade and has no clearly defined wider relationship with the EU, such as in security matters.

Phase 2: transition deal or extension of Article 50's two-year period

A successful deal here (and one was provisionally agreed in March 2018) would see agreement for the UK and EU to enter into a period where they have more time to agree the many details of a new UK–EU relationship and during which the UK, although no longer a member of the EU, would be able to trade with the single market on something akin to EEA terms. Instead of a transition, agreement could be reached to extend Article 50 but this would mean the UK remains a member of the EU, something many in the UK would find unacceptable and which would cause problems for the EU. Without an agreement to a transition period the UK would leave the EU having agreed an Article 50 deal but not a new relationship. If negotiations over a transition or during it went nowhere or broke down then this would lead to what has been termed a 'cliff edge Brexit'. As with a 'chaotic Brexit' or 'no deal Brexit' this would see the UK coming to terms with the 'hard Brexit' of WTO rules.

Phase 3: A new relationship deal

The options here range from the UK's desired 'cake' option, membership of the EEA through to some as yet unspecified 'deep and special partnership' or relying on WTO terms. This entails the full range from 'soft Brexit' (membership of such things as the EEA) through to 'hard Brexit' (WTO). Agreement over a broad-ranging new relationship (that is, a mixed agreement) would not be straightforward and could require the approval of a large number of national and regional parliaments across the EU, possibly some referendums, and the UK Parliament. This new relationship is also likely to be about more than trade, involving some political and security cooperation.

Further readings

John Armour and Horst Eidenmüller (eds), *Negotiating Brexit* (Hart Publishing, 2017). A broad-ranging discussion of the many different aspects of the Brexit negotiations.

John H. Barton, Judith L. Goldstein, Timothy E. Josling and Richard H. Steinberg, *The Evolution of the Trade Regime: Politics, Law, and Economics of the GATT and the WTO* (Princeton University Press, 2006). Offers a good introduction to the WTO and the complexities of modern international trade.

Roger Bootle, *Making a Success of Brexit and Reforming the EU* (Hodder and Stoughton, 2017). An update of Bootle's *The Trouble with Europe*, the book offers not only an analysis of Britain and Brexit, but also where it leaves the EU.

Tony Connelly, *Brexit and Ireland: The Dangers, the Opportunities, and the Inside Story of the Irish Response* (Penguin, 2017). An acclaimed analysis of how the Irish have approached the single biggest economic and foreign policy challenge to their country since 1945.

Desmond Dinan, Neil Nugent and William E. Paterson (eds), *The European Union in Crisis* (Palgrave, 2017). This wide-ranging overview shows how Brexit has been one of a series of crises facing the EU in recent years.

Jennifer Hillman and Gary Horlick (eds), *Legal Aspects of Brexit: Implications of the United Kingdom's Decision to Withdraw from the EU* (Institute of International Economic Law, 2017). An edited overview of the wide range of legal issues connected to Brexit, covering such matters as international trade negotiations through to the implications for the English Premier League.

Patricia Mindus, *European Citizenship after Brexit: Freedom of Movement and Rights of Residence* (Palgrave, 2017). An in-depth analysis of the many questions Brexit has posed about European citizenship.

Tim Oliver (ed.), *Europe's Brexit: EU Perspectives on Britain's Vote to Leave.* (Agenda 2018). Explores how the other 27 EU member states and the EU's institutions responded to the UK's renegotation, referenudm campaign and vote to leave.

Dalibor Rohac, *Towards an Imperfect Union: A Conservative Case for the European Union* (Rowman and Littlefield, 2016). A free market analysis of the EU that shows how much the EU has done to break down trade barriers in Europe, but also how far it still has to go.

Uta Staiger and Benjamin Martill (eds), *Brexit and Beyond: Rethinking the Futures of Europe* (UCL 2018). Offers a broad-ranging analysis from a large number of experts on how Brexit fits into a changing EU.

SEVEN

Brexit, Britain, Europe and the world

Introduction

This final chapter looks at the processes through which Brexit connects with the rest of the world. As the chapter shows (see Table 7.1), Britain will need to work through such issues as what Brexit means for its international power, security, trading relationships and its strategy for managing these. The idea of Britain embracing the wider world and leaving behind the EU was one put forward by a number of Eurosceptics. What that entails, as the chapter shows, is far from clear and Britain faces a number of choices as to what sort of player in the world it tries to be. Choices will also need to be made about the ways in which the UK and the EU will cooperate with one another on international matters. Both sides have expressed an interest in pushing forward on foreign, security and defence matters, but how to do so is far from clear. EU–UK cooperation will depend in large part on what a post-Brexit EU tries to do on its own in the foreign, security and defence fields. As the chapter explores, the EU's efforts in these areas have in the past been limited by the UK's unwillingness to fully engage. Will Britain's withdrawal mean cooperation in these areas now advances more quickly? This will be shaped by how other powers, such as Russia and China, respond to an EU post Brexit. A great deal will also depend on the reaction of the US, not least under the leadership of President Trump. If Trump's victory was, as he put it, 'Brexit plus, plus, plus' then does his election and Brexit herald a change in both Western politics, especially towards globalisation? The chapter shows that whether it is in trade or security, both the UK and the EU face significant challenges in coming to terms with a world in which Europe (Britain included) will increasingly matter a lot less.

Table 7.1: The world and Brexit processes

Processes	Participants	Issues
Britain in a multipolar world	UK, WTO and non-EU states	Seeking new trade links, agreeing schedules at the WTO, defining Britain's role in the world, UK–US relations
UK–EU cooperation in the world	UK, EU27 (especially France and Germany), EU institutions	How to continue cooperation on foreign, security and defence matters, UK and Europe in transatlantic relations
The EU in a multipolar world	EU, UK, USA Russia, China	The EU in the world, Russian and Chinese views of Brexit and Europe's place, Western unity

Britain in a multipolar world

Seeking new trade links

Theresa May has said she wants the UK to rediscover its heritage 'as a great global trading nation', including with key emerging markets such as India and China. This fits with a long-standing vision of the UK as a global player, one that at times can hark back to Britain as an imperial power, but one which also reflects a desire to exploit the UK's modern international links in terms of trade, demographics, culture and security. One of the first decisions of May's new government in 2016 was to establish a Department for International Trade (DIT), under the leadership of Liam Fox. Since its establishment, the UK has discussed, informally, trade deals with a number of countries. Discussions have been informal because no agreements can be formally negotiated or ratified while the UK is a member of the EU and its customs union. One of the things the EU does for its member states is negotiate trade agreements. As a customs union, and one of the largest markets in the world, its combined weight means it can often be in a stronger position to negotiate at a global level.

At the same time, the EU's size and complexity mean it can also be somewhat slow and difficult to negotiate with.

The UK's new relationship with the EU will be a key factor in negotiating trade agreements with others. Trade agreements cannot be seen in isolation from one another, but as a series of overlapping and interconnected deals that shape one another. Until the rest of the world knows what relationship (as discussed in Chapter Six) the UK has with the EU, its biggest trading partner, they will be unsure of what new relationship they can seek with the UK and how it fits with their own relationship with the EU. Only then can other states 'be clear about the baseline from which to measure the value of any preferences in the UK market' (Holmes, Rollo and Winters 2016, R24).

It should be remembered that trade deals are a means to facilitate economic links and development between countries, and as such should not be seen as an end in themselves. What then does Britain seek from them? More than anything it seeks the maintenance and minimal disruption to existing trade relationships. Disrupted supply chains, whether in industry or agriculture, would be costly. There have been doubts as to whether on leaving the EU, the UK will remain a party to the 60 trade agreements the EU has negotiated with other states. If these states do not agree to simply replicate their agreement for the UK on a bilateral basis, then the UK could find it loses access to the benefits of these agreements. British politicians have outlined several other reasons for seeking new trade agreements, in addition to the need to maintain existing trading relations.

First, the EU might be a large player in trade negotiations but its size and the number of states and interests it has to take into account can make it slow to negotiate. Freed from this, the UK could be more nimble in seeking negotiations, not least with emerging markets in Asia and the Commonwealth, who will generate most of the world's economic growth over the next few decades. This would allow the UK to pursue a UK-specific vision on trade. Second, new trade deals can compensate for any losses to the UK from leaving the EU, although this is more in the longer term because in the short term they will struggle to help with any immediate problems or losses for the UK's trade from leaving the EU. Third, as noted earlier, they can play a part in restructuring the UK's political economy to whatever end the UK government hopes to see the UK economy move towards. Fourth, they can lower prices, benefiting British consumers and producers, but also potentially hurting some UK companies exposed to international competition.

At the same time that informal talks have begun with multiple states on bilateral trade agendas, the DIT has also opened discussions with the 164-member body of the WTO over the UK's post-Brexit terms of membership. The WTO is the body that governs international trade, setting rules by which all members trade with one another. The UK's current membership is governed by its status within the EU, with Brussels making commitments on trade tariffs and quotas on behalf of the 28 member states. The DIT has been seeking to replicate, as much as possible, the UK's current schedule of commitments to the WTO. On leaving the EU, these obligations would then serve as the baseline from which the nation would negotiate new trade agreements. While these WTO negotiations contain significant opportunities, they also have risks. If the UK fails to achieve a new schedule of WTO commitments, the country's trading arrangements would be severely disrupted. Yet again, a key difficulty for the UK is that, under the terms of the UK's EU membership, the UK can only engage in informal talks with other WTO members until a Brexit deal is in place.

The challenges and opportunities of trade deals

Trade deals can be extremely complex with slow-moving negotiations and can take a long time to have any effect. The EU's trade deal with Canada, CETA, was first outlined in 2004 with negotiations concluding in 2014. The problem of slow-moving negotiations can apply especially to advanced forms of trade agreement that go beyond negotiations over tariffs. Most tariffs are already at historically low levels, with tariffs between the US and the EU averaging about 1.6 per cent. Overcoming differences in regulatory approaches, what are called 'non-tariff barriers' (NTBs), can be complex and politically difficult but can also deliver bigger gains given they can add substantially to the costs of goods (some estimates suggest up to 13 per cent) and even more for services (up to 30 per cent in some areas). These costs can be reduced through such approaches as 'mutual recognition' but this and other methods can be more efficiently applied if part of a broader deal. TTIP, for example, sometimes described as the first 21st-century trade deal, has been contentious because of concerns that it would affect NTBs connected to the health sector (an issue of especial note in the UK), food safety and data protection. Discussions about some form of transatlantic trade deal have been going on for decades, with several previous attempts failing because of opposition from both sides of the Atlantic. TTIP emerged in the first decade of the 21st century and while at first it was heralded as a potential breakthrough in international trade, it soon became mired in political controversy in both Europe and the US. With traditional tariffs between the US and EU already quite low, the aim was to attempt to find a way to reduce NTBs. But as noted above, this has proved contentious in a large number of states. It had been hoped that negotiations would be concluded by the end of 2014, but by 2018 no clear end was yet in sight.

The UK could also find that the trade deals it seeks get caught up in the domestic politics of the other countries. The UK's own domestic politics may slow them down due to opposition to the lowering of standards or demands that standards be raised, or because of groups that successfully lobby to prevent such deals in order to protect their interests. The prospect of a UK–US trade agreement, for example, is one where there are many areas ripe for agreement, such as lowering or eliminating remaining tariffs on goods, but also for many potential disagreements, such as over harmonising financial services regulations or agreeing on data protection provisions. There is also Donald Trump's commitment to 'America First', which could complicate any hopes the UK has that the US will make concessions. The idea, therefore, of developing a UK-specific vision to international trade is one that could take a long time to realise. So too could it take a long time for any effects from a trade deal to be felt. A good example here is TTIP. In 2013 it was estimated that the EU economy could be €120 billion larger (0.5 per cent of its GDP) and the US economy €95 billion larger (0.4 per cent of its GDP) if TTIP, the largest trade deal ever negotiated, was successfully ratified and implemented by 2017. But that gain would have been by 2027, meaning a gradual build-up over 10 years (European Commission 2013).

Britain faces a challenge in finding how much power and weight it has in international trade negotiations. The EU's size gives it a superpower status in the world of trade, but like any superpower it can be slow moving and inefficient. While the UK is one of the world's largest economies, it may find itself squeezed by the much larger power of the US, EU, China and other countries such as Japan.

As several studies have shown, in trade negotiations – especially when it comes to settling disputes – market size equals power (Bièvre, Poletti and Yildirim 2016). It is also not clear what Britain will be able to offer on its own that it cannot within the EU. Slashing tariffs may attract some trade deals, but tariffs are already low by historic standards. This would also do little to advantage the UK in negotiations over NTBs, which are especially relevant for a country such as the UK, which has a service-based economy. Studies have highlighted that the slow pace of trade deals and the UK's economic needs mean these deals are unlikely to quickly compensate for any reduction in UK–EU trading links such as from the UK leaving the EU's single market (Ebell 2016).

Finally, Britain also lacks the experience of negotiating such deals, not having had to do so since it joined the EU. Given the scale of the negotiations Britain's trade negotiators have been asked to undertake, it is likely than in time they will become some of the world's most experienced. Until then, however, Britain could find itself vulnerable, taken advantage of and having to prioritise negotiations with a select few countries.

Searching for a role

Debate about Brexit has often focused on trade, especially UK–EU trade deals, which will play an important part in underpinning the UK's place in the world. At the same time, Brexit offers a range of uncertainties, dangers and opportunities for the UK's wider strategic place in the world, an outlook that combines economics with a broader set of issues related to security, politics, identity and risks. Since 1945 Britain has based its strategic place in the world on sustaining close alliances with both Europe and the US. Managing this has rarely been easy, and Brexit tests it further by putting into question the nature of the relationship with Europe within a Western order defined by the US and EU. That this has happened at the same time as the election of Donald Trump has added an extra element of confusion by raising doubts about the reliability of the UK–US relationship. It has also raised questions about the UK's ability to remain united, not least over Scotland (home of the UK's nuclear deterrent) and Northern Ireland.

As told in Chapter Two, in 1962 former Secretary of State Dean Acheson claimed that Britain had lost an empire and not yet found a role. There have been numerous attempts by UK decision makers to think through its role, sometimes known as 'strategising'. A key part of this, since 2008 has been the publication by the UK government of a series of national security strategies and strategic defence and security reviews (Gaskarth 2014). Brexit offers another chance to review Britain's role, and below are set out several roles it could now choose from (Kitchen and Oliver 2017). Each is an ideal-type, meaning they are set out here in a very pure form. Each should be assessed against three markers. First, whether it allows the UK to respond to the international risks it and its allies will face, something likely to be taken into account as the government reviews the UK's 2015 National Security Strategy and Strategic Defence and Security Review. Second, the ways in which the US and the rest of Europe – the UK's main allies – will react to it. Third, whether the economy of the UK can provide the taxes and trading links to underpin it and if the British people will support it.

'Switzerland with nukes'

This would be an isolationist option in which Britain would retreat from both European and global security, and economic and political commitments. The focus of Britain's defence would be entirely on the British Isles, with few if any overseas military commitments. Immigration and economic policies would both be hostile to open markets and free movement, favouring protectionism and therefore designed to please domestic audiences concerned about the threats to the UK from immigration and globalisation and the security challenges they bring. Overseas aid would be slashed or abolished altogether. Such a course carries the risk of being deeply unpopular with allies, assuming Britain's defence can be territorial in basis, reducing Britain's competitiveness and wealth through protectionism, and lowering Britain's soft power.

A 'pivot' away from Europe

As part of this role the UK would focus on building economic, security and political relations with the world beyond Europe, in particular with emerging powers in Asia. It would also align closely with such efforts by the US. This would reflect how global power has been shifting away from the North Atlantic. The idea of 'pivoting' from Europe to Asia is something the Obama administration attempted for the US. That the US found it difficult to do so serves as a warning for the UK, which, compared with the US, does not have as extensive a network of trading, security and political links in areas such as the Pacific or Asia. It also risks being dependent on the policy positions of the US government, which under Donald Trump have not been as clearly focused as those of previous presidents. Turning away from Europe risks overlooking the fact that, as a European state, Britain's foremost concern is European security. Britain's strategic climate is shaped largely by developments in Europe and its place in the world. Europe is, as Churchill once said, 'where the weather comes from'.

A UK–EU 'special relationship'

Under this role the UK would work to ensure that Theresa May's idea of a 'deep and special partnership' is deeper and more special than that with the US. Britain would therefore commit to a relationship in security, economics and politics that keeps the UK as deeply connected to the EU as possible without rejoining; although it is under this role that rejoining the EU would be a possibility. Such a role would raise difficult questions about the role of NATO, would be largely dependent on the rest of the EU reciprocating and would require new institutions, perhaps some form of UK–EU treaty, to be established to define it. Britain would also be required to reverse a policy that has over the past two decades seen it shift diplomatic and military resources from Europe towards other areas of the world, not least towards emerging powers. Britain would therefore have to commit new defence and diplomatic resources to elsewhere in Europe or contribute to EU military missions around the world. It would also require strong domestic support, which would be a challenge given Britain's vote to leave the EU.

A global European balancer

British policy makers have long sought to make Britain both a European and global power, which would continue under this 'balancer' role. It would combine some of the 'UK–EU special relationship' and the 'pivot away from Europe'. The UK's military would be configured to deal with a full range of conflicts around the world; Britain would seek to lead global trade negotiations and build new relations with emerging powers while maintaining existing ones. It would be the most ambitious role in terms of scope and cost. It therefore raises questions about over-stretch. Other powers might view it sceptically given Britain's struggle to negotiate its exit from the EU. They might also wonder if the British public would support such a role given the potential costs.

Adrift and lost at sea

This would not necessarily be a role, more the outcome of a failure to articulate and pursue a clear strategy. The UK would 'muddle through' events through an ad hoc mix of commitments to European security, pursuing global links while also being isolationist and protectionist in some areas. Britain's defence capabilities would be confused and degraded; trade deals pursued without adequate thought to any overall strategy; and allies left feeling the UK had become unreliable thanks to it falling back on an impulsive outlook.

The UK–US special relationship

Where do Brexit and the above options leave the UK–US relationship? When discussing the 'special relationship' we need to remember that for both sides it is 'a' special relationship. Both have multiple special relationships, such as US–Israel and UK–Ireland. For the foreseeable future the relationships that will be most special for both are the ones they face the most difficult but important long-term questions over: US–China and UK–EU. Nevertheless, the UK–US 'special relationship' is defined by three core areas: intelligence, special forces and nuclear weapons. Other factors such as demographics, religion, culture, law, politics, economics and much more also make it 'special'. But it is these three areas that are protected from any tensions and arguments, for example between presidents and prime ministers. It is through these three links that the two countries trust one another in ways they do not trust others.

For Britain, the maintenance of this relationship has been vital to its foreign policy, with the pursuit of intimate links to the heart of US government often a key aim. When in 2000, George W. Bush was elected US president, there were concerns in London that he would pursue an isolationist agenda in US foreign policy. This, the British government worried, could weaken NATO and the security of Europe. In response Prime Minister Tony Blair followed President Bill Clinton's outgoing advice to 'hug them close'. Blair's Chief of Staff, Jonathan Powell, put it more bluntly when he advised Sir Christopher Meyer, the British Ambassador to the US to 'get up the arse of the White House and stay there'.

Similar concerns about the Trump presidency

In Donald Trump the UK–US relationship has entered a period of deep uncertainties, in part because of the president's own impulsive and poorly defined strategic outlook, but also because Brexit further complicates Britain's options. The UK could become an 'awkward inbetweener', dependent on how the larger US–EU relationship moves forward and in particular what the US does. As discussed further below, it is important not to overlook the similarities in the Brexit and Trump votes. Nevertheless, despite any similarities, Trump's election has posed problems for the UK's decision makers and those elsewhere in Europe. In losing the UK, the EU finds itself between a weakened EU rock that will soon be bereft of Britain and a Trump hard place. Europe is confronted with the dilemma of having contracted out its defence to the US to such an extent that it has left itself reliant on a political system and president over which it has little control and, in President Trump, a man in whom it has little faith.

The degree of control Britain has over relations with the US is also questionable. Such a question would arise with any US administration. It is now largely dependent on whether President Trump's more extreme positions are moderated by the US political system. A lot hangs on how Trump behaves, something that is often difficult to predict given his erratic behaviour and inconsistencies in the things he says (Quinn 2017). Trump's 'America First' stance may also present obstacles for the UK in seeking trade deals. Trump has hinted at being open to a trade deal with a UK outside the EU. But that contrasts with his overall protectionist stance. While he might leave an opening for Britain (albeit one Britain is not necessarily guaranteed a good deal over, given that, as trade negotiators often point out, there are no special relationships in trade negotiations), his wider attitude to international relations, which mixes protectionism, sovereignty and retreat of US commitments, risks much larger damage to the global system of which Britain's government remains a committed member. Britain's hopes of securing global trade deals depend on the rest of the world being open to such approaches. Should the US abandon its lead in these areas then the system could fragment, close or see other countries and organisations – China or the EU – attempt to lead.

UK–EU cooperation in the world

As touched on in Chapter Two, as the EU has enlarged it has extended cooperation beyond trade and internal matters to include foreign, security and defence cooperation. The EU's member states have since the early 1970s sought to use their combined economic might to pursue certain international goals. This has been largely (but not entirely) undertaken through intergovernmental arrangements (and therefore largely separated from the EU's supranational institutions such as the European Commission) such as the Common Foreign and Security Policy (CFSP) and the Common Security and Defence Policy (CSDP), both of which emerged in the 1990s.

Cooperation on external relations, of course, goes beyond these two areas and covers a wide range of areas including trade policy, international aid, cooperation over environmental matters, immigration, borders, asylum, cross-border policing, and justice cooperation. The EU is the world's leading international aid donor. Its economic power has allowed its member states to play leading roles in such agreements as those over Iran's nuclear deal. It has also struggled to play an effective role, as seen over its failures to adopt united and strong positions towards such conflicts as those in Libya and Ukraine. EU efforts to create and deploy military forces might have been limited compared to those of NATO, but the EU has deployed and run a number of overseas operations. These are overseen in a largely intergovernmental manner, with coordination undertaken by the EU's High Representative of the Union for Foreign and Security Policy, who is also a vice-president of the European Commission.

The UK has been at the forefront both of pushing the EU in these areas and resisting them. In the aforementioned Review of the Balance of Competences the UK government assessed Britain's participation in the CFSP as being strongly in the UK's interests. It was efforts in 1998 by Tony Blair and French President Jacques Chirac that led to the setting up of the CSDP, which they hoped would change a situation where fragmented European defence spending produces little by way of deployable power. However, the UK has also often been unwilling or uneasy about what integration in these areas could lead to. In particular, successive British governments have worried that the CSDP could threaten NATO. For that reason the UK has also often been a key block to further progress.

EU–UK international cooperation post Brexit

One of the EU's responses to Brexit has been to attempt to focus on efforts at cooperation in foreign, security and defence matters (Whitman 2016). In the months following Britain's vote, proposals were put forward for deepening cooperation in these areas, with EU leaders sensing an opportunity from the UK's departure to move forward on proposals without fear of UK objections or vetoes. Progress could be made on such matters as the European Defence Agency (EDA), which is intended to facilitate better defence industrial cooperation, and in the setting up of a permanent EU military operational headquarters so that in future the EU can avoid having to depend on either member states or NATO to provide such a facility. Hopes have also been expressed that the EU can lead in coordinating logistics, medical assistance, satellite data, and air–lift capabilities, and by creating a combined defence research and procurement budget under the EDA.

Cooperation could move forward in differentiated ways, with some member states moving ahead while others decline to do so, which the EU terms 'permanent structured cooperation'. However, at a time when, because of crises in the Eurozone and Schengen, integration has been tested as never before, it might seem strange that the EU should attempt to move forward in an area that touches directly on a range of national sensitivities such as sovereignty, neutrality and commitments to NATO. Furthermore, the EU's efforts in this area have been modest at best. The EU's capabilities, such as the 'EU Battlegroups' (set up after 2005 and made up on a rotational basis by member states' armed forces) have never been deployed on the crisis–stabilising missions they are designed for. Nevertheless, the intention has been to build cooperation in these areas, which presents the UK with a series of questions about what it will do in response.

By leaving the EU the UK will lose direct access to the decision making over CFSP and CSDP matters. As discussed in Chapter One, the geopolitics of Europe is Britain's primary foreign policy concern. How the EU develops its place in the world will therefore be of direct concern to the UK. Not only does Brexit mean the UK can no longer be able to use the rest of the EU to amplify its place in the world, but nor will the UK government be able to directly involve itself in negotiations over common matters of concern such as EU sanctions against countries such as Russia, although if the UK is outside the EU's customs union then it will be able to impose sanctions on whoever it wants. The UK would move from a decision maker to a decision shaper based on the outside. This would place extra strains on UK diplomatic resources given the shift over the past decade to focus resources on emerging powers and less on influencing decisions across Europe outside of Brussels.

It should come as no surprise then that the UK government has expressed a strong desire to continue cooperation with the EU on foreign, security and defence matters. This has been reciprocated to some extent by other EU governments who recognise that the EU is losing one of its two major military powers. Failure to cooperate in these areas could also see the UK and EU face significant difficulties in policing and intelligence cooperation. As former head of MI6, Sir John Sawers, warned, the main concern here is that Brexit could disrupt the exchange of data and that Britain will find itself outside of the EU's main decision-making bodies that shape the rules about exchanging such data (Elwes 2018). At the same time, there are costs and benefits to both sides from any possible future relationship, with trade-offs being, again, an inevitable choice to be faced by the UK. Choices are complicated by the fact that existing setups such as the EEA or free trade deals do not come with any significant arrangements for cooperation on foreign, security and defence matters.

Richard Whitman (2016) has outlined three scenarios for how cooperation might develop (see Table 7.2). The first would see the UK as an 'integrated player' whereby an EU+1 format would be established that allowed UK ministers to participate in decision making, and whereby the UK would hold associate membership of such organisations as the EDA. This would also allow the EU more direct access to the UK's capabilities. It would also be a part of the aforementioned 'UK–EU special relationship' scenario. A second scenario would revolve around the UK being an 'associated partner', mirroring the existing setup with Norway. The UK would align itself with EU positions, which would be facilitated by dialogues, rather than membership and a place at the decision-making table. The UK would not have direct influence over EU decision making but could opt to work with the EU in certain areas when needs necessitated such cooperation. Finally, the UK could be a 'detached observer', with minimal formal connections with EU decision making and policies in these areas. The UK would have a great deal of freedom but could expect the least degree of influence in any of the three scenarios. Such a scenario would fit with the idea of the UK pivoting away from Europe, especially if that meant working closely with the US. This might also lead to competition and divergence.

Europe and transatlantic relations

For the US and the EU (Britain included), the most important of their international relationships remains the transatlantic one. The current relationship owes its existence to the Second World War and the Cold War, conflicts that bound the US and Europe together (Hanhimaki, Schoenborn and Zanchetta 2012). Shared values of liberal democracy and free-market capitalism, and a history of political, cultural and ethnic links, provided a set of values and economic interests that helped bind the two sides together in the struggles against fascism and communism, which outlasted the end of the Cold War. The economic and military links remain extensive (Wicket 2018). Attempts to agree the TTIP reflected hopes on both sides – and especially in the UK – to more closely combine their economic might and through this shape the emerging global economic order. US–EU trade in goods and services amounted to US\$1.5 trillion in 2012. Foreign direct investment in one another amounted to US\$2.2 trillion (or about 50.3 per cent) of total US investment abroad, and US\$1.6 trillion (or about 62 per cent) of EU investments. NATO also remains the world's pre-eminent alliance, with combined US and European NATO defence spending in 2016 totalling US\$918.3 billion (The Economist 2017). The US military commitment to Europe has been an essential component of European integration. Despite their differences, including several US–EU trade wars, the two sides have worked together

Table 7.2: Future scenarios for UK–EU, CFSP and CSDP relations

	Battlegroups	European Defence Agency	Working groups	Political and Security Committee	CSDP		Foreign Affairs Council membership
					Civilian operations	Military operations	
Full EU membership	YES	YES	YES	YES	YES	YES	YES
Integrated player	YES	ASSOCIATE MEMBER	NO	SPECIAL STATUS (cooperation on selected agenda)	YES	YES	SPECIAL STATUS (in-Council cooperation on selected agenda)
Associated PARTNER	Permanent participation	Administrative Agreement	NO	NO	Framework Participation Agreement		NO (Norway model – foreign policy synchronisation on 'dialogue' basis)
Detached observer	NO	NO	NO	NO	Case-by-case basis	NO	NO

Source: Whitman (2016, R48).

more often than with others to shape global governance and international trade, and on agreements such as relations over security concerns surrounding Iran and Ukraine.

Despite the closeness, the relationship faces four challenges, with Brexit an integral factor to be taken into account in each (Oliver and Williams 2016). First, US attention has for some time been moving away from Europe and towards emerging powers, and in some cases towards disengagement and withdrawal (Posen 2013). This has added to fears in Europe that the US is a declining power.

Second, there is long-standing US frustration at Europe's low levels of defence spending. This has gone so far as to raise questions about the viability of NATO, something Donald Trump has strongly hinted at but which has been raised across the US political spectrum. Rising defence spending elsewhere in the world means the US is increasingly disinclined to commit resources and attention to a Europe that will not pay its way. While the UK has been one of the few NATO members to meet the alliance's goal of each member spending 2 per cent of GDP on defence, this has not been easy. Brexit will mean only 18 per cent of NATO defence spending will come from EU states, although that increases to only 25 per cent if the UK is included. In 2016, 72 per cent of NATO defence spending was by the US, a figure that in 1990 was 60 per cent (T. Oliver 2017b). US investments in military technologies and new equipment also mean that interoperability with European forces, which have not received such investments, is a growing concern. NATO might endure, but it might become irrelevant (Williams 2013).

Third, as touched on above, Europe's fragmented and declining defence capabilities are a reflection of the lack of European and EU unity and cooperation. The EU has often adopted a 'civilian power' outlook, which is one where it pursues its interests through economic, diplomatic and cultural means. This has left it vulnerable in a world where hard power still matters a lot. Europe seems to be in decline, inward looking because of crises such as the Eurozone and Brexit, and therefore incapable of doing much to reverse this and so assert its place internationally.

Fourth, both the US and Europe have seen a rise in nationalist, populist and inward-looking agendas, which have been driven in part by growing unease among electorates at the economic, social and political effects of globalisation, liberalisation and immigration. Brexit and Trump's election are products of this. It is important, however, to note that these developments have exploited rifts in transatlantic relations, not caused them.

The EU in a multipolar world

The global context in which Brexit is unfolding is one where emerging powers are increasingly asserting and perhaps challenging the liberal international order created by the US and the rest of the West post 1945 and after the end of the Cold War. Debates about where this will take the world range from arguments that emerging powers are attempting to contest and replace the system (Russell Mead 2014) through to arguments that they have accepted and embraced the existing order and tensions are due to their attempts to raise their profile within it (Ikenberry 2011). Two countries that are at the heart of these debates, and which are also often raised in debates about the wider impact of Brexit, are Russia and China.

Russian views

Geopolitical calculations have long figured prominently in Russian government and political thinking on international matters (Wohlforth and Zubok 2017). Britain's withdrawal from the EU has therefore been viewed by some Russians as a sign of the EU's weakness and decline in size and clout. This contrasts with the EU's own outlook, which has tended to look beyond the importance of hard power and geopolitics, focusing more on what some have termed a 'post-modern' outlook on international affairs (including the 'civilian power' outlook mentioned previously). Recent events, most notably in Ukraine and Crimea, have served to remind the EU that traditional thinking on international affairs – about borders, sovereignty and nationalism – remain strong. As mentioned in Chapter Three, there have been concerns that Russia involved itself in the EU referendum campaign as part of a wider strategy to sow division and doubt into Western politics (Bradshaw 2017).

This geopolitical outlook does not mean that Russian decision makers welcomed Brexit. Britain's withdrawal would take with it the EU country that has been among the strongest supporters of EU sanctions on Russia. Yet Russia's economy remains heavily dependent on the success of an EU and European market place. Russian interests in the UK are also not insignificant, not least in London's financial and service sectors. Any fragmentation of the European market place or weakening of London's economy might not necessarily benefit Russia.

At the same time, some in Russia did view the possibility of Brexit as a way of dampening further the EU's normative power, which had already suffered because of the problems in the Eurozone and Schengen (Gromyko 2015). It helped buttress their argument that the EU was declining because it had abandoned traditional values such as Christianity, the family, national pride, and respect for law and order, and had instead embraced an uncontrollable and unstable agenda connected to diversity. While this might be contrasted with Russia's own significant internal problems, this portrayal, not least in Russian media, did find a receptive audience across Europe, especially among supporters of some populist and nationalist parties. These debates were felt very clearly in Ukraine, where Britain's debate about withdrawing from the EU ran up against views of the EU as a source of modernisation and European identity (Getmanchuk 2015).

Whether British decision makers will notice this, however, offers a final note of comparison with Russia. Britain and Russia are both former superpowers that have passed through periods of profound decline. Both have continued – sometimes succeeding – to 'punch above their weight' in international affairs. They show the limits for anyone who hopes that either will easily accept a reduced or changed place in the world.

Chinese views

China's views of Brexit can be broken down into economics and strategic relations. China found itself aligned with both Japan and the US when during the referendum campaign it stated that it would prefer the UK to remain in the EU. China's prime concern was the economic uncertainties Brexit could bring for UK-Chinese relations, the UK economy and the rest of the EU. Full-market access to the EU has been one of the positives for China in UK–EU relations. For the UK, playing the role of gateway to the EU's single market was a selling point to China along with Britain's well-regulated, stable and open economy, which Chinese investors could rely on. British governments have made increasing efforts to court China, with Chinese investment in a range of infrastructure projects (Heathrow airport, high-speed rail projects and Hinkley Point nuclear power station) and across industry, making China an ever-present aspect of UK life.

The potential for Brexit to change this has been an abiding concern for China, and not simply with regard to the UK. China, like the US and other large powers, has relations with Europe that are both multilateral with the EU and bilateral with the various member states. China–German relations, in particular, have been very close as a result of both being leading industrial and exporting economies. The potential for Brexit to turn the UK and EU inwards has been something that Chinese officials have worried about. Britain, for example, has been a strong supporter of China being granted 'market economy status', something others in the EU have been uncertain about. And while the British government has gone to great lengths since the referendum result to make clear that the UK remains an open, international economy, this contrasts with parts of the UK's referendum debate – not least those that were anti-immigration and globalisation – which did not pass unnoticed in China.

Any future trade negotiations with the UK are likely to run into the thorny issue of immigration and visas, something that has already arisen with regard to UK–India relations. They are also likely to be shaped by whatever deal the UK is able to secure over future relations with the EU. The UK's referendum also reminded decision makers in China that its relations with powers such as the UK and other members of the EU cannot be built on trading and investment links alone. Chinese President Xi had put a great deal of effort into developing close relations with the UK, efforts that had led to a range of closer economic links. This has only taken relations so far. Delays and doubts over the Hinkley Point C nuclear power station – which is to be developed in a deal involving France and China – along with doubts and suspicions about investments by Chinese state-owned companies, show the relationship remains dogged by questions of trust.

The motives and interest of the UK and China are not necessarily the same, with differences over human rights, rule of law and relations with the US being sticking points, to say nothing of continued historical prejudices on both sides. The same can be said to overhang China–EU relations in a broader sense. Some form of larger strategic partnership would be needed if relations were to become more stable. Brexit may not help create the conditions for this because Britain's own strategic outlook is now uncertain. For example, closer UK–US relations under President Trump may come with US demands over how far UK–China relations can develop in terms of trade deals and investments, and certainly over any attempts to build a strategic partnership.

Brexit and a changing West

As has been touched on several times, the studying of Brexit offers a way to analyse more than just the UK. It also casts a light on developments across Europe and the wider West, not least in terms of political economy. Locating Brexit in trends in Western politics reveals a context that includes fears about the potential disintegration or stagnation of the EU, the rise of populists, the financial crisis and failure of technocratic elites, growing frustrations among publics who feel excluded from the mainstreams of their society, and tensions between large swathes of society and global metropolises such as London or New York.

Here Brexit itself can be seen as a symptom of a wider crisis in Western democratic capitalism identified by authors such as Wolfgang Streeck (2016). As Burgoon, Oliver and Trubowitz (2017) argue, the past few years has seen the decline in a post-Cold War solidarity found in both Europe and the US that saw decision makers in both push forward an agenda of globalisation entailing freer movement of people, goods, services, capital and ideas across national boundaries. Support for that agenda increased from the 1970s to the 1990s, but since the early

2000s has declined across the West. This has happened at both the level of national policy and at the level of party politics, a development closely linked to the rise of populist politics in Europe and the US.

Figure 7.1: US and European policy support for globalisation

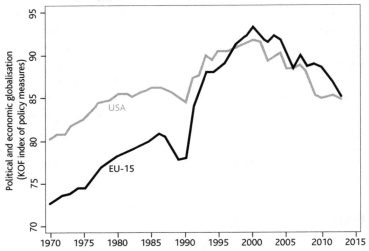

Source: Burgoon, Oliver and Trubowitz (2017).

This does not mean the EU, transatlantic cooperation and Western internationalism are dead. The US, the UK and the rest of Europe remain each other's key partners. However, in understanding why Brexit happened, what is now unfolding within the UK, in UK–EU relations, within the remaining EU and in the wider West, it is clear that some of the political economic agendas that have sustained the relationships are being challenged in ways the leaders of each cannot ignore. The biggest challenge the UK, the rest of the EU, and the US face in addressing these common problems will be finding solidarity in a common purpose to overcome them (Oliver and Williams 2017). The alternative is one in which decision makers on both sides of the English Channel, across Europe and on either side of the North Atlantic instead pursue purely inward-looking policies. That could end with their driving themselves further apart, fragmenting Western leadership and in turn damaging the global institutions to which they have committed themselves since 1945.

Further readings

William Drozdiak, *Fractured Continent: Europe's Crises and the Fate of the West* (W.W. Norton, 2017). Examines the problems facing Europe as part of a wider set of problems facing the West.

Robert Falkner, 'Europe and the World: Rethinking Europe's External Relations in an Age of Global Turmoil', *International Politics*, 54(4), July 2017. This is a special issue put together by the Dahrendorf Forum, which looks at how the world views Europe and its global place. Includes perspectives from the US, China, Russia, the Middle East and elsewhere.

Andrew Gamble, *Between Europe and America: The Future of British Politics* (Palgrave, 2003). One of the best histories that combines that of the UK, the British Empire, debates about Britain's political economy and the country's repeated attempts to bridge relations between Europe and the US.

Jamie Gaskarth, *British Foreign Policy: Crises, Conflicts and Future Challenges* (Polity Press, 2013). A comprehensive introduction to British foreign policy.

Stephan Keukeleire and Tom Delreux, *The Foreign Policy of the European Union* (Palgrave Macmillan, 2014). Provides a good introduction to studying the EU's place in the world.

Nicholas Kitchen, *Investing for Influence: Report of the LSE Diplomacy Commission* (2015, LSE IDEAS). Assesses the options facing the UK and what capabilities and diplomatic networks are needed to pursue them.

David Owen and David Ludlow, *British Foreign Policy After Brexit* (Biteback, 2017). Owen, a former Labour foreign secretary, SDP leader and supporter of Leave, and Ludlow, a former diplomat who supported Remain, offer their thoughts on what Brexit means for Britain in the world.

Gideon Rachman, *Easternisation – War and Peace in the Twenty First Century* (Bodley Head, 2017). A leading columnist at the *Financial Times*, Rachman sets out the debate about the rise of Asia and what it could mean (including the possibility of war) for the Western order.

David Sanders and David Patrick Houghton, *Losing an Empire, Finding a Role: British Foreign Policy since 194* (Palgrave, 2016). An update of a classic study of UK foreign policy, which applies several theoretical approaches.

Paul Welfens, *An Accidental Brexit: New EU and Transatlantic Economic Perspectives* (Palgrave Macmillan, 2017). Examines both the causes of Brexit and its possible implications for the UK, Europe and the transatlantic relationship.

Conclusion

As highlighted throughout, Brexit is not a single event, a single process, solely about Britain or the country's departure from the EU, or something that will be over in a short period of time. To appreciate this better the conclusion returns to the 15 questions set out in the introduction, which look into the causes, consequences and meaning of Brexit.

Causes

1. Why do you think 51.9 per cent of those who voted chose Leave?

As set out in Chapter Four, 51.9 per cent of Britons who voted backed Leave for a number of reasons. They were unconvinced by David Cameron's renegotiation of the UK–EU relationship, not least over the question of immigration, an issue that motivated a large number of Leave voters. While many voters had concerns about the economic impact, these were insufficient to overcome the various (and sometimes contradictory) messages put out by the various Leave campaigns (whose leaders were also more effective at getting their message across than the Remain campaign's leaders), a media environment dominated by Leave, and perceptions by many voters that the country was headed in the wrong direction not only in its membership of the EU, but also in socio-cultural and socio-economic ways.

As a result, is it possible to identify a single reason or a closely interconnected series of causes behind the vote for Leave? As discussed in Chapter Four the Leave vote was the outcome of a combination of factors connected to the effectiveness of the Leave campaigns, socio-cultural and socio-economic reasons, views of the incumbent government and the state of domestic UK politics, and the legacy of historically weak levels of support for membership of the EU. That the EU was passing through a period of profound crisis made it a particularly difficult sell. Having identified the causes behind the vote for Leave the question becomes one of how to implement it, which remains contested and something covered in question 11.

2. Why do you think 48.1 per cent of those who voted chose Remain?

Despite the close result, most analysis of the referendum result has focused on those Britons who voted Leave. Remain voters can therefore be overlooked. As with Leave voters, Remain voters were a combination of different groups and outlooks. No single reason can be put forward for why just under half the electorate who voted did so for continued membership of the EU. As Chapter Four showed, Remain voters were younger, better qualified, more comfortable with immigration and a multicultural society, and more likely to identify as British than English. Some Remain voters were motivated by a commitment to the ideals of European integration, but many more reflected a long-standing British attitude towards the EU of seeing Britain's membership as an economic relationship that benefited the country.

Remaining in the EU also appeared to be a status quo option, posing less risk to Britain's economy, security and place in the world. The extent to which Remain was a status quo option depends on how the EU, with Britain as a member, would have changed in the years following the vote. While a Remain vote would not have seen the degree of changes that have unfolded in the UK and EU as they have begun to come to terms with the Leave vote, it could still have led to Britain facing some big changes at a later date or over a longer period of time. For example, a new EU treaty or further efforts at integration would more than likely have led to renewed debates about the implications of Britain's participation in the EU, potentially triggering another referendum.

3. Was Britain destined to leave the EU?

As Chapter Two showed, Britain's relationship with the EU has often been difficult. This has played out in UK–EU relations and in UK politics where the issue of Europe has split political parties, toppled prime ministers, and was a key factor behind the emergence of a new political party: UKIP. Factors such as Britain's late membership, different experiences in the Second World War, the legacy of empire, and a different political and constitutional model to that used elsewhere in Europe have added to the tensions. But Britain was not the only country to join late (or to have had problems getting in), to have had problems adjusting to membership, or to have experienced fractious debates about membership and over issues such as immigration from elsewhere in the EU. Nor was it the country most badly affected by the crises in the Eurozone and Schengen.

If some of the commonly identified causes behind a Leave vote can be found elsewhere in the EU then why did Britain vote to leave? Was it a combination of such factors coming together in ways not found elsewhere in other states? A key factor might be that membership of the EU has also never been the only role British decision makers have sought for their country in the world, providing a wider public sense that other options existed for the UK outside the EU. The context in which the referendum happened – an unpopular EU, austerity at home in the UK, the continuing effects on many parts of the UK of the Great Recession that began in 2007, high levels of scepticism towards the elite, and growing levels of dissatisfaction at the direction of the country – did not help the Remain campaign because of the status quo it represented.

That leads to a question of how long Britain could remain a fully committed member given the aforementioned differences, the low levels of support, the lack of pro-European voices and a transactional approach. Historians might one day conclude that the referendum result was the consequence of a process of disengagement from the EU that dates back over a longer period. But does that mean the UK and EU could not have found another way of managing their relationship?

4. What effect has Britain's membership of the EU had on it and vice versa?

The complexity of the Brexit negotiations has highlighted how interconnected the UK has become with the EU over the course of its 45 years of membership. As covered in Chapter Six, the EU has had to face the prospect of the departure of one of its largest member states. Whether as 'an awkward partner' or a 'quiet European' the UK has had an effect on the EU.

A list could be drawn up of the ways in which the UK has shaped the EU and the EU has shaped the UK. For each item on the list, however, it would be necessary to take into account the extent to which the UK or EU was responsible as opposed to other member states or wider European or global trends. Such a list could also be shaped by political outlooks on whether the effect of the UK or the EU has been positive or negative. For example, Britain has often been portrayed as being one of the leading backers of EU enlargement. But by widening the Union, enlargement may also have weakened it because Britain was also a keen advocate of ensuring the EU's central institutions remained weak. Whether these developments are good or bad depends on your views of European integration.

Another way in which the effect could be considered is by thinking about the counterfactual of what the UK and EU would look like today had Britain not joined in 1973 (T. Oliver 2016b). That would require an analysis of the extent to which such a UK would have found itself drawn towards the EU and how, outside the formal membership structures, the UK would have shaped the EU.

5. Should David Cameron have called the referendum or was there another way to handle what he termed Britain's 'European Question'?

As Chapter Three covered, David Cameron called the referendum for a number of reasons. As political tools, referendums in the UK are called largely by the government of the day. While their use in British politics has grown, Britain does not have as strong a tradition of direct democracy as found in some other democracies. Britain's democracy has instead been based on parliamentary sovereignty, with all key decisions taken by a governing party (or coalition) that commands a majority in the House of Commons.

The problem facing Cameron was that he felt he could not command such a majority on the issue of Britain's EU membership because large numbers of his backbenchers were prepared to rebel. What other way forward was there for Cameron? And was he being too ambitious when he set out to have the referendum settle Britain's European question when, as discussed in Chapter Two, the relationship is shaped and strained by historic and structural factors that a referendum could not change, not least that the UK–EU relationship has always been one in a perpetual state of flux?

Perhaps answers lie in Scotland's debate about its relationship with the UK. As Mitchell (2014) has argued, the 'Scottish question' – one of party politics, identity, constitution and political economy – cannot be answered through independence or through remaining in the UK. The Scottish question, like Britain's European one, will be reframed for each new generation. As in Scotland's debate, the obstacles to Britain answering its European question are considerable, but they can be managed through a debate about the type of country Britain is and wants to be. That requires a longer-term debate that avoids an attempt at a quick fix of a referendum. This is not to argue that referendums cannot play an important role in such a debate. But if the European question is to be better managed then referendums need to be seen as means to an end, not ends in themselves.

Consequences

6. Has the EU referendum settled or changed Britain's 'European Question'?

As question 5 alluded to, there is no simple way to answer the 'European question'. Instead it is a matter of managing it as it evolves. The referendum result has turned the question into primarily one of how to deliver Brexit and a UK–EU relationship with the UK outside of the EU. That entails two very complex challenges. First, a successful new UK–EU relationship. Success here will come in finding a way through the negotiations and in implementing new economic, political, social and security relationships.

Second, in delivering changes to the UK that address some of the causes of the Leave vote. As discussed in Chapters Four and Five, it is possible to identify a number of socio-economic and socio-cultural concerns that fuelled support for Leave. Failure to address these could doom Brexit in the eyes of millions of voters. Addressing them will be about more than negotiating a new UK–EU relationship. They will require considerable domestic changes that touch on the UK's constitutional arrangements, identity, party politics, political economy, welfare, responses to globalisation, and place in a changing Europe and transatlantic relationship. That leads to the question at the heart of the Brexit debate: what type of country does Britain want to be?

7. What does Brexit mean for the rest of the EU?

Britain's vote to leave the EU adds to the questions facing the EU over what type of union it wants to be. The EU is *sui generis*. It is not a state or nation but nor is it strictly an international treaty-based organisation, having long since moved beyond this to be something that sits between the two. Its guiding principles, such as 'an ever closer union' can be interpreted in a number of ways. Its history has been one of integration but also, especially in recent years, growing resistance to integration.

Britain's vote to leave was an unprecedented and key moment in the EU's history, but one that sits alongside several other challenges such as those over the future of the Eurozone or Schengen. As Chapter Six covered, in conjunction with these other challenges Britain's departure could shift the EU's balance of power, direction and unity. The EU was resilient in protecting its unity during the first stages of the Brexit negotiations, but how long might this last? Brexit is a long-term process that forever changes both Britain and the EU; it is not simply one that lasts the two years set out in Article 50. Understanding the consequences of Brexit for the EU is therefore not simply about what happens during the negotiations, but what influence Britain as a non-EU European state and the experience of facing Brexit will have on the EU as the years pass.

8. How have non-EU Europe and the rest of the world responded to Brexit?

Brexit has been seen to be both a consequence of wider political trends and a development that has had and will continue to have profound consequences outside of Britain and Europe. Many will think of the links between Brexit and the election of Donald Trump, and there are similarities and differences between the two, as discussed in Chapter Seven. Brexit could be seen as a development that heralds further such developments.

From the perspective of other powers such as Russia or China, Brexit signals different things. It can be taken to show that fragmentation is not something Europe has overcome and could face more of in future. What shapes the views of these states is not only their bilateral relations with the UK or the EU, but the debates within them about their place and that of Europe's (Britain included) in a changing global world order. Britain's leaders have long sought to play a leading role shaping this order, and a key question for the likes of the US, Russia and China will be the extent to which post-Brexit Britain will be able to do so.

9. What have been the UK's and EU's strategies for Brexit and how should they be approved and scrutinised?

A strategy is a combination of ends, ways and means with an assessment of the degree of risk involved and which takes into account the likely strategy of an opponent. As Chapter Five discussed, the UK government's approach to the first stages of the Brexit negotiations has often been seen as falling short of a coherent strategy, in large part because it has struggled to define the end it seeks in Brexit. But has the EU done any better given it also faces some challenging questions about how to change as the UK withdraws? It is also important not to overlook the fact that Brexit, as a process, means both the UK and EU will need to adapt their strategies as they move forward. Britain's government might have struggled with its strategy for negotiating Brexit, but will it – or any governments that follow – do a better job at managing the changes to Britain's society, economy and place in the world that Brexit brings about? How might the UK's and EU's strategies look in 10 or 20 years' time?

Finally, who is to scrutinise and approve these strategies? The consequences of a flawed strategy can be costly, for example financially, politically or in terms of international reputation. Yet the debate can often be poisonous and divisive. Those in the UK who have challenged or questioned Brexit have been accused of being 'saboteurs' or 'mutineers', while those pushing for Brexit have been ridiculed as dooming Britain to irrelevance and driving it off a cliff. Given the importance of Brexit for the UK it is important not to lose sight of the importance of debate and scrutiny.

The process by which Brexit is approved also raises awkward questions. Did the referendum sanction a Brexit of a specific type? As touched on in Chapter Five, the Brexit narrative remains far from settled in terms of what sort of Brexit Britain should pursue in terms of UK–EU relations and in terms of what type of country it wants to be as it addresses the causes behind the Brexit vote. How well aligned will be the strategies for Brexit and what country Britain wants to be? Are the strategies for Brexit to be settled by government, Parliament or the people in another referendum or through elections? For each of these, how is such approval to fit with the process of negotiating Brexit with the EU or the UK's own constitutional setup where elected representatives in places such as Scotland or Greater London also demand a say?

10. Who wins and loses from Brexit?

It is easy to discuss the consequences of Brexit in broad-brush ways but on closer inspection it soon becomes clear that Brexit will produce winners and losers in many different ways. There will be winners and losers at the international, European, national, regional, local and individual levels. These wins and losses can also be understood in many ways such as from economic, political, social, security and ideological perspectives.

As noted in Chapter Six, Brexit may benefit some states in the EU while weakening others. Some economic projections forecast that Leave voters will lose out economically more than those who voted Remain. The heart of the UK's economy, London, could be hit by Brexit, but its diversified economy could mean it rebounds faster than elsewhere and continues to grow apart from the rest of the country. But when will these wins or losses happen? Some of the losses and gains will only become apparent over a longer period of time. Time might also better reveal the opportunity costs of Brexit. An opportunity cost is the benefit that could have been gained had other courses been taken over Brexit. For example, would it have been better for the UK to remain in the EU or to have pursued some other strategy for negotiating Brexit?

How then can the harm versus good of Brexit be assessed? Brexit has consumed the time and attention of many in British government. Could this time, effort and resources have been put to a better use on domestic, European or international matters? And who – individuals, groups, communities, companies, countries and so forth – have won and lost as a result of this? Finally, who wins and loses from Brexit is not guaranteed to be the result of a fair contest or end in a fair result. Whether it is states or individuals, who wins and who loses will be heavily influenced by differences in wealth, access to information, degree of political power, or membership of networks that others are excluded from. Is Brexit therefore going to strengthen, weaken or change in anyway the inequalities in the UK?

Meaning

11. 'Brexit means Brexit' means what?

As Brexit unfolds the meaning of 'Brexit' will change and remain a subject of much debate. This means that, as touched on throughout the book, there is no set definition of what Brexit means. This does not mean decision makers and others will not try to define it. That means that in order to analyse Brexit one must always seek clarity as to what is meant by it by those who use the term.

As discussed in Chapter Five, when Theresa May said 'Brexit means Brexit' she was accused of being deliberately unclear in order to buy herself negotiating room. When she finally did set out her ideas for what Brexit should mean, many others were quick to point out some of the inconsistencies and that it remained unclear as to how she would deliver on her definition. For example, she has spoken of her desire to create a 'deep and special partnership' with the EU, but what new relationship Brexit leads to is not for Britain alone to define given the EU also has a say.

If Brexit was to 'take back control' as some Leave campaigners argued, then does the meaning of Brexit lie in the degree of control leaving the EU delivers? But control for whom, over what? When and how will it compare to the control exercised by remaining members of the EU and other states around the world such as Canada or Japan? Will it mean Britain can drop all the regulations and laws the EU requires as part of its single market, or will the pull of the EU as Britain's biggest trading partner limit the degree of control Britain has? And what then of international regulations? To what extent will Britain be bound by these or, outside of the EU, be able to shape them at the international level on its own?

Finally, is Brexit about taking back control from a British elite whom many Leave voters felt had left them behind or forgotten about them? Was it to be control over immigration? Is Brexit about control for the Westminster Parliament or for any UK government that with a majority in the House of Commons can do largely what it wants?

12. What theoretical approach best explains and analyses Brexit?

Analysis of Brexit can be consumed by the latest developments and lose sight of the bigger picture. A longer-term and more systemic view of developments is needed. This is where theory comes in. The point of using theories is not necessarily to be speculative, although some speculation is inevitable with a topic so much in flux as Brexit. Rather it is important to ask what established bodies of theories can reveal about Brexit and the likely consequences of it. This can apply to areas ranging from domestic through to international politics or economic factors through to the role of gender.

13. How can the success or failure of Brexit be measured?

As discussed for question 10, who wins and loses from Brexit will depend on the level or sector being examined and the time frame involved. But how can such wins or losses be measured? How can the consequences of something as big as Brexit be measured, not least when, as touched on in discussing question 6, one of the outcomes of a 'successful Brexit' would be to address the causes of such a vote.

Would Brexit be deemed a success or failure if Britain in 10 years' time was a poorer but fairer society? Could this be adequately measured? Should success or failure be measured in terms of levels of trade between the UK and the EU or between the UK and other markets around the world? Can opinion polling point to whether the British people (or others elsewhere) feel Brexit has been a success or failure? Will the success or failure be judged in election outcomes such as a UK general election? Will Brexit be deemed a success if the projections of economic costs from leaving as put forward by the Remain campaign do not come to pass? But will it be deemed a failure if the promises of the Leave campaign fail to materialise? And what would it mean if the effects of Brexit are negligible?

14. Is Brexit a 'critical juncture' for the UK and/or the EU?

The opposite to a negligible outcome mentioned at the end of the previous question would be for Brexit to turn out to be a 'critical juncture'. This is a term that historians sometimes use when they identify an event or decision in the history of a country that profoundly changed it. As the opening paragraph of Chapter One made clear, Brexit is important because so much is potentially at stake. This certainly applies to the UK and perhaps also to the EU and others. If Brexit leads to profound changes to Britain's society, constitution, unity, economy and place in the world then that would make it a critical juncture.

It could also matter if Brexit were not a 'critical juncture'. If leaving the EU did not lead to significant change to Britain then it would raise questions about the effect of being a member of the EU. It could also raise questions about whether anything much had been done to address the causes of Brexit, such as the socio-economic and socio-cultural concerns outlined in Chapter Four.

As has already been raised in this conclusion, a great deal here depends on time. Therefore, this is a question only answered in hindsight, but whether that will be sooner or later depends on the types of changes Brexit brings about.

15. Is Brexit something that is unique to the UK or something symptomatic of wider trends?

As discussed throughout the book, Britain's vote to leave the EU not only has implications for the rest of the EU and others, but also raises questions and debates about them and their links and similarities with the UK. It is possible to see common themes in the UK's vote for Leave and political developments elsewhere in the EU, most notably rising levels of Euroscepticism and the 'constraining dissensus' that has held back recent attempts at European integration. It is also possible to see it as part of wider political trends across the world, such as the election of Donald Trump and rising support for populism, authoritarian politics and scepticism about the benefits of such developments as globalisation. There is a need, however, to be careful as to how far these comparisons and similarities are taken. Brexit cannot be explained without reference to the UK's unique historical, economic and political relations with the rest of the EU. The way the referendum was called in the UK, and the context within which it took place, also help explain the result, these being factors that may not necessarily play out the same way elsewhere. That does not mean the publics of other member states of the EU might not vote for their member state to leave the EU. The British people voted for Leave despite living in the member state least affected by the crises in the Eurozone and Schengen.

It is also possible to see in the way Brexit has unfolded wider trends in how states have become interconnected and how they try to manage their interconnected relationships. The process of separating the UK from the EU has shown the depth of the institutional and economic links that bind EU member states together. Britain's ability to chart its own course in the world is constrained not only by these links, but also by the wider economic, political and institutional arrangements that govern transatlantic relations and the wider international order. Britain's ability to shape these is being tested by Brexit. The extent to which Britain's experiences can be translated to others, however, varies considerably. Again, the UK's unique circumstances – its island nature, political setup, history, economic, security and social links – mean the way it has faced withdrawing from the EU is not necessarily the way in which any other EU member state could go about it.

The Brexicon glossary

Below in a glossary-style format are listed the most common forms of Brexit and some other Brexit and EU-related terms used in the book and the broader Brexit debate. There are many other terms, such as 'Remoaner' and 'Brexodus', which can be found in Oliver's *Now! That's what I call Brexit!* (2016).

Acquis – the complete body of EU treaties, laws, CJEU case law, declarations and resolutions adopted by the EU, measures relating to the CFSP and Justice and Home Affairs, and international agreements concluded by the EU.

Article 49 – the article of the EU's treaties that sets out how a country can join the EU.

Article 50 – the article of the EU's treaties that sets out how a member state can exit the EU.

Article 218 – the article of the EU's treaties that sets out how the Union can reach agreement with third countries and international organisations over the relationship between them.

Association Agreement – a treaty between the EU and a non-EU country that, as set out in Article 217 of the EU's treaties, may establish 'an association involving reciprocal rights and obligations, common action and special procedure'. This can cover matters such as political, trade, security, and cultural and social links.

Chaotic Brexit/no deal Brexit/no plan Brexit/cliff edge Brexit – a Brexit where the UK–EU negotiations collapse or run out of time, with the UK leaving the EU without a deal over its exit or a new relationship.

Common Travel Area – the UK, Republic of Ireland, the Channel Islands, and the Isle of Man form a common travel area where a person who has legally passed immigration control into one of these four can then freely enter any of the other parts of the area.

Customs union – a group of states that have agreed to charge a common external tariff. Once goods have entered the customs union they may move freely within the union without further tariffs being applied.

Equivalence – under 'mutual recognition' both sides accept and recognise each other's standards and regulations. But if only one side recognises the other's standards and regulations, this is termed 'equivalence'.

Europeanisation – a term used to describe a number of processes by which the EU shapes its member states, the member states shape the EU, and EU member states shape each other.

Frictionless border – a border (sometimes referred to as a 'seamless frictionless border' or an 'invisible border') between the Irish Republic and the UK that entails no physical stops and customs checks.

Good Friday Agreement – also known as the Belfast Agreement, it was a two-part deal agreed in 1998 between most of Northern Ireland's political parties (a multi-party agreement) and between the UK and Irish governments (an international agreement), which underpins the Northern Ireland peace process.

Great Repeal Bill – now known as the EU Withdrawal Bill, it is the key piece of UK legislation necessary to implement Brexit in British law. It repeals the 1972 European Communities Act, which took Britain into the EU. It also copies all existing EU legislation into domestic UK law.

Hard Brexit – a form of Brexit in which the UK cuts most of its links with the EU. This would entail leaving both the single market and customs union and could, in the most severe sense, involve no new relationship deal with the EU.

Harmonisation – the goal of harmonisation in trade negotiations is to standardise regulations so as to provide uniformity between countries.

Henry VIII clauses – powers that allow the UK government to use secondary legislation to repeal or amend primary legislation, sometimes without further parliamentary scrutiny.

Intergovernmentalism – usually contrasted with supranationalism, it is a process where decisions are made between governments without relinquishing sovereignty.

Most favoured nation (MFN) – a WTO rule that requires members to apply the same tariff schedules to all other WTO members with which they do not have free trade agreements.

Mutual recognition – an approach to trade in which two countries mutually accept each other's rules or procedures by which products are assessed and evaluated for compliance. This is often agreed through a mutual recognition agreement.

Non-tariff barriers (see also '**tariffs**') – any barriers to the import and export of goods or services that are not traditional tariffs. They can include regulations, rules of origin and quotas.

Parliamentary sovereignty – that the UK Parliament is the supreme legal authority in the UK and that only it can create or repeal any law.

Passporting – allows any firm registered within the EEA to do business in any other EEA state without needing further authorisation or licences from those other countries.

Premature Brexit – a unilateral hard Brexit that happens before the end of the two-year Article 50 time frame because of a failure to agree to a deal or because of a collapse of all negotiations.

Regulatory alignment – a process whereby the UK would continue to follow the rules and regulations of the EU.

Regulatory divergence – a process whereby the UK would diverge from EU rules and regulations. Some have called for 'managed divergence' whereby the UK and the EU continue regulatory alignment in some areas, but the UK is permitted to diverge from future rules in others, in which case the EU would curtail market access in such areas.

Rules of origin – the rules used in international trade to define the country of origin of a product.

Single market – an association of countries trading goods, capital and services with each other without borders, tariffs or regulatory obstacles. The EU's single market aims to break down barriers to trade through the free movement of goods, services, capital and labour.

Soft Brexit – a Brexit that sees the UK remain as close as possible to the EU and the EU's single market, for example through being in the EEA.

Supranationalism – usually contrasted with intergovernmentalism, it is a process by which non-nation state institutions such as the European Commission or CJEU make decisions independent of national governments who are then obliged to accept these decisions.

Tariffs (see also '**non-tariff barriers**') – a tax or duty set by a country or customs union on imports or exports between countries.

Third country – a country that is not a member of the EU.

Timed-out Brexit – a hard Brexit because of a failure to reach an agreement by the end of the two-year time frame of Article 50.

Unanimity – a requirement that all EU countries when meeting in the Council agree to a proposal for it to move forward.

WTO terms – In some hard Brexit scenarios, Britain would trade with the EU under the rules set by the World Trade Organization, which limits the levels of tariffs on goods.

Timelines of UK–EU relations and Brexit

Key dates in the development of the EU, other European organisations and the UK–EU relationship

Date	Event
19 September 1946	In a speech in Zurich, Sir Winston Churchill calls for a United States of Europe.
1949	The Council of Europe is founded by the Treaty of London.
4 April 1949	The North Atlantic Treaty Organization (NATO) is founded.
18 April 1951	Treaty of Paris is signed establishing the European Coal and Steel Community between France, Germany, Italy, the Netherlands, Belgium and Luxembourg.
3 September 1953	European Convention on Human Rights enters into force. The European Court of Human Rights is established in 1959.
25 March 1957	The Treaty of Rome is signed establishing the European Economic Community and the European Atomic Energy Community.
4 January 1960	The European Free Trade Association is formed with Austria, Denmark, Norway, Portugal, Sweden, Switzerland and the UK.
15 January 1963	Britain's first application (submitted on 1 August 1961 by the Conservative government of Harold Macmillan) to join the EEC is blocked by President de Gaulle.
27 November 1967	Britain's second application, submitted by the Labour government of Harold Wilson, to join is again blocked by President de Gaulle.
1 July 1968	EEC members agree a customs union, removing all import duties between them.
27 October 1970	'European Political Cooperation' is launched as the foreign ministers of the six founding members, meeting in Luxembourg, adopt the Davignon Report, which laid the foundations for coordinating the foreign policies of the EEC member states.
1 January 1973	Britain joins the EEC. Denmark and Ireland also join. Norway decides not to following a referendum.
7 June 1975	Labour Prime Minister Harold Wilson secures a renegotiated UK–EEC relationship and Britain votes 67 per cent to 33 per cent to remain in the EEC.
3 July 1975	The Organization for Security and Co-operation in Europe (OSCE) is established.

Date	Event
1977	Customs duties between the nine EC members are completely abolished.
13 March 1979	The European Monetary System (EMS) and Exchange Rate Mechanism (ERM) are established.
4 May 1979	Conservatives win general election, Margaret Thatcher becomes prime minister.
1979	First direct elections to the European Parliament.
1 January 1981	Greece joins the EEC.
27 June 1984	EEC agrees to a UK rebate.
14 June 1985	Schengen Treaty is signed, abolishing borders between members.
1 January 1986	Spain and Portugal join the EEC.
17/28 February 1986	The Single European Act is signed, in Luxembourg and the Hague.
20 September 1988	Margaret Thatcher delivers her Bruges speech.
1990	Fall of the Berlin Wall, Germany is reunified, with East Germany becoming a part of the EEC.
8 October 1990	Britain joins the ERM.
1991–2001	Wars are fought in the former Yugoslavia. The EU, NATO, OSCE and others are involved throughout.
17 September 1992	Britain and Italy forced out of the ERM.
7 February 1992	Treaty of Maastricht is signed, creating the EU.
1 January 1995	Austria, Sweden and Finland join the EU.
2 May 1997	Labour win the general election. Tony Blair appointed prime minister.
2 October 1997	Treaty of Amsterdam signed.
2 October 2000	Charter of Fundamental Rights is established.
26 February 2001	Nice Treaty signed.
1 January 2002	Euro replaces currencies in 12 member states, having been launched as a currency in 1999.
2003	Convention on the Future of Europe prepares a draft constitutional treaty.
31 March 2003	EU deploys first troops under the European Security and Defence Policy.
1 May 2004	10 new member states join the EU: Cyprus, Czech Republic, Estonia, Hungary, Latvia, Lithuania, Malta, Poland, Slovakia, and Slovenia.
2005	Constitutional treaty is abandoned after rejection in referendums in France and the Netherlands.
1 January 2007	Romania and Bulgaria join the EU.
13 December 2007	Lisbon Treaty signed and is ratified by 2009.
2007–2008	Global financial crisis.
2009	A crisis begins in the Eurozone.

Date	Event
9 December 2011	David Cameron vetoes a fiscal compact, causing the rest of the EU to establish it via a separate treaty.
1 July 2013	Croatia joins the EU.
23 January 2013	David Cameron delivers his Bloomberg speech in which he commits the Conservative Party to an in/out referendum, which is later included in the party's 2015 general election manifesto.
2015	The EU faces a migration crisis.

The UK–EU renegotiation, referendum and Brexit negotiations

Date	Event
8 May 2015	The Conservative Party under the leadership of David Cameron wins a majority in the general election.
25 June 2015	David Cameron informs the rest of the EU that he will seek a renegotiated relationship to be put to the British people in an in/out referendum.
October 2015	David Cameron informs the European Council and the House of Commons of the four sets of reforms he is seeking.
10 November 2015	David Cameron sets out his aims for reform in a letter to Donald Tusk, President of the European Council.
17 December 2015	The EU Referendum Act, which enables a referendum to be held, is given Royal Assent.
2 February 2016	Donald Tusk and the European Council set out their proposals for the renegotiation.
18-19 February 2016	European Council meeting agrees to a UK–EU renegotiation in four areas.
22 February 2016	David Cameron announces the date of the referendum.
15 April 2016	Official referendum campaigning begins.
23 June 2016	Referendum held.
24 June 2016	David Cameron announces his resignation as prime minister. The EU releases a statement on the outcome of the referendum.
28–29 June 2016	European Council meeting.
13 July 2016	Theresa May becomes leader of the Conservative Party and is appointed prime minister.
20 July 2016	Britain agrees to relinquish its next rotating presidency of the European Council, which it was due to hold from July to December 2017.
2 October 2016	Theresa May tells the Conservative Party Conference that she will introduce a 'Great Repeal Bill' to repeal the European Communities Act 1972 and that it will be the government's, not Parliament's, decision to trigger Article 50 and that it will do so before the end of 2017.

Date	Event
October 2016	Legal challenge in Northern Ireland over whether the Northern Ireland Assembly must give its consent to leaving the EU, the Northern Ireland High Court eventually rules against. Scottish First Minister, Nicola Sturgeon, announces legislation for a second independence referendum.
8 November 2016	Donald Trump wins the US presidential election.
13 November 2016	UK High Court rules that the UK government cannot use royal prerogative powers to trigger Article 50. Government appeals to the Supreme Court.
5–8 December 2016	UK Supreme Court hears the government's appeal against the High Court's ruling on triggering Article 50.
7 December 2016	House of Commons votes to respect the outcome of the referendum by 461 to 89.
3 January 2017	UK Permanent Representative to the EU, Sir Ivan Rogers, resigns. Sir Tim Barrow, the then UK ambassador to Russia, is appointed to replace him.
17 January 2017	Theresa May delivers her Lancaster House speech in which she sets out her plan for leaving the EU, including 12 priorities for the UK's Brexit objectives.
24 January 2017	The UK Supreme Court rejects the UK government's appeal against the High Court ruling and states that primary legislation is required to trigger Article 50. Also rules that the UK Parliament is not required to seek the consent of devolved legislatures.
26 January 2017	In response to the Supreme Court's decision, the UK government publishes the European Union (Notification of Withdrawal) Bill.
2 February 2017	UK government publishes a Brexit White Paper setting out its strategy for exiting the EU.
9–10 March 2017	European Council in Brussels.
13 March 2017	Parliament passes the European Union (Notification of Withdrawal) Bill. It gains Royal Assent on 16 March.
29 March 2017	Theresa May writes to Donald Tusk to inform him of the UK's intention to leave the EU, thus triggering Article 50.
31 March 2017	European Council publishes draft Brexit negotiation guidelines for the EU27.
18 April 2017	Theresa May calls an early general election, which MPs approve on 19 April.
29 Apr 2017	EU27 leaders meet at a special European Council and unanimously adopt guidelines for Brexit negotiations.
7 May 2017	Second round of French presidential elections sees Emmanuel Macron elected president.
31 May 2017	Irish High Court rejects a legal challenge over the revocability of Article 50 notification.
8 June 2017	UK general election produces a hung parliament.
26 Jun 2017	Conservative–DUP agreement reached that secures a minority Conservative government.
19 June 2017	Formal negotiations on the UK withdrawal begin.

Date	Event
24 September 2017	Federal elections in Germany see Angela Merkel returned as chancellor but with reduced levels of support.
8 December 2017	UK and EU negotiators agree a text to conclude Phase 1 of the Brexit negotiations.
14–15 December 2017	UK and EU leaders agreed there had been sufficient progress in Phase 1 of the Brexit negotiations for negotiations to move on to Phase 2.

2018 and onwards

Date	Event
First half of 2018	Parliament expected to pass the EU Withdrawal Bill (once known as the 'Great Repeal Bill').
22-23 March 2018	Deal agreed on UK's transition, the Phase 2 negotiations. Phase 3 negotiations – over a new relationship – began.
Autumn 2018	Date by which the UK–EU negotiating time frame aims to have concluded negotiations over the UK's exit.
Late 2018	UK Parliament presented with the deal agreed with the EU.
Late 2018	European Parliament votes on the Article 50 deal. If the European Parliament gives its consent then the Council votes by super-qualified majority vote on whether to conclude deal.
29 March 2019	If two-year time frame of Article 50 is adhered to then this will be when the UK formally leaves the EU (midnight Central European Time).
30 March 2019– 31 December 2020	21 month transition period, as proposed in the March 2018 Phase 2 agreement.
June 2019	European Parliament elections.
7 May 2020	Elections for the London Mayor and Greater London Assembly.
3 November 2020	US presidential election.
31 December 2020	Date on which the transition period is due to end.
6 May 2021	Elections to the Scottish Parliament and Welsh Assembly.
May 2022	UK general election. Northern Ireland Assembly elections due on 5 May 2022.

Sources: Data from Walker (2017) inter alia.

Bibliography

Armour, John and Horst Eidenmüller. 2017. *Negotiating Brexit.* Hart Publishing.

Armstrong, Kenneth. 2017. *Brexit Time: Leaving the EU – Why, How and When?* CUP.

Ashcroft, Michael. 2016. *How the United Kingdom voted on Thursday... and why.* 24 June. https://lordashcroftpolls.com/2016/06/how-the-united-kingdom-voted-and-why/

Ashcroft, Michael and Kevin Culwick. 2016. *Well, You Did Ask ... Why the UK Voted to Leave the EU.* Biteback.

Audickas, Lukas, Oliver Hawkins and Richard Cracknell. 2017. *UK Election Statistics: 1918–2017. Number CBP7529.* House of Commons Library.

Bailey, David and Leslie Budd. 2017. *The Political Economy of Brexit.* Agenda.

Banks, Aaron. 2016. *The Bad Boys of Brexit.* London: Biteback.

Barnett, Anthony. 2017. *The Lure of Greatness: England's Brexit and America's Trump.* Unbound.

Barton, John H., Judith L. Goldstein, Timothy E. Josling and Richard H. Steinberg. 2006. *The Evolution of the Trade Regime: Politics, Law and Economics of the GATT and the WTO.* Princeton University Press.

BBC. 2016a. *EU referendum: The result in maps and charts.* 24 June. http://www.bbc.com/news/uk-politics-36616028.

BBC. 2016b. *EU vote: Where the cabinet and other MPs stand.* 22 June. http://www.bbc.com/news/uk-politics-eu-referendum-35616946.

Begg, Iain. 2017. *How much will Brexit cost?* 19 May. http://ukandeu.ac.uk/how-much-will-brexit-cost/.

Bellamy, Richard. 2018. 'Would a Second Brexit Referendum Be Legitimate – and If So, When?' In *The Referendum Challenge to the EU.* EUI.

Bennett, Owen. 2016. *The Brexit Club.* Biteback.

Benton, Meghan. 2017. *Safe or Sorry? Prospects for Britons in the European Union after Brexit.* Migration Policy Institute.

Bickerton, Chris. 2016. *The European Union: A Citizens Guide.* Penguin.

Bièvre, Dirk De, Arlo Poletti and Aydin Yildirim. 2016. 'About the Melting of Icebergs. Political and Economic Determinants of Dispute Initiation and Resolution in the WTO'. In Manfred Elsig, Bernard Hoekman and Joost Pauwelyn (eds), *Assessing the World Trade Organization: Fit For purpose.* CUP.

Bogdanor, Vernon. 2005. 'Footfalls Echoing in the Memory. Britain and Europe: The Historical Perspecte'. *International Affairs* 81(4).

Booker, Christopher and Richard North. 2005. *The Great Deception: Can the European Union Survive?* Continuum.

Bootle, Roger. 2017. *Making a Success of Brexit and Reforming the EU.* Hodder and Stoughton.

Bradshaw, Ben. 2017. 'Business of the House'. *Hansard*, 19 October: 1014.

British Journal of Politics and International Relations. 2017. First special issue on Brexit 19 (3).

British Journal of Politics and International Relations. 2017. Second special issue on Brexit 19 (4).

Brunet, Luc-Andre. 2017. *Forging Europe: Industrial Organisation in France, 1940–1952.* Palgrave Macmillan.

Burgoon, Brian, Tim Oliver and Peter Trubowitz. 2017. 'Globalization, Domestic Politics and Transatlantic Relations'. *International Politics* 54(4).

Business for Britain. 2015. *Change, or Go: How Britain Would Gain Influence and Prosper Outside an Unreformed EU.* Business for Britain.

Butler, David and Uwe Kitzinger. 1976. *The 1975 Referendum.* Macmillan.

Cabinet Office. 1959. *Study of Future Policy, 1960–1970.* Cabinet Office.

Cameron, David. 2015. 'The future of the EU and the UK's relationshjip with it'. 10 Downing St. 23 January. https://www.gov.uk/government/speeches/eu-speech-at-bloomberg.

Carl, Noah. 2017. *What Sort of Brexit Deal Does the British Public Want? A Review of Evidence So Far.* UK in a Changing Europe.

Cato the Younger. 2017. *Guilty Men: Brexit Edition.* Biteback.

Checkel, Jeffrey. 2001. 'From Meta- to Substantive Theory? Social Constructivism and the Study of Europe'. *European Union Politics* 2(2): 219–249.

Clarke, Harold, Matthew Goodwin and Paul Whiteley. 2017. *Brexit: Why Britain Voted to Leave the European Union.* CUP.

Clegg, Nick. 2017. *How to Stop Brexit (and Make Britain Great Again).* Vintage.

Clements, Ben. 2017. *The referendums of 1975 and 2016 illustrate the continuity and change in British Euroscepticism.* 31 July. http://blogs.lse.ac.uk/brexit/2017/07/31/the-referendums-of-1975-and-2016-illustrate-the-continuity-and-change-in-british-euroscepticism/.

Connelly, Tony. 2017. *Brexit and Ireland: The Dangers, the Opportunities and the Inside Story of the Irish Response.* Penguin.

Court of Justice of the European Union. 2017. 'Annual Report 2016'. https://curia.europa.eu/jcms/upload/docs/application/pdf/2017-03/ra_jur_2016_en_web.pdf.

Crafts, Nicholas. 2016. 'The Impact of EU Membership on UK Economic Performance'. *The Political Quarterly* 87(2): 262–268.

Curtice, John. 2017. 'Why Leave Won the UK's EU Referendum'. *Journal of Common Market Studies* 55(S1): 19–37.

Daddow, Oliver. 2012. 'The UK Media and "Europe": From Permissive Consensus to Destructive Dissent'. *International Affairs* 88(6): 1219–1236.

Daddow, Oliver and Tim Oliver. 2016. 'A not so awkward partner: the UK has been a champion of many causes in the EU'. *LSE Brexit blog.* 15 April. http://blogs.lse.ac.uk/brexit/2016/04/15/a-not-so-awkward-partner-the-uk-has-been-a-champion-of-many-causes-in-the-eu/.

De Vries, Catherine E. 2017. 'Benchmarking Brexit: How the British Decision to Leave Shapes EU Public Opinion'. *Journal of Common Market Studies* 55(S1): 38–53.

Dhingra, Swati, Stephen Machin and Henry G. Overman. 2017. *The Local Economic Effects of Brexit.* LSE Centre for Economic Performance.

Dhingra, Swati, Hanwei Huang, Gianmarco I.P. Ottaviano, João Paulo Pessoa, Thomas Sampson and John Van Reenen. 2017. *The Costs and Benefits of Leaving the EU: Trade Effects.* LSE Centre for Economic Performance.

Dinan, Desmond, Neil Nugent and William E. Paterson (eds). 2017. *The European Union in Crisis.* Palgrave.

Djankov, Simeon. 2017. *The City of London after Brexit.* https://piie.com/publications/policy-briefs/city-london-after-brexit.

Donnelley, Brendan. 2005. 'The Euro and British Politics'. *European Policy Brief,* September.

Drozdiak, William. 2017. *Fractured Continent: Europe's Crises and the Fate of the West.* W.W.Norton.

Dunt, Ian. 2016. *Brexit: What the Hell Happens Now?* Canbury Press.

Ebell, Monique. 2016. 'Assessing the Impact of Trade Agreements'. *National Institute Economic Review* 238: R31–R41.

Economist, The. 2017. *Military spending by NATO members.* 16 February. 2017. https://www.economist.com/blogs/graphicdetail/2017/02/daily-chart-11.

Electoral Commission. 2016. *EU Referendum Results.* https://www.electoralcommission.org.uk/find-information-by-subject/elections-and-referendums/past-elections-and-referendums/eu-referendum/electorate-and-count-information.

Elwes, Jay. 2018. 'Former MI6 Head John Sawers: Brexit Could Pose Long-term Problems for British Security'. *Prospect,* 14 February.

Emerson, Michael. 2016. 'Which model for Brexit?' *CEPS.* https://www.ceps.eu/system/files/SR147%20ME%20Which%20model%20for%20Brexit.pdf.

European Commission. 2013. *Transatlantic Trade and Investment Partnership: The Economic Analysis Explained.* European Commission.

Evans, Geoffrey and Anand Menon. 2017. *Brexit and British Politics.* Polity Press.

Falkner, Robert. 2017. 'Europe and the World: Rethinking Europe's External Relations in an Age of Global Turmoil'. *International Politics* 54(4).

Farrell, Jason and Paul Goldsmith. 2017. *How to Lose A Referendum: The Definitive Story of Why the UK Voted for Brexit.* Biteback.

Ford, Robert and Matthew Goodwin. 2014. *Revolt on the Right: Explaining Support for the Radical Right in Britain.* Routledge.

Foreign and Commonwealth Office. 2014. December. https://www.gov.uk/guidance/review-of-the-balance-of-competences.

Fossum, John Erik and Hans Petter Graver. 2018. *Squaring the Circle of Brexit: Could the Norway Model Work?* Policy Press.

Gamble, Andrew. 2003. *Between Europe and America: The Future of British Politics.* Palgrave.

Garton-Ash, Timothy. 2001. 'Is Britain European?' *International Affairs* 77(1).

Gaskarth, Jamie. 2013. *British Foreign Policy: Crises, Conflicts and Future Challenges.* Polity Press.

Gaskarth, Jamie. 2014. 'Strategizing Britain's Role in the World'. *International Affairs* 90(3): 559–581.

Geddes, Andrew. 2013. *Britain and the European Union.* Macmillan.

George, Stephjen. 1998. *An Awkard Partner: Britain in the European Community.* OUP.

Getmanchuk, A. 2015. *Ukraine: Brexit would damage Ukranian hopes for a European future.* http://blogs.lse.ac.uk/brexit/2015/12/04/views-on-the-uks-renegotiation-russia-ukraine-and-turkey/.

Gibbon, Gary. 2017. *Breaking Point: The UK Referendum on the EU and Its Aftermath.* UCP.

Glencross, Andrew. 2016. *Why the UK Voted for Brexit.* Palgrave.

Goodwin, Matthew and Caitlin Milazzo. 2015. *Britain, the European Union and the Referendum: What Drives Euroscepticism?* Chatham House.

Goodwin, Matthew and Oliver Heath. 2016. 'The 2016 Referendum, Brexit and the Left Behind: an Aggregate-level Analysis of the Result'. *Political Quarterly* 87(3): 323–332.

Grant, Charles. 2016. *How Leave Outgunned Remain: The Battle of the 'Five Ms'.* 25 June. http://www.cer.eu/insights/how-leave-outgunned-remain-battle-five-ms.

Green, David Allen. 2017. *Brexit: What Everyone Needs to Know.* OUP.

Green, Stephen. 2017. *Brexit and the British.* UCP.

Gromyko, A. 2015. *Russia: A New Twist for an Awkward Partnership.* http://blogs.lse.ac.uk/brexit/2015/12/04/views-on-the-uks-renegotiation-russia-ukraine-and-turkey/.

Guerrina, Roberta and Hailey Murphy. 2016. 'Strategic Silences in the Brexit Debate: Gender, Marginality and Governance'. *Journal of Contemporary European Research* 12(4).

Haas, Ernst. 1958. *The Uniting of Europe: Political, Social and Economic Forces, 1950–1957.* Stevens.

Halligan, Liam and Gerald Lyons. 2017. *Clean Brexit: Why Leaving the EU Still Makes Sense – Building a Post-Brexit Economy for All.* Biteback.

Hammond, Andrew and Tim Oliver. 2017. *The 14 Brexit Negotiations.* Strategic Update. LSE IDEAS.

Hanhimaki, Jussi, Benedict Schoenborn and Barbara Zanchetta. 2012. *Transatlantic Relations Since 1945: An Introduction.* Routledge.

Hannan, Daniel. 2016a. *What Next: How to Get the Best from Brexit.* Head of Zeus.

Hannan, Daniel. 2016b. *Why Vote Leave.* Head of Zeus.

Hanretty, Chris. 2016. 'The EU referendum: how did Westminster constituencies vote?'. *Medium.* 29 June. https://medium.com/@chrishanretty/the-eu-referendum-how-did-westminster-constituencies-vote-283c85cd20e1

Hanretty, Chris. 2017a. 'Areal Interpolation and the UK's Referendum on EU Membership'. *Journal of Elections, Public Opinion and Parties* 27(4): 466–483.

Hanretty, Chris. 2017b. *Final estimates of the Leave vote, or 'A real interpolation and the UK's referendum on EU membership'.* March 24. https://medium.com/@chrishanretty/final-estimates-of-the-leave-vote-or-areal-interpolation-and-the-uks-referendum-on-eu-membership-5490b6cab878.

Hassan, Gerry and Russell Gunson (eds). 2017. *Scotland and the UK after Brexit. A Guide to the Future.* Luath Press.

Hawkins, Oliver. 2017. *Migration Statistics.* SN06077, House of Commons Library.

Hayward, Katy. 2017. 'Into Thin Eire: Britain's Exit from the EU Could Undo 40 Years of Progress on the Island of Ireland'. *International Politics and Society*,http://www.ips-journal.eu/regions/europe/article/show/into-thin-eire-1947/

Heffernan, Richard. 2003. 'Prime Ministerial Predominance? Core Executive Politics in the UK'. *British Journal of Politics and International Relations* 5(3).

Hennig, Benjamin and Danny Dorling. 2016. 'In Focus: The EU Referendum'. *Political Insight* 7(2).

Hillman, Jennifer and Gary Horlick. 2017. *Legal Aspects of Brexit: Implications of the United Kingdom's Decision to Withdraw from the EU.* Institute of International Economic Law.

Hix, Simon. 2015a. *Brits know less about the EU than anyone else.* 27 November. http://blogs.lse.ac.uk/europpblog/2015/11/27/brits-know-less-about-the-eu-than-anyone-else/.

Hix, Simon. 2015b. 'Is the UK Marginalised in the EU?'. *UK in a Changing Europe.* http://ukandeu.ac.uk/explainers/is-the-uk-marginalised-in-the-eu-2/.

Hix, Simon and Sara Hagemann. 2015. 'Is the UK a winner or loser in the EU Council?' *The Guardian.* 2 November. https://www.theguardian.com/world/datablog/2015/nov/02/is-uk-winner-or-loser-european-council.

Holmes, Peter, Jim Rollo and L. Alan Winters. 2016. 'Negotiating the UK's Post-Brexit Trade Arrangements'. *National Institute Economic Review* 238: R22–R30.

Hooghe, Liesbet and Gary Marks. 2009. 'A Postfunctionalist Theory of European Integration: From Permissive Consensus to Constraining Dissensus'. *British Journal of Political Science* 39: 1–23.

House of Commons Library. 2018a. *A Guide to the EU Budget.* House of Commons Library.

House of Commons Library. 2018b. *Brexit: A Reading List of Post-EU Referendum Publications by the UK Parliament and the Devolved Assemblies.* House of Commons Library.

House of Commons Public Administration Select Committee. 2008. *Parliamentary Commissions of Inquiry.* HC473, Public Administration Select Committee, House of Commons.

House of Commons Treasury Select Committee. 2016. *The Economic and Financial Costs and Benefits of the UK's EU membership.* HC122:House of Commons.

House of Lords European Committee. 2017. *Brexit and the EU Budget.* HL Paper 125. House of Lords.

HM Treasury. 2016. https://www.gov.uk/government/uploads/system/uploads/attachment_data/file/590488/PU2027_EU_finances_2016_print_final.pdf

HM Treasury. 2017. European Union Finances 2016: statement on the 2016 EU Budget and measures to counter fraud and financial mismanagement. CM 9400, February, 12.

Hug, Adam. 2014. *Renegotation, Reform and Referendum: Does Britain Have a European Future?* Foreign Policy Centre.

Ikenberry, G. John. 2011. 'The Future of the Liberal World Order: Internationalism after America'. *Foreign Affairs* 90(3): 56–68.

Ipsos Mori. 2016. *European Union Membership – Trends.* 15 June. https://www.ipsos.com/ipsos-mori/en-uk/european-union-membership-trends.

James, Scott and Lucia Quaglia. 2017. *Brexit and the Limits of Financial Power in the UK.* Global Economic Governance Programme.

Johnson, Boris. 2013. 'We must be ready to leave the EU if we don't get what we want'. *Daily Telegraph*, 12 May.

Kaufmann, Erik. 2016. *Brexit Voters: NOT the left behind.* 24 June. http://www.fabians.org.uk/brexit-voters-not-the-left-behind/.

Kenealy, Daniel, John Peterson and Richard Corbett. 2015. *The European Union: How Does It Work?* OUP.

Keukeleire, Stephan and Tom Delreux. 2014. *The Foreign Policy of the European Union.* Palgrave Macmillan.

Kitchen, Nicholas. 2015. *Investing for Influence: Report of the LSE Diplomacy Commission.* LSE IDEAS.

Kitchen, Nicholas and Tim Oliver. 2017. 'Written evidence submitted by Dr Tim Oliver and Dr Nicholas Kitchen'. *House of Commons Defence Select Committee Inquiry into UK–US relations.* 7 March.

Krastev, Ivan and Mark Leonard. 2010. *The Spectre of a Multipolar Europe.* European Council on Foreign Relations.

Krotz, Ulrich and Richard Maher. 2016. 'Europe's Crisis and the EU's "Big Three"'. *West European Politics* 39(5): 1053–1072.

Lawton, Chris and Robert Ackrill. 2016. *Hard Evidence: how areas with low immigration voted mainly for Brexit.* 8 July. https://theconversation.com/hard-evidence-how-areas-with-low-immigration-voted-mainly-for-brexit-62138.

MacShane, Denis. 2016. *How Britain Left Europe.* I.B.Tauris.

MacShane, Denis. 2017. *Brexit, No Exit: Why (in the End) Britain Won't Leave Europe.* I.B.Tauris.

May, Theresa. 2017. 'The government's negotating objectives for exiting the EU'. *Prime Minister's Office.* 17 January. https://www.gov.uk/government/speeches/the-governments-negotiating-objectives-for-exiting-the-eu-pm-speech.

McCormick, John. 2014. *Understanding the European Union: A Concise Introduction.* Palgrave Macmillan.

McGowan, Lee. 2017. *Preparing for Brexit: Actors, Negotiators and Consequences.* Palgrave.

Menon, Anand. 2016. 'Uniting the United Kingdom'. *Foreign Affairs.* 6 July. Menon, Anand. 2017. *A Successful Brexit: Four Economic Tests.* UK in a Changing Europe.

Menon, Anand. 2018. 'Is it possible to reverse Brexit?'. *The Guardian.* 16 February. https://www.theguardian.com/commentisfree/2018/feb/16/possible-reverse-brexit-second-referendum?CMP=Share_iOSApp_Other.

Menon, Anand and Brigid Fowler. 2016. 'Hard or Soft? The Politics of Brexit'. *National Institute Economic Review* 238: R4–R12.

Menon, Anand and John-Paul Salter. 2016. 'Brexit: Initial Reflections'. *International Affairs* 92(6): 1297–1318.

Menon, Anand and Jonathan Portes. 2017. 'The Debate about a BREXIT Transition Is a Phoney War'. *Prospect,* 17 August.

Milward, Alan. 1992. *The European Rescue of the Nation-State.* Routledge.

Mindus, Patricia. 2017. *European Citizenship After Brexit: Freedom of Movement and Rights of Residence.* Palgrave.

Mirrorme22 Nilfanion: English and Scottish council areas TUBS: Welsh council areas Sting: Gibraltar, 2016 [CC BY-SA 3.0 (https://creativecommons.org/licenses/by-sa/3.0)], via Wikimedia Commons.

Mitchell, James. 2014. *The Scottish Question*. OUP.

Moravcsik, Andrew. 1998. *The Choice for Europe: Social Purpose and State Power from Messina to Maastricht*. Cornell University Press.

Moravcsik, Andrew. 2001. 'Bringing Constructivist Integration Theory Out of the Clouds: Has it Landed Yet?' *European Union Politics* 2(2): 226–240.

Morphet, Janice. 2017. *Beyond Brexit: How to Assess the UK's Future*. Policy Press.

Mount, Harry. 2017. *Summer Madness: How Brexit Split the Tories, Destroyed Labour and Divided the Country*. Biteback.

Nicolaidis, Kalypso. 2017. 'Brexit Arithmetics'. In John Armour and Horst Eidenmüller (eds), *Negotiating Brexit*. Hart Publishing.

Office for National Statistics. 2018. *Who does the UK trade with?* 3 January. https://visual.ons.gov.uk/uk-trade-partners/.

Oliver, Craig. 2016. *Unleashing Demons: The Inside Story of Brexit*. Hodder and Stoughton.

Oliver, Tim. 2013. *Europe without Britain: Assessing the Impact on the EU of a UK Withdrawal*. Stiftung Wissenschaft und Politik.

Oliver, Tim. 2015. 'To Be or Not to Be in Europe: Is That the Question? Britain's European Question and an In/out Referendum'. *International Affairs* 91(1): 77–91.

Oliver, Tim. 2016a. *Now That's What I Call Brexit! Delving into the Brexicon*. 22 December. http://blogs.lse.ac.uk/brexit/2016/12/22/now-thats-what-i-call-brexit-delving-into-the-brexicon-of-brexit/.

Oliver, Tim. 2016b. 'What If Britain Had Voted to Leave the EEC in 1975?' In Duncan Brack and Iain Dale (eds), *Prime Minister Corbyn: and Other Things That Never Happened*. Biteback.

Oliver, Tim. 2017a. *Britain's Brexit Strategy: Lions Misled by Donkeys*. 28 September. http://www.dahrendorf-forum.eu/britains-brexit-strategy-lions-misled-by-donkeys/.

Oliver, Tim. 2017b. 'Never Mind the Brexit? Britain, Europe, the World and Brexit'. *International Politics* 54(4): 519–532.

Oliver, Tim. 2017c. *We need to talk about the London question*. 10 May. https://constitutioon-unit.com/2017/05/10/we-need-to-talk-about-the-london-question/.

Oliver, Tim. 2018. *Europe's Brexit: EU Perspectives on Britain's Vote to Leave.* Agenda.

Oliver, Tim and Michael Williams. 2016. 'Special Relationships in Flux: Brexit and the Future of the US-EU and US-UK Relationships'. *International Affairs* 92(3): 547–567.

Oliver, Tim and Michael Williams. 2017. *Making the 'Special Relationship' Great Again?* LSE IDEAS.

Outhwaite, William. 2017. *Brexit: Sociological Responses.* Anthem Press.

Owen, David and David Ludlow. 2017. *British Foreign Policy After Brexit.* Biteback.

Oxford Review of Economic Policy. 2017. 'The Economics of Brexit: What Is at Stake?' *Oxord Review of Economic Policy* 33(S1): S1–S3.

Peston, Robert. 2017. *WTF.* London: Hodder & Stoughton.

Peterson, John. 2009. 'Policy Networks'. In Antje Wiener and Thomas Diez (eds), *European Integration Theory.* OUP.

Pinder, John and Simon Usherwood. 2013. *The European Union: A Very Short Introduction.* OUP.

Pisani-Ferry, Jean, Norbert Rottgen, Andre Sapir, Paul Tucker and Guntram B. Wolff. 2017. *Europe After Brexit: A Proposal for a Continental Partnership.* Brugel.

Political Quarterly. 2016. 'Up for Grabs? Key Issues in the Negotiations about Britain's Membership in the EU.' 87(2).

Political Quarterly. 2016. 87(3).

Pollack, Mark. 2009. 'The New Institutionalism and European Integration'. In Antje Wiener and Thomas Diez (eds), *European Integration Theory.* OUP.

Portes, Jonathan. 2016. 'Immigration after Brexit'. *National Institute Economic Review* R13–R21.

Posen, Barry. 2013. 'Pull Back: The Case for a Less Activist Foreign Policy'. *Foreign Affairs* 92(1): 116–128.

Prosser, Chris, Jon Mellon and Jane Green. 2016. *What mattered most to you when deciding how to vote in the EU referendum?* July. http://www.britishelectionstudy.com/bes-findings/what-mattered-most-to-you-when-deciding-how-to-vote-in-the-eu-referendum/#.WetMkROCxbU.

Putnam, Robert. 1988. 'Diplomacy and Domestic Politics: The Logic of Two-level Games'. *International Organization* 42(3): 427–460.

Quinn, Adam. 2017. *Trump as Brexit Britain's BFF? Remember: for him talk is cheap.* http://ukandeu.ac.uk/trump-as-brexit-britains-bff-remember-for-him-talk-is-cheap/.

Rachman, Gideon. 2017. *Easternisation – War and Peace in the Twenty First Century.* Bodley Head.

Rapport, Aaron. 2017. 'Cognitive Approaches to Foreign Policy Analysis'. *Oxford Research Encyclopedia of Politics.* March. http://politics.oxfordre.com/view/10.1093/acrefore/9780190228637.001.0001/acrefore-9780190228637-e-397.

Renwick, Alan. 2017. 'Citizens' Assembly on Brexit: Summary Report'. *Citizens' Assembly.* September. http://citizensassembly.co.uk/wp-content/uploads/2017/10/CAB-summary-report.pdf.

Richards, Lindsay and Anthony Heath. 2017. *'Two Nations'? Brexit, inequality and social cohesion.* 6 June. https://www.britac.ac.uk/blog/%E2%80%9Ctwo-nations%E2%80%9D-brexit-inequality-and-social-cohesion.

Roberts, Dan. 2017. 'Brexiters nowhere to be seen as UK raises white flag over EU divorce bill'. *The Guardian*, 29 November.

Rohac, Dalibor. 2016. *Towards an Imperfect Union: A Conservative Case for the European Union.* Rowman and Littlefield.

Rosamond, Ben. 2000. *Theories of European Integration.* Palgrave.

Rosamond, Ben. 2016. 'Brexit and the Problem of European Disintegration'. *Journal of Contemporary European Research* 12(4).

Rosenbaum, Martin. 2017. *Local voting figures shed new light on EU referendum.* 8 February. http://www.bbc.com/news/uk-politics-38762034.

Russell, Meg and Daniel Gover. 2017. *Legislation at Westminster: Parliamentary Actors and Influence in the Making of British Law.* OUP.

Russell Mead, Walter. 2014. 'The Return of Geopolitics: the Revenge of the Revisionist Powers'. *Foreign Affairs.* May/June. Rutter, Jill and Julian McCrae. 2016. *Brexit: Organising Whitehall to Deliver.* Institute for Government.

Sanders, David and David Patrick Houghton. 2017. *Losing an Empire, Finding a Role: British Foreign Policy since 1945.* 2nd edition. Palgrave.

Schimmelfennig, Frank. 2015. 'The European Union as a System of Differentiated Integration: Interdependence, Politicization and Differentiation'. *Journal of European Public Policy* 22(6): 764–782.

Shipman, Tim. 2016. *All Out War: The Full Story of How Brexit Sank Britain's Political Class.* William Collins.

Simms, Brendan. 2016. *Britain's Europe: A Thousand Years of Conflict and Cooperation.* Allen Lane.

Smith, Julie. 2017. *The UK's Journey into and out of the EU: Destinations Unknown.* Routledge.

Springford, John. 2016. *Brexiting yourself in the foot: why Britain's Eurosceptic regions have most to lose from EU withdrawal.* 13 June. http://www.cer.eu/insights/brexiting-yourself-foot-why-britains-eurosceptic-regions-have-most-lose-eu-withdrawal.

Sriskandarajah, Danny and Catherine Drew. 2006. *Brits Abroad: Mapping the Scale and Nature of British Emigration.* IPPR.

Staiger, Uta and Benjamin Martill. 2017. *Brexit and Beyond: Rethinking the Futures of Europe.* UCL.

Streeck, Wolfgang. 2016. *How Will Capitalism End?* Verso.

Swales, Kirby. 2016. *Understanding the Leave Vote.* NatCen and UK in a Changing Europe.

Tierney, Stephen. 2014. *Constitutional Referendums: The Theory and Practice of Republican Deliberation.* OUP.

Travis, Alan. 2017. 'Net migration to UK shows largest annual fall since records began'. *The Guardian*, 30 November.

United Nations Department of Economic and Social Affairs. 2015. *Migrant Stock: The 2015 Revision.* United Nations Department of Economic and Social Affairs.

Walker, Nigel. 2017. *Brexit Timeline: Events Leading to the UK's Exit from the European Union.* Briefing Paper, House of Commons Library, London: 13.

Wall, Stephen. 2012. *The Official History of Britain and the European Community, Volume II: From Rejection to Referendum, 1963–1975.* Routledge.

Weaver, Matthew. 2017. 'Brexit is reversible even after date is set, says author of article 50.' *The Guardian.* 10 November. https://www.theguardian.com/politics/2017/nov/10/brexit-date-is-not-irreversible-says-man-who-wrote-article-50-lord-kerr

Webber, Douglas. 2014. 'How Likely Is It that the European Union Will Disintegrate?' *European Journal of International Relations* 20(2): 341–365.

Welfens, Paul. 2017. *An Accidental Brexit: New EU and Transatlantic Economic Perspectives.* Palgrave Macmillan.

Wendt, Alexander. 1992. 'Anarchy Is What States Make of It: The Social Construction of Power Politics'. *International Organization* 46(2): 391–425.

Whitman, Richard. 2016. 'The UK and EU Foreign, Security and Defence Policy after Brexit: Integrated, Associated or Detached?' *National Institute Economic Review* 28.

Wicket, Xenia. 2018. *Transatlantic Relations: Converging or Diverging?* Chatham House.

Williams, Michael. 2013. 'Enduring, But Irrelevant? Britian, NATO and the Future of the Atlantic Alliance'. *International Affairs* 50(3): 360–386.

Wohlforth, William C. and Vladislav M. Zubok. 2017. 'An Abiding Antagonism: Realism, Idealism and the Mirage of Western-Russian Partnership after the Cold War'. *International Politics* 54(4): 405–419.

YouGov. 2016. 'How Britain voted'. 27 June. https://yougov.co.uk/news/2016/06/27/how-britain-voted/'

Young, Hugo. 1998. *This Blessed Plot: Britain and Europe from Churchill to Blair.* Overlook Press.

Index